ARGONAUT CONFERENCE

January-February 1945

PAPERS
AND
MINUTES OF MEETINGS
ARGONAUT CONFERENCE

EDITED AND PUBLISHED BY THE
OFFICE, U.S. SECRETARY
OF THE COMBINED CHIEFS OF STAFF
1945

Published by Books Express Publishing
Copyright © Books Express, 2011
ISBN 978-1-780394-02-2

Books Express publications are available from all good retail and online booksellers. For publishing proposals and direct ordering please contact us at: info@books-express.com

TOP SECRET

TABLE OF CONTENTS

PAPERS

C.C.S.		PAGE
320/35	Allocation of Zones of Occupation in Germany . . . . . *(Memorandum by the United States Chiefs of Staff)*	1
320/37	Allocation of Zones of Occupation in Germany . . . . . *(Note by the Secretaries)*	9
417/11	Operations for the Defeat of Japan . . . . *(Memorandum by the United States Chiefs of Staff)*	11
452/37	Operations in Southeast Asia Command . . . . *(Note by the Secretaries)*	15
452/38	Operations in Southeast Asia Command . . . . *(Note by the Secretaries)*	18
625/14	Levels of Supply of All Petroleum Products in All Theaters *(Report by a Combined ad hoc Committee)*	21
660/3	Estimate of the Enemy Situation — Europe (as of 23 January 1945) . . . . *(Report by the Combined Intelligence Committee)*	27
746/8	Shipping Agreement . . . . *(Memorandum by the United States Chiefs of Staff)*	45
746/10	Over-All Review of Cargo Shipping . . . . *(Report by the Combined Military Transportation Committee and the Combined Shipping Adjustment Board)*	54
746/11	Over-All Review of Cargo and Troop Shipping Position for the Remainder of 1945 . . . . *(Report by the Combined Military Transportation Committee and the Combined Shipping Adjustment Board)*	57

TOP SECRET

TABLE OF CONTENTS

PAPERS

C.C.S.		PAGE
747/7 ARGONAUT	Allocation of Resources between India-Burma and China Theaters . . . . *(Memorandum by the British Chiefs of Staff)*	101
755/3	Provision of LVT's for the Mediterranean . . . . *(Memorandum by the United States Chiefs of Staff)*	103
755/4	Provision of LVT's for the Mediterranean . . . . *(Memorandum by the British Chiefs of Staff)*	105
761/3	SCAEF Report on Strategy in Northwest Europe . . . . *(Note by the Secretaries)*	107
761/6	Strategy in Northwest Europe . . . . *(Note by the Secretaries)*	122
765/1	Subjects for Consideration at the Next U.S.-British-U.S.S.R. Staff Conference . . . . *(Memorandum by the United States Chiefs of Staff)*	125
765/4	Subjects for Consideration at the Next U.S.-British-U.S.S.R. Staff Conference . . . . *(Memorandum by the Representatives of the British Chiefs of Staff)*	128
765/8	Agenda for Next U.S.-British Staff Conference . . . . . *(Memorandum by the Representatives of the British Chiefs of Staff)*	129
768/1 ARGONAUT	Equipment for Allied and Liberated Forces . . . . . . *(Memorandum by the United States Chiefs of Staff)*	131

TOP SECRET

TABLE OF CONTENTS

PAPERS

C.C.S.		PAGE
768/2	Equipment for Allied and Liberated Forces *(Memorandum by the British Chiefs of Staff)*	134
772	Planning Date for the End of the War with Germany *(Memorandum by the British Chiefs of Staff)*	135
773/2	Transfer of Tactical Air Forces from SACMED to SCAEF *(Memorandum by the British Chiefs of Staff)*	139
773/3	Operations in the Mediterranean *(Note by the Secretaries)*	141
774/1	U-Boat Threat During 1945 *(Memorandum by the British Chiefs of Staff)*	145
774/3	U-Boat Threat During 1945 *(Note by the Secretaries)*	152
775	Basic Undertakings in Support of Over-All Strategic Concept *(Memorandum by the British Chiefs of Staff)*	155
776/3	Report to the President and Prime Minister *(Note by the Secretaries)*	157
777/2	Reciprocal Agreement on Prisoners of War *(Note by the Secretaries)*	175
778/1	Liaison with the Soviet High Command over Anglo-American Strategic Bombing in Eastern Germany *(Note by the Secretaries)*	181

TOP SECRET

TABLE OF CONTENTS

MESSAGES

		PAGE
COSSEA 200	Directive to Supreme Allied Commander, Southeast Asia .	19
FAN 477	Bombline in Eastern Europe and the Balkan Area between the Allied and Soviet Armies	185
FAN 501	Directive to the Supreme Allied Commander, Mediterranean	142
NAF 841	Equipping Additional Greek Forces	188
SCAF 179	Development of Operations in Northwest Europe . . .	109
SCAF 180	Appreciation and Plan of Operations in Northwest Europe	116
SCAF 194	Revised Paragraphs (A) and (B) to Plan of Operations in Northwest Europe	123
S-77211	General Eisenhower's Confirmation and Amplification of SCAF 194	124

TOP SECRET

TABLE OF CONTENTS

MINUTES OF MEETINGS

ARGONAUT CONFERENCE

	PAGE
C.C.S. 182d Meeting (Malta)	191

    Procedure for the Conference

    Agenda for the Conference

    German Flying Bomb and Rocket Attacks

    Strategy in Northwest Europe

    Coordination of Operations with the Russians

    The Combined Bomber Offensive

    Planning Date for the End of the War with Germany

    Planning Date for the End of the War with Japan

    The U-Boat Threat

C.C.S. 183d Meeting (Malta)	205

    Operations in the Mediterranean

    Strategy in Northwest Europe

    Planning Date for the End of the War with Germany

    Operations in Southeast Asia Command

    Allocation of Resources between the India-Burma and China Theaters

    Estimate of the Enemy Situation — Europe

    Bombing of U-Boat Assembly Yards and Operating Bases

TOP SECRET

TABLE OF CONTENTS

MINUTES OF MEETINGS

ARGONAUT CONFERENCE

PAGE

C.C.S. 184th Meeting (Malta) 215

    Strategy in the Mediterranean

    Equipment for Allied and Liberated Forces

    Operations in Southeast Asia Command

    Allocation of Resources between the India-Burma and China Theaters

    Pacific Operations

    U-Boat Threat

    Bombing of Assembly Yards and Operating Bases

    Strategy in Northwest Europe

C.C.S. 185th Meeting (Malta) 225

    Equipment for Allied and Liberated Forces

    Review of Cargo Shipping

    Levels of Supply of Petroleum Products in U.K. and Northwest Europe

    Transfer of Tactical Air Forces from SACMED to SCAEF

    Provision of LVT's for the Mediterranean

    U-Boat Threat

    Basic Undertakings

    Interim Report to the President and Prime Minister

TOP SECRET

TABLE OF CONTENTS

MINUTES OF MEETINGS

ARGONAUT CONFERENCE

	PAGE
C.C.S. 186th Meeting (Yalta)	233

    Levels of Supply of Petroleum Products in U.K. and Northwest Europe

    Planning Date for the End of the War against Germany

    Provision of LVT's for the Mediterranean

    Allocation of Zones of Occupation in Germany

    Basic Undertakings

    Liaison with the Soviet High Command over Anglo-American Strategic Bombing in Eastern Germany

    Next Meeting, Combined Chiefs of Staff

C.C.S. 187th Meeting (Yalta)	239

    Levels of Supply of All Petroleum Products in All Theaters

    Over-All Review of Cargo Shipping

    Reciprocal Agreement on Prisoners of War

    Equipment for Greek Forces

    Final Report to the President and Prime Minister

    Operations on the Western Front

C.C.S. 188th Meeting (Yalta)	247

    Draft Final Report to the President and Prime Minister

    Liaison with the Soviet High Command with Regard to Strategic Bombing in Eastern Germany

    Concluding Remarks

TOP SECRET

TABLE OF CONTENTS

MINUTES OF ARGONAUT

TRIPARTITE MILITARY MEETINGS

	PAGE
First Tripartite Military Meeting (Yalta)	251

    Coordination of Offensive Operations

        European Theater
        Mediterranean Theater

    Movement of German Forces from Norway

    Use of Artillery and Air in Future Operations

    Liaison Arrangements

    Naval Operations in Support of the Land Offensive

    Date of the End of the War with Germany

    Future Business

Second Tripartite Military Meeting (Yalta) 267

    Bombline and Liaison Arrangements

    Coordination of Offensive Operations

    Exchange of Information with Regard to River-Crossing Technique and Equipment

    Bases for U.S. Strategic Bomber Forces in the Vienna-Budapest Area

    Provision of Soviet Airfields for Damaged British Night Bombers

    Enemy Intelligence

    Pacific Operations

    VLR Bomber Operations against Japan

    Operations in Burma and China

    Future Business

TOP SECRET

TABLE OF CONTENTS

MINUTES OF ARGONAUT

PLENARY MEETINGS

	PAGE
First Plenary Meeting, U.S.A.-Great Britain (Malta)	287

    Report to the President and Prime Minister
        Basic Undertakings
        The U-Boat War
        Operations in Northwest Europe
        Strategy in the Mediterranean
        The War Against Japan

Second Plenary Meeting, U.S.A.-Great Britain (Yalta) 295

    Report to the President and Prime Minister
    Entry of Russia in the War Against Japan
    Continuation of the Combined Chiefs of Staff
        Organization after the End of the War

Tripartite Plenary Meeting (Yalta) 299

    Situation on the Eastern Front
        Probable Enemy Action
        Shifting of Enemy Troops
        Russian Intentions
    Operations on the Western Front
    Bomber Offensive
    Situation in Italy
    Submarine Warfare
    Coordination of Winter Offensives

INDEX 311

TOP SECRET

C.C.S. 320/35
C.C.S. 320/37

ALLOCATION OF ZONES OF OCCUPATION IN GERMANY

Reference:

CCS 186th Meeting, Item 5

On 5 February 1945 the United States Chiefs of Staff proposed a revised draft agreement for the American control of the Bremen-Bremerhaven enclave (Enclosure "A" to C.C.S. 320/35) in lieu of the draft agreement proposed in the appendix to Enclosure "B."

The Combined Chiefs of Staff in their 186th Meeting amended and approved the draft agreement proposed in the appendix to Enclosure "B," which was subsequently circulated on 6 February as C.C.S. 320/37.

TOP SECRET

C.C.S. 320/35　　　　　　　　　　　　　　　　　　　　　　　5 February 1945

COMBINED CHIEFS OF STAFF

ALLOCATION OF ZONES OF OCCUPATION IN GERMANY

References:

a. CCS 320/33
b. CCS 320/34

Memorandum by the United States Chiefs of Staff

1. With regard to the draft agreement concerning the Bremen-Bremerhaven area proposed by General Macready in the attached letter to Mr. McCloy (Enclosure "B"), the United States Chiefs of Staff prefer that the final agreement exist on one sheet of paper and recommend that the Combined Chiefs of Staff approve Enclosure "A."

2. As regards the numerous points proposed in General Macready's letter it appears to the United States Chiefs of Staff that such matters which cannot be agreed to by the local commanders of the Zones of Occupation should be referred at that time to the Combined Chiefs of Staff for decision. There will be undoubtedly some problems of overlapping authority and conflicting interests which will have to be resolved under the policy of coordination and cooperation.

3. It has been our understanding that the draft agreement as proposed by Lord Halifax and Mr. McCloy and as modified by the British Chiefs of Staff does not involve the question of command of the Bremen-Bremerhaven area. Such command, with the full authority that is inherent in command, must rest with the American commander of the Bremen-Bremerhaven area, as subordinate of the American commander of the Southwestern Zone. It is intended, however, that in the normal administration of the Bremen-Bremerhaven area the American commander thereof will, in accordance with the draft agreement, conform to the general policy pursued in the administration of the British Zone as qualified in the phrasing of the draft agreement.

TOP SECRET

4. If the British Chiefs of Staff prefer to retain the wording of the agreement attached to General Macready's letter it is acceptable to the United States Chiefs of Staff provided the British Chiefs of Staff indicate their concurrence to the above interpretation of the draft agreement.

5. The United States Chiefs of Staff urge that this matter be completed before the end of the present conference.

TOP SECRET

ENCLOSURE "A"

(Paragraph numbers conform to the attachment to General Macready's letter. Underlining and *italicizing* represent amendments to that attachment.)

1. The Bremen *and* - Bremerhaven *enclave* Area as shown on the attached map will be under complete American control including military government and responsibility for disarmament and demilitarization *but will be generally administered as a subdistrict of a larger British controlled area*. It is understood that the American military government will conform to the general policies pursued in the administration of the *larger district* British Zone, subject always to the right of the American commander to vary the administration of the *enclave* Bremen-Bremerhaven Area in any particular that he may find necessary on military grounds.

2. The United States Chiefs of Staff agree to permit necessary access by the British to offices, and necessary use of available installations, situated in the Bremen-Bremerhaven Area, which provide services essential to British administration of the British Zone of Occupation.

2. 3. The U.S. interest in transit passage from the Bremen-Bremerhaven Area to the Southwestern Zone is so dominant and the British interest in possible movement through the American Zone to Austria so evident that obligation to carry stores and personnel for the one government through the zone controlled by the other is mutually recognized. To better achieve *responsible* responsive service, each military zone commander will accept a Deputy Controller for United States (or British) requirements of Movement and Transport from the other to assist in the coordination of the movement and transport involved in such essential traffic.

3. 4. The map *referred to is* attached is the same as that attached to C.C.S. 320/29.

Words underlined are proposed additions.
Words italicized are proposed deletions.

Enclosure "A"

TOP SECRET

ENCLOSURE "B"

BRITISH JOINT STAFF MISSION
OFFICES OF THE COMBINED CHIEFS OF STAFF
WASHINGTON

General Staff   20 January 1945

Hon. J. J. McCloy,
Assistant Secretary of War,
Room 4E886 Pentagon Bldg.,
Washington, D. C.

Dear Mr. McCloy:

BREMEN ENCLAVE

1. I am now glad to be able to inform you that the British Chiefs of Staff are prepared to accept the formula which was arrived at our meeting in the War Department on the 5th January subject to the American Chiefs of Staff confirming their interpretation of one or two points.

For convenience I attach a copy of the formula with two small amendments inserted which I have underlined. These amendments are proposed in order to ensure that the British and American interpretations of the formula are the same.

2. I think you will agree that the interpretation by the British Chiefs of Staff as indicated by these amendments is correct. With regard to the amendment in paragraph 2 the British Chiefs of Staff understand the "Deputy Controller" to be an officer deputed to a functional control office situated outside his national zone, which controls the agents of that office situated within his national zone. He controls such agents only, and does not, in the absence of the "Controller" assume authority over any other portion of the area within the sphere of that Controller.

Enclosure "B"

TOP SECRET

3. The British Chiefs of Staff would also like confirmation that administrative questions such as wage rates, which raise points of principle, will necessarily fall into line with the general policies of the Governments or of the Control Commission.

4. The British Chiefs of Staff understand that the proposed formula will have to be read in conjunction with paragraph 7 of C.C.S. 320/34* which will in practice be modified by the principles enunciated in the formula.

It would appear that such modification, however, will be in favor of American interests and providing that it is understood that paragraph 7 of C.C.S. 320/34 is modified by the formula, the British Chiefs of Staff do not consider it necessary to amend C.C.S. 320/34.

5. If you can confirm that the American Chiefs of Staff agree the interpretation of the formula in paragraphs 1 to 4 above, the British Chiefs of Staff propose:

(a) That the American and British Chiefs of Staff respectively issue instructions that the United States group, and the British element, of the Control Council for Germany should jointly proceed forthwith with the detailed planning of the arrangements in connection with the Bremen enclave.

(b) That the American and British Chiefs of Staff should issue instructions that the naval elements of the two Control Council groups should examine the extent of the naval command to seaward referred to in paragraph 7 (b) of C.C.S. 320/33* and should submit their joint proposals to the Navy Department and Admiralty.

(c) That the American Chiefs of Staff should now recommend that the United States Government ratify the occupation protocol for Germany (E.A.C. (44) 12th Meeting).

(d) That the American Chiefs of Staff should now approve:

(i) Paragraphs 1 to 6 of C.C.S. 320/33.

(ii) C.C.S. 320/34.

---

* Not published herein.

Enclosure "B"

TOP SECRET

6. If the United States Chiefs of Staff agree the above proposals, perhaps you will initiate the issue by the United States Chiefs of Staff of the appropriate instructions in accordance with paragraph 5 above.

                            Yours sincerely,

                            /s/ G. N. MACREADY

1 Attachment

Enclosure "B"

TOP SECRET

APPENDIX TO ENCLOSURE "B"

(ATTACHMENT)

THE BREMEN ENCLAVE

1. The Bremen and Bremerhaven enclave as shown on the attached map will be under complete American control including military government <u>and responsibility for disarmament and demilitarization</u> but will be generally administered as a subdistrict of a larger British controlled area. It is understood that the American military government will conform to the general policies pursued in the administration of the larger district subject always to the right of the American commander to vary the administration of the enclave in any particular that he may find necessary on military grounds.

2. The U.S. interest in transit passage from the Bremen area to the southwestern zone is so dominant and the British interest in possible movement through the American zone to Austria so evident that obligation to carry stores and personnel for the one government through the zone controlled by the other is mutually recognized. To better achieve responsible service, each military zone commander will accept a <u>Deputy Controller for United States (or British) requirements</u> of Movement and Transport from the other to assist in the coordination of the movement and transport involved in such essential traffic.

3. The map referred to is that attached to C.C.S. 320/29.

(ATTACHMENT)

Appendix to Enclosure "B"

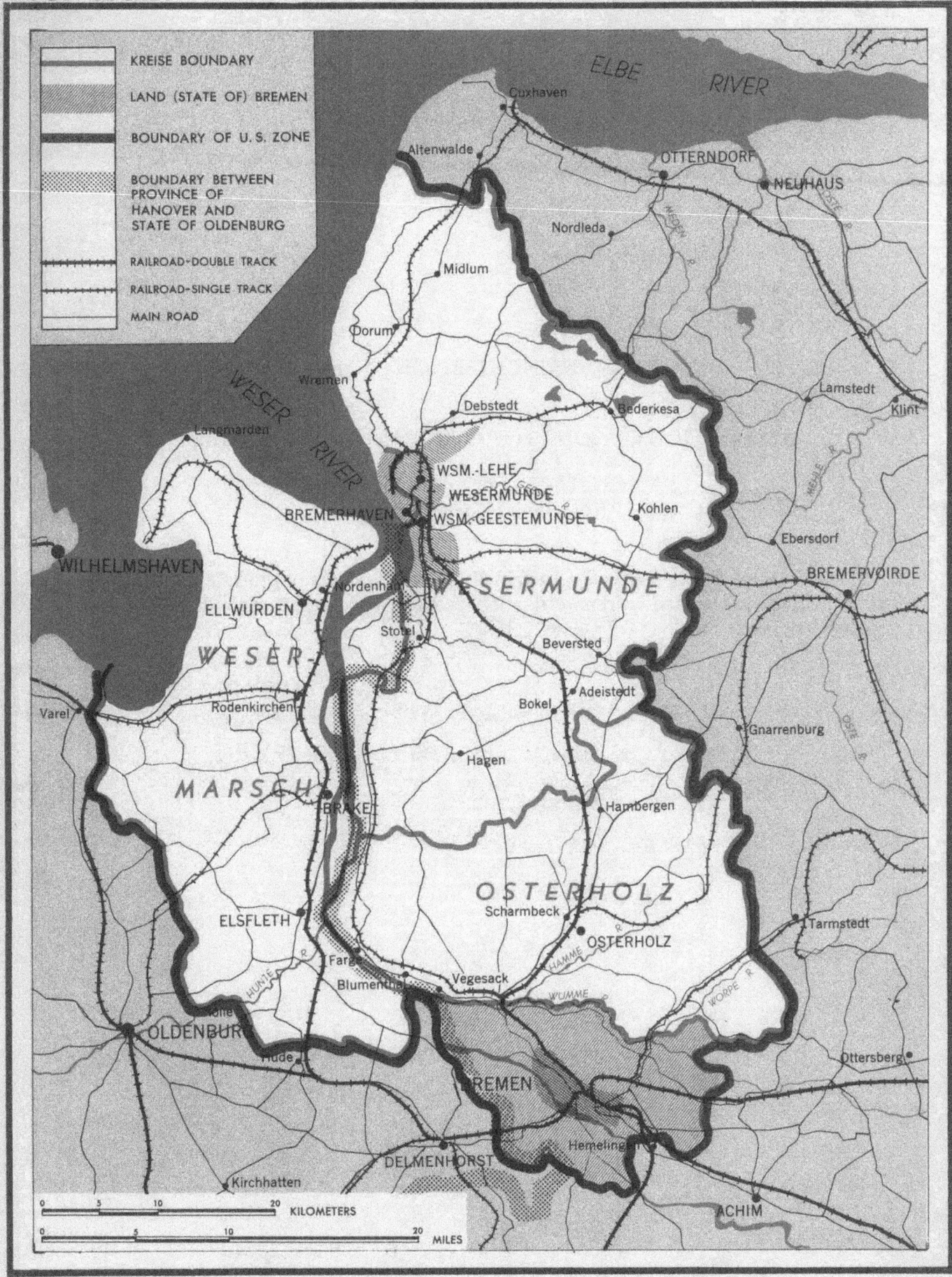

TOP SECRET

C.C.S. 320/37　　　　　　　　　　　　　　　　　　　　　　　　6 February 1945

COMBINED CHIEFS OF STAFF

ALLOCATION OF ZONES OF OCCUPATION IN GERMANY

Note by the Secretaries

    The Combined Chiefs of Staff, in their 186th Meeting on 6 February 1945, approved the attached agreement with respect to the Bremen and Bremerhaven enclave.

A. J. McFARLAND,

A. T. CORNWALL-JONES,

Combined Secretariat.

TOP SECRET

ENCLOSURE

THE BREMEN ENCLAVE

1. The Bremen and Bremerhaven enclave as shown on the attached map will be under complete American control including military government and responsibility for disarmament and demilitarization. It is understood that the American military government will conform to the general policies pursued in the administration of the British zone subject always to the right of the American commander to vary the administration of the enclave in any particular that he may find necessary on military grounds.

2. The U.S. interest in transit passage from the Bremen area to the southwestern zone is so dominant and the British interest in possible movement through the American zone to Austria so evident that obligation to carry stores and personnel for the one government through the zone controlled by the other is mutually recognized. To better achieve responsive service, each military zone commander will accept a Deputy Controller for (United States/British) requirements of Movement and Transport from the other to assist in the coordination of the movement and transport involved in such essential traffic.

3. The map referred to is that attached to C.C.S. 320/29.*

---

* C.C.S. 320/29 is not published herein but reference map is reproduced facing page 8.

TOP SECRET

C.C.S. 417/11

OPERATIONS FOR THE DEFEAT OF JAPAN

References:

CCS 184th Meeting, Item 5
2d Tripartite Military Meeting, Item 7
CCS 776/3, Paragraph 15

C.C.S. 417/11, dated 22 January 1945, was circulated by the United States Chiefs of Staff for the information of the Combined Chiefs of Staff and was noted in their 184th Meeting.

TOP SECRET

C.C.S. 417/11   22 January 1945

COMBINED CHIEFS OF STAFF

OPERATIONS FOR THE DEFEAT OF JAPAN

Memorandum by the United States Chiefs of Staff

1. The agreed over-all objective in the war against Japan has been expressed as follows (C.C.S. 417/9*):

To force the unconditional surrender of Japan by:

(1) Lowering Japanese ability and will to resist by establishing sea and air blockades, conducting intensive air bombardment, and destroying Japanese air and naval strength.

(2) Invading and seizing objectives in the industrial heart of Japan.

2. The United States Chiefs of Staff have adopted the following as a basis for planning in the war against Japan:

The concept of operations for the main effort in the Pacific is (C.C.S. 417/10):

a. Following the Okinawa operation to seize additional positions to intensify the blockade and air bombardment of Japan in order to create a situation favorable to:

b. An assault on Kyushu for the purpose of further reducing Japanese capabilities by containing and destroying major enemy forces and further intensifying the blockade and air bombardment in order to establish a tactical condition favorable to:

c. The decisive invasion of the industrial heart of Japan through the Tokyo Plain.

---

* *OCTAGON* Conference book, page 38.

TOP SECRET

3. The following sequence and timing of operations have been directed by the United States Chiefs of Staff and plans prepared by theater commanders:—

Objectives	Target Date
Continuation of operations in the Philippines (Luzon, Mindoro, Leyte)	—
Iwo Jima	19 February 1945
Okinawa and extension therefrom in the Ryukyus	1 April-August 1945

4. Until a firm date can be established when redeployment from Europe can begin, planning will be continued for an operation to seize a position in the Chusan-Ningpo area and for invasion of Kyushu-Honshu in the winter of 1945-1946.

5. Examination is being conducted of the necessity for and cost of operations to maintain and defend a sea route to the Sea of Okhotsk when the entry of Russia into the war against Japan becomes imminent. Examination so far has shown that the possibility of seizing a position in the Kuriles for that purpose during the favorable weather period of 1945 is remote due to lack of sufficient resources. The possibility of maintaining and defending such a sea route from bases in Kamchatka alone is being further examined.

6. The United States Chiefs of Staff have also directed examination and preparation of a plan of campaign against Japan in the event that prolongation of the European war requires postponement of the invasion of Japan until well into 1946.

TOP SECRET

C.C.S. 452/37

C.C.S. 452/38

OPERATIONS IN SOUTHEAST ASIA COMMAND

References:

CCS 183d Meeting, Item 5
CCS 184th Meeting, Item 4
1st U.S.-U.K. Plenary Meeting, Item *e.*
CCS 747/7 (ARGONAUT)
CCS 776/3, Paragraph 16

In C.C.S. 452/35, dated 30 January 1945, the British Chiefs of Staff proposed a draft directive to the Supreme Allied Commander, Southeast Asia. The United States Chiefs of Staff replied on 31 January (C.C.S. 452/36) accepting the proposed directive subject to agreement by the Combined Chiefs of Staff with the policy as set forth therein regarding U.S. resources in the India-Burma Theater.

The Combined Chiefs of Staff in their 184th Meeting considered C.C.S. 452/35, C.C.S. 452/36 and C.C.S. 747/7 (ARGONAUT), a memorandum by the British Chiefs of Staff with regard to the allocation of resources between the India-Burma and China Theaters. After discussion, the Combined Chiefs of Staff amended and approved the policy contained in C.C.S. 452/36 (subsequently circulated as C.C.S. 452/37); approved the directive to the Supreme Allied Commander, Southeast Asia as amended to draw his attention to the agreed policy set forth in C.C.S. 452/37 (approved directive subsequently circulated as C.C.S. 452/38); and took note that the British Chiefs of Staff withdraw C.C.S. 747/7 (ARGONAUT).

TOP SECRET

C.C.S. 452/37 1 February 1945

COMBINED CHIEFS OF STAFF

OPERATIONS IN SOUTHEAST ASIA COMMAND

Note by the Secretaries

In their 184th Meeting on 1 February 1945, the Combined Chiefs of Staff approved the policy set forth in the enclosure.

                                  A. J. McFARLAND,
                                  A. T. CORNWALL-JONES,
                                  Combined Secretariat.

ENCLOSURE

The primary military object of the United States in the China and India-Burma Theaters is the continuance of aid to China on a scale that will permit the fullest utilization of the area and resources of China for operations against the Japanese. United States resources are deployed in India-Burma to provide direct or indirect support for China. These forces and resources participate not only in operating the base and the line of communications for United States and Chinese forces in China, but also constitute a reserve immediately available to China without permanently increasing the requirements for transport of supplies to China.

The United States Chiefs of Staff contemplate no change in their agreement to SACSEA's use of resources of the U.S. India-Burma Theater in Burma when this use does not prevent the fulfillment of their primary object of rendering support to China including protection of the line of communications. Any transfer of forces engaged in approved operations in progress in Burma which is contemplated by the United States Chiefs of Staff and which, in the opinion of the British Chiefs of Staff, would jeopardize those operations, will be subject to discussion by the Combined Chiefs of Staff.

TOP SECRET

C.C.S. 452/38　　　　　　　　　　　　　　　　　　　　20 February 1945

COMBINED CHIEFS OF STAFF

OPERATIONS IN SOUTHEAST ASIA COMMAND

Note by the Secretaries

1. In their 184th Meeting on 1 February 1945, the Combined Chiefs of Staff approved the directive to the Supreme Allied Commander, Southeast Asia, contained in C.C.S. 452/35, subject to the addition of a paragraph drawing his attention to the policy set out in C.C.S. 452/37.

2. The directive, as dispatched, is circulated for information.

　　　　　　　　　　　　　　　　　　　　　　A. J. McFARLAND,
　　　　　　　　　　　　　　　　　　　　　　R. D. COLERIDGE,
　　　　　　　　　　　　　　　　　　　　　　Combined Secretariat.

TOP SECRET

ENCLOSURE

From: British Chiefs of Staff

To: Headquarters, Southeast Asia Command

No: COSSEA 200 (CM-IN-3376)

3 February 1945

Following to SACSEA has been approved by Combined Chiefs of Staff.

Begins 1. Your first object is to liberate Burma at the earliest date. (To be known as operation *LOYALIST*.)

2. Subject to the accomplishment of this object your next main task will be the liberation of Malaya and the opening of the Straits of Malacca. (To be known as operation *BROADSWORD*.)

3. In view of your recent success in Burma, and of the uncertainty of the date of the final defeat of Germany, you must aim at the accomplishment of your first object with the forces at present at your disposal. This does not preclude the despatch of further reinforcements from the European Theatre should circumstances make this possible.

4. You will prepare a programme of operations for the approval of the Combined Chiefs of Staff.

5. In transmitting the foregoing directive the Combined Chiefs of Staff direct your attention to the agreed policy in respect of the use in your theatre of United States resources deployed in the India-Burma Theatre.*

Ends

---

* Enclosure to C.C.S. 452/37.

SECRET

C.C.S. 625/14

LEVELS OF SUPPLY OF ALL PETROLEUM PRODUCTS IN ALL THEATERS

References:

CCS 185th Meeting, Item 4
CCS 186th Meeting, Item 2
CCS 187th Meeting, Item 2
CCS 776/3, Paragraph 21

In C.C.S. 625/10 (ARGONAUT), dated 1 February 1945, the British Chiefs of Staff requested agreement of the Combined Chiefs of Staff to the minimum stock levels of supply proposed therein for Northwest Europe.

C.C.S. 625/11 (5 February) circulated a reply from the Combined Administrative Committee in response to a directive from the Combined Chiefs of Staff as agreed in their 185th Meeting.

In C.C.S. 625/12, dated 6 February, the United States Chiefs of Staff submitted certain comments on the proposals set forth in C.C.S. 625/10 (ARGONAUT).

C.C.S. 625/13 (7 February) circulated the report by a combined *ad hoc* committee appointed by the Combined Chiefs of Staff in their 186th Meeting.

The Combined Chiefs of Staff in their 187th Meeting amended and approved the enclosure to C.C.S. 625/13. The agreement for levels of supply of all petroleum products in all theaters as amended and approved was circulated as C.C.S. 625/14.

SECRET

C.C.S. 625/14 8 February 1945

COMBINED CHIEFS OF STAFF

LEVELS OF SUPPLY OF ALL PETROLEUM PRODUCTS IN ALL THEATERS

Note by the Secretaries

In their 187th Meeting, the Combined Chiefs of Staff amended the agreement set forth in the enclosure to C.C.S. 625/13. The agreement as amended and approved by the Combined Chiefs of Staff is enclosed herewith.

A. J. McFARLAND,
A. T. CORNWALL-JONES,
Combined Secretariat.

ENCLOSURE

AGREEMENT ON LEVELS OF SUPPLY OF ALL PETROLEUM PRODUCTS IN ALL THEATERS

1. The theater level should equal operating level plus emergency reserve level.

2. Each level shall be expressed in days of forward consumption. The rate of forward consumption used takes into account the size and degree of activity of the consuming forces as estimated by the theater commanders or other appropriate authorities.

3. The operating level provides the working stock required to be in the theater to provide for planned operations. It represents the number of days of supply to sustain the theater at the expected rate of consumption during the maximum interval which may exist between sustaining shipments. Experience has shown that all theaters (except ice-bound ports for which special levels must be established) can be assured of such a shipment at least every 30 days.

4. The emergency reserve level is intended to provide for unexpectedly high rates of consumption, destruction of stocks and handling facilities, and interruption of supply due to enemy action. It is based on the number of days or average number of days necessary to make emergency replacements from the principal port or ports of embarkation to the points of consumption in a theater of operation, and it includes loading time, voyage time, unloading time, and theater distribution time. Theater distribution time provides for the products which are necessarily absorbed and immobilized in the internal theater distribution system and takes account of variations in the different theaters.

It is considered that an emergency reserve level based on emergency replacement time in each theater is adequate to meet any contingency that might arise until special provision can be made for additional supplies.

5. The theater level of petroleum products shall include all bulk and packed stocks in the theater except those products which are (a) en route to the theater prior to discharge ashore, unless held as stock afloat, (b) issued

SECRET

to civilian garages, retailers and other small consumers, (c) issued to actual consuming units (aircraft, vehicles, ships, craft, and so forth) or issued to dumps forward of Army rear boundary in combat zone.

6. The following theater levels expressed in days of forward consumption have been agreed upon for the supply of all petroleum products for military services and essential civilian use:—

THEATER	Operation Level	Emergency Reserve Level	Theater Level	
Northwest Europe and U.K.*				
Admiralty				
Fuels	30	60	90	
War Office and European Theater of Operations, U.S. Army				
Motor Transport Fuels	30	30	60	
Air Ministry				
100 Octane	30	35	65	
Other Grades	30	35	65	
Others				
Motor Spirit	30	45	75	
Other White	30	60	90	
Gas/Diesel	30	60	90	
Fuel Oil	30	60	90	
Lubricants	30	150	180	
Central Mediterranean	30	40	70	
Middle East	30	30	60	) see para-
Persia and Iraq	30	30	60	) graph 6 *a*.
South & East & West Africa	30	30	60	)
Southeast Asia Command (Including India-Burma)	30	55	85	
China Theater	30	55	85	
Southwest Pacific	30	55	85	
South Pacific	30	45	75	
Central Pacific	30	50	80	
Alaska	30	30	60	) see para-
North America	30	25	55	) graph 6 *b*.
Latin America	30	30	60	

* Emergency level for this theater takes special cognizance of the complexity of the distribution systems.

a. In these theaters the theater level for aviation spirit will be 75 days instead of 60.

b. Within the Alaskan, North American, and other applicable theaters special levels over and above the theater level will be necessary for ice-bound areas.

c. It is agreed that the above theater levels except as noted for Northwest Europe and U.K. will not apply to stocks of lubricating oils and greases which are subject to special considerations, particularly in areas where blending or packing takes place. The stocks required consequently vary considerably between theaters but normally approximate to 180 days consumption needs.

7. As some theaters have insufficient tankage to accommodate stocks at theater level, consideration will be given to the holding of a proportion of the reserves for these theaters in other areas which have surplus storage capacity available and are suitably placed strategically for this purpose.

8. Priority for providing supplies and allocating tankers shall be accorded to the maintenance of the emergency reserve levels in all theaters with the balance of all theater levels to be accumulated as rapidly as practicable thereafter, each theater taking its proportionate share of any shortage in supplies and tankers.

After all theater levels have been attained, any surplus supplies should be stored, under the control of the owner or as otherwise agreed upon, in available tankage nearest to the source of supply or where it appears most desirable strategically.

Theater stocks in excess of the theater level, unless permitted by specific agreement of the Combined Chiefs of Staff, shall be reduced promptly to authorized levels by appropriate allocation of supplies and/or tankers.

9. If priorities among theaters become necessary they will be determined by the Combined Chiefs of Staff.

10. The Army-Navy Petroleum Board and appropriate British authorities will be the agencies of the Combined Chiefs of Staff primarily charged with the proposal to the Combined Chiefs of Staff of any required revision of the levels of supply of petroleum products in any or all theaters and the principles governing these levels.

SECRET

C.C.S. 660/3

ESTIMATE OF THE ENEMY SITUATION—EUROPE
(as of 23 January 1945)

Reference:

CCS 183d Meeting, Item 6

The Combined Chiefs of Staff took note of C.C.S. 660/3 in their 183d Meeting.

SECRET

C.C.S. 660/3   24 January 1945

COMBINED CHIEFS OF STAFF

ESTIMATE OF THE ENEMY SITUATION—EUROPE
(as of 23 January 1945)

Note by the Secretaries

The enclosed estimate of the enemy situation in Europe as of 23 January 1945, prepared by the Combined Intelligence Committee in accordance with paragraph 5 of C.C.S. 765/2,* is submitted for consideration.

                                         A. J. McFARLAND,
                                         A. T. CORNWALL-JONES,
                                         Combined Secretariat.

---

* Not published herein.

SECRET

ENCLOSURE

ESTIMATE OF THE ENEMY SITUATION—EUROPE
(as of 23 January 1945)

Report by the Combined Intelligence Committee

THE PROBLEM

1. To estimate the enemy situation in Europe.

DISCUSSION

2. See "Appendix."

CONCLUSIONS

3. Germany's fundamental situation is relatively weak and deteriorating in comparison with the basic military and economic resources of her enemies. However, by skillfully applying available resources in selected efforts, Germany's leaders can, in favorable circumstances, achieve a local and temporary superiority of immediately available strength.

4. The Germans intend to conduct an active defense on interior lines with a view to preventing a concerted attack upon the Reich, and to launch an all-out submarine assault against Allied shipping. By this strategy they hope to wear out their enemies before exhausting their own resources, to gain time for the development of anticipated dissensions among them, and so to gain ultimately an acceptable peace.

5. In Poland, Silesia, and East Prussia the Germans are now under powerful assault by the Red Army. To avert a fatal collapse of that front they must reinforce it with ground and air strength drawn from elsewhere. Withdrawals from the West would be dangerous in the face of strong Allied pressure, while

Enclosure

SECRET

withdrawals from Italy would be seriously hampered by continued Allied pressure there. It is evident, therefore, that Germany has most to fear from a full-scale, coordinated Allied assault on all fronts.

6. Although German resources are inadequate for a prolonged defense of the Reich against a determined, simultaneous assault on all fronts and in the air, the Germans can postpone the decision by fanatical refusal to accept defeat and skillful employment of such resources as they have. This factor and the lack of a firm basis for estimating the scale and timing of concerted Allied offensive efforts make any estimate of the probable time of German collapse highly speculative and probably misleading.

Enclosure

APPENDIX

DISCUSSION

1. *General Strategic Situation*. During the summer of 1944 the Germans, under concerted attack from the west, south, and east for the first time, were compelled to abandon the concept of *Festung Europa* and were driven back upon the Reich itself in such fashion as to put in question their ability to rally for a final stand at or near its frontiers. They succeeded, however, in stabilizing their fronts and even recovered sufficiently to seize a temporary initiative in the West.

This recovery was not the result of any change in Germany's fundamental situation, which is weak and deteriorating in comparison with the basic military and economic resources of her enemies. However, by skillfully applying available resources in selected efforts, Germany's leaders can, in favorable circumstances, achieve a local and temporary superiority of immediately available strength.

The radical reduction of her occupational commitments and lines of communication, the diminution in intensity of the pressure maintained against her as compared to that exerted during the summer, and the advantage of operating on interior lines have enabled the Germans to mobilize and concentrate their resources with the urgency of desperation. The bold and concentrated application of these resources in the Ardennes offensive, although achieving no decisive results, did relieve pressure on a vital area, and, in its spoiling effect, prevent a full-scale assault in the West in coordination with the Soviet offensive in the East.

The Germans intend to conduct an active defense on interior lines utilizing to the full the Westwall and other strong defensive positions as bases for operations designed to engage their enemies in detail with a view to preventing a concerted attack upon the Reich. They also intend to launch an all-out submarine assault against Allied shipping. By such strategy they hope to wear out their enemies before exhausting their own resources, to gain time for the development of anticipated dissensions among them, and so to gain ultimately an acceptable peace.

In Poland, Silesia, and East Prussia the Germans are now under powerful assault by the Red Army. To avert a fatal collapse of that front they must reinforce it with ground and air strength drawn from elsewhere. Withdrawals from the West would be dangerous in the face of strong Allied pressure, while withdrawals from Italy would be seriously hampered by continued Allied pressure there. It is evident, therefore, that Germany has most to fear full-scale, coordinated Allied assault on all fronts.

2. *Political and Psychological Factors.* One of the strongest elements in the German strategic situation continues to be the political and psychological forces which have united the majority of the German people behind the total war effort. This support derives from effective Nazi control of every aspect of German life, from the strong basic patriotism of the German people in defense of the Fatherland and from increased acceptance of the following ideas:

a. Unconditional surrender involves the destruction of the German nation. Only the Nazi regime has the power and determination to prevent this.

b. Continued resistance will permit the emergence of conflicts among the Allies and out of these conflicts Germany will obtain an acceptable peace.

German acceptance of *a.* above has been strengthened by the publicity given to reported Allied plans for post-war treatment of Germany. The effect of this upon the German soldier has been to convince him not only that the fate of Germany is at stake, but that he must resist or be enslaved.

The effectiveness of *b.* above has been strengthened by the following developments:

(1) Allied failure to end the war at early dates publicly announced by Allied officials.

(2) Inter-Allied political friction as evidenced in the Polish and Greek situations.

The German winter offensive did have the effect of stimulating German confidence in the Wehrmacht, but its failure to achieve decisive results and the opening of the Soviet offensives are undoubtedly undermining this confidence.

There is, however, little sign that the mass of the German people has the inclination, the energy, or the organization to break the Nazi grip and to take

SECRET

active steps to end the war. Since the failure of the attempted putsch of 20 July 1944, the likelihood of popular revolt has become increasingly remote. The military and conservative opposition represented in the putsch has been disorganized and discouraged by its aftermath, and at present collaboration between the Party and the Army appears to be effective, despite a certain measure of mutual distrust.

Underground opposition of German workers is not strong enough to constitute an effective political force prior to German collapse, and conciliatory measures toward foreign workers have somewhat lessened the potential threat from that group.

While antagonisms, susceptible to development by Allied psychological warfare, clearly exist within the Nazi state, none of these antagonisms is at present strong enough to endanger the national cohesion, or to elude the strict, efficient Nazi control apparatus.

3. *Economic Factors.* Possible expansion of specific items of German war production cannot reduce substantially the present marked Allied superiority in the production rates of almost all categories of military matériel. Territorial losses, bomb damage, and other factors will continue to cause a decline in the general level of German production.

However, materials in process, and stocks on hand, as well as further reduction of long-term uses of scarce materials, may cushion and postpone the military effects of Germany's economic deficiencies. Moreover, the existence of a straitened and inferior economic situation does not necessarily result in a corresponding inferiority in relative military strength at the front. Germany's matériel requirements are subject to wide fluctuations depending mainly upon the length of supply lines and the nature and extent of actual operations. Any statement of Germany's economic ability to meet her military "requirements" depends not so much upon comparison with Allied production as upon the actual rates of matériel expenditure which are imposed upon Germany. This latter factor is always problematical since it depends largely upon Allied operations and upon the skill of German leaders in resisting with a minimum expenditure of material.

In most categories of equipment recent wastage rates exceed current production levels. However, unless there is an Allied breakthrough with exploitation into a key industrial area, we believe there will be no general critical deterioration of Germany's economic ability to support her armed forces during

Appendix

the next six months, provided that the rate of wastage imposed upon Germany is not much greater than that of the last six months of 1944. Should the Red Army occupy Upper Silesia, Germany's position would be greatly weakened. Even if, however, the Germans succeed in retaining both Upper Silesia and the Ruhr, with over-all production declining and given the continuance of a rate of wastage at least equal to that of the last six months, the gap between production and wastage will progressively widen, with the result that in future the German Army, except in certain critical items which may even improve, will be less well equipped than it is today.

With these factors in mind, the German economic position in certain important categories may be summarized as follows:

a. Monthly *oil* production which reached 1,360,000 metric tons in April of 1944 was reduced to 310,000 tons in September and has now recovered to a rate of more than 400,000 tons, without prospect of further substantial increase. Only the most drastic reduction of military and civilian commitments, aided by economies resulting from the loss of large occupied areas, plus the most extreme conservation measures makes possible the reduction of consumption to about the present production level. Although the present oil position permits vigorous defensive warfare, including limited counter-offensives, it is equally true that the oil position reduces the effectiveness of the German armed forces especially in any situation requiring tactical mobility over a broad area. This is one of the major factors which limits German strategic offensive capabilities, and their ability to deal with a future Allied breakthrough. Germany's future oil position depends not only upon the rate of expenditure, but upon future bomb damage to German oil production and storage facilities and upon the extent to which the Germans can recuperate from damage. If they could disperse and protect their remaining oil facilities, the Germans might be able in the future to effect some reduction in damage from bombing. On the other hand, their ability to repair damage is progressively decreasing.

b. Raw materials shortages, notably in ferro-alloys, which will effect a reduction in the quality of some steels, will be felt over an ever-wider field of production, even though the military effects of such shortages can be partially postponed and minimized by planning production in terms of Germany's most pressing combat needs and at the expense of her longer range position.

Appendix

SECRET

c. Aircraft production has continued to increase in spite of bomb damage, which, however, has prevented a much greater planned increase. Because aircraft production has to a large extent been dispersed or placed underground, its future reduction by bombing attack will become progressively more difficult.

d. Tank production has increased from 450 a month in July, 1944, when air attacks on engine and gear works ceased, to possibly 550 a month now.

e. Production of most categories of *weapons* and *ammunition* will face growing difficulties. The effects of these difficulties on the fighting fronts will depend upon the rate of attrition incurred.

f. U-boat production is increasing.

The civilian supply position, although increasingly tight, is unlikely directly to cause military difficulties or to precipitate a civil revolt, but may cause some political difficulties and further reduce labor efficiency.

4. *Manpower.* Germany's lack of fully fit men aged 17 to 37 constitutes one of her critical weaknesses. Her position in regard to older and less fit manpower is not so severely strained. As a result of the heavy attrition suffered since 1941, the number of fully fit young men remaining in the entire German population is substantially less than that required to maintain the German armed forces according to their former standards, and a considerable proportion of them must be deferred for occupational reasons. This deficiency in fully fit young manpower has been met to some extent by the maintenance of elite units at standard strength and quality, and by the extensive use of foreigners and less fit Germans, not only in rear establishments, but in other combat units and in every possible individual role.

The heavy attrition suffered by the German Army during the summer of 1944 was substantially offset by a contraction of the area of German occupation which permitted the absorption of line-of-communications personnel into combatant units as replacements. Some further absorption of such personnel may occur as a result of further withdrawals but at the maximum would not be comparable to the gains of 1943-1944. By the same token, the possibilities of further recruitment or impressment of foreigners are now strictly limited. The German population itself has already been thoroughly combed over, except for German womanpower, which has not yet been fully exploited.

Appendix

SECRET

Thus, while the German Army can still find replacements among older and less fit Germans, and, directly or indirectly, by the impressment of foreigners, its opportunities in this regard are decreasing. In any case, it cannot fully replace in kind heavy losses of fully fit young Germans, and consequently its combat effectiveness must progressively decline in the face of heavy attrition.

5. *Ground Forces.* The estimated divisional composition of German ground strength as of mid-October and mid-January is set forth below:—

	October	January
Panzer-type	47	50
Field	127	121
Limited employment	85	113
Static	7	7
Totals	266	291

The indicated net gain of 25 divisions during the three-month interval resulted from the disbandment of 14 divisions, the formation of 6 new divisions, and the reconstitution of 33 divisions previously destroyed or at least badly mauled and out of action. The indications are that, as a general rule, the numerical strength of the existing divisions has been brought up approximately to the reduced tables of organization. Some 10 additional divisions are believed to be now in the process of formation or reconstitution.

The German Army is experiencing some stringencies in the provision of important items, such as tanks, field artillery, signal equipment, and particularly motor transport and fuel. The effect of these stringencies is to limit the German Army's freedom of action, but none of them is likely to have a decisive effect upon the strategic situation in the predictable future. Although the number of tanks and assault guns has declined, new types have shown increased effectiveness.

In such a situation as has now arisen, imposing heavy attrition of manpower, the Germans face a choice between replacement of casualties in active divisions and the formation of new or reconstituted divisions. In the predictable future it is probable that they will attempt to keep active and experienced divisions up to minimal effective strength, while forming and training new or reconstituted divisions so far as the tempo of the war may permit. The over-all effect would be a further decline in the actual strength of the Army, whether or not there were a decline in the number of divisions. The effective combat

Appendix

SECRET

strength of the German Army will decline to a greater extent than the numerical strength owing to the high proportion of permanent casualties among fit Germans of military age. It is probable, however, that so far as manpower is concerned, the Army can be maintained as an effective combat force for at least six months, provided that it does not meet with military disaster in the field.

6. *Air Forces.* The operational strength of the German Air Force is approximately the same as that of mid-1944, although some fluctuations have taken place in the intervening period. During that period, however, there has been a considerable increase in stored reserves. In composition, the German Air Force has been expanding the forces equipped with single-engine fighters, particularly at the expense of long-range bombers. In disposition, it has been assigning an increasing proportion of its fighter strength for operations in the West. Until the opening of the German counteroffensive on 16 December, the increase in the single-engine fighter force was used to strengthen the air defense of Germany against strategic bombing. After 16 December a large proportion of this force was transferred and disposed for cooperation with ground forces in the western battle area. However, in view of its numerical inferiority on the Eastern Front, the German Air Force has already transferred a substantial number of units from the Western Front to meet the new Soviet offensive.

During the last two months the German Air Force has altered its policy of conservation and has intermittently put up a considerable effort for short periods both in defense of Germany against strategic bombing and in cooperation with the ground forces. However, in face of Allied superiority, it has been unable to sustain a high scale of effort and it has only been able to put up these intermittent bursts of high activity by taking advantage of the restrictions of operations by bad weather which have enabled it to replace losses and improve serviceability.

From the long-term point of view, if there is a continuation of present production rates and only short intermittent periods of high activity, the German Air Force will continue to expand in numerical strength, which will be mainly in the single-engine fighter and fighter-bomber categories. There will also be an improvement in performance and fire-power. Furthermore an increasing proportion of its aircraft will be jet-propelled, which by virtue of their superior performance in comparison with conventional types may so increase the effectiveness of German fighter forces as to constitute a serious threat to Allied daylight air operations.

Appendix

SECRET

These developments, if not offset by other factors, would by the spring of 1945 increase the effectiveness of the German Air Force beyond that of the spring of 1944. We believe, however, that the over-all shortage of fuel, and the lack of pilots of a high degree of quality, training and experience will continue to impair the operational efficiency of the German Air Force and so prevent its effectiveness from surpassing that of the spring of 1944.

Hence, though the German Air Force will retain the capability of delivering damaging blows, particularly if surprise is achieved or targets are insufficiently defended, it will remain incapable of exercising more than a local and limited influence on the course of military operations.

7. *Naval Forces.* After the failure of U-boats to interrupt *OVERLORD* there has been, until recently, a comparative lull in the campaign. Activity in construction has continued and the highest priority has been given to the production by prefabricated methods of two new, improved types with high submerged speeds. The enemy has used the lull to work up his new boats, to refit old-type boats and incorporate structural improvements in them, and to give his commanders and crews experience during work-up patrols in operating close inshore and in the use of "schnorkel" and other new equipment.

The number of sinkings by submarines has recently been steadily increasing, probably as a result of:

a. Increased skill and confidence in the use of "schnorkel" and other new equipment;

b. The improvement in morale, due mainly to the ineffectiveness of our anti-submarine countermeasures; and

c. The wish to embarrass our supply lines during the recent German land offensive.

This increase in sinkings must be expected to continue, since the new technical developments have increased the U-boats' potential for offensive action and have considerably reduced the effectiveness of our present naval and air countermeasures, especially in shallow coastal waters.

Germany now possesses a growing fleet of new U-boats which, though in commission and fully worked up, have not yet been used operationally. It is not known why she has not already used these boats, since there is no information to suggest that any serious technical delays have occurred. There is evidence that she intends to start a major offensive with them not later than mid-March, and that she expects to obtain spectacular results.

Appendix

SECRET

In this new offensive the Germans may intend to operate their boats as follows:

    a. The new large type in packs with the object of annihilating Atlantic convoys. If pack tactics are not successful they will be redeployed in coastal waters.

    b. The small type in coastal waters off the east and southeast English coast and off Belgium.

    c. The old type boats to be so stationed as to cause the maximum dispersion of our anti-submarine forces.

The potential U-boat threat must be regarded as severe. It may lead to so large an increase in shipping losses as to prejudice the maintenance and build-up of our forces in Europe and to accentuate the existing shortage of shipping for other requirements.

The degree of success achieved in this new offensive will depend on:

    a. Our success in developing new technique in anti-submarine measures;

    b. The extent to which submarine construction may be disrupted by Allied action; and

    c. The morale of U-boat crews as influenced by the general war situation.

New technical developments in mines and torpedoes may, as in the past, also prove of material value to the enemy. Minelaying and the operations of one-man torpedoes, explosive motor boats, and such weapons, will probably continue, especially against our continental ports and their approaches.

All major surface units are in south Norway or the Baltic. Though these units may continue to play some part in delaying further deterioration of the situation in this area, it is most unlikely that they will be able to exert any appreciable influence elsewhere. German light surface forces in all other areas have been reduced to negligible strength.

    8. *Long-Range Weapons.* Attacks by air-launched and ground-launched flying bombs and by long-range rockets are likely to continue on a steadily increasing scale.

Appendix

SECRET

No radically improved types of these weapons are expected to be used for such attacks at any rate during the next few months.

It is possible that the Germans may increase the scale of long-range rocket and flying-bomb attacks against continental targets, particularly Antwerp, at the expense of the effort against the United Kingdom. In any event the continuation of long-range rocket attacks against the United Kingdom would depend on the retention by the Germans of the Hague area. The remote possibility exists that sporadic attacks might be launched against the eastern coast of the United States and Canada, and the Panama Canal.

9. *The Situation by Fronts.*

a. Norway. The Germans are gradually withdrawing from northern Norway. The indications are that, after a temporary stand at the Lyngsfjord line, they will withdraw to a line covering the Trondheim area and seek to hold there. Further withdrawal would jeopardize their U-boat campaign, as well as other strategic and economic interests.

After this withdrawal, and with appreciation that strong Allied operations against southern Norway would be unlikely, the Germans might undertake to hold the area from Trondheim southwards with six to eight divisions. Eight to six divisions in addition to those already withdrawn would thus become available for use elsewhere. However, judged by past experience, difficulties of sea transport would prevent their withdrawal complete with their heavy equipment at a faster rate than two to three a month. At best, therefore, Germany could evacuate some six additional fully equipped divisions from Norway before 1 April.

b. Western Front. Aided by fixed fortifications, favorable terrain, hastily assembled fresh forces, and Allied logistical difficulties, the Germans were able to check the Allied pursuit at or near their frontier and to stabilize the front. Although subsequently compelled to give ground in certain areas, they were able to maintain their front unbroken without employing strategic reserves being prepared for a countereffort. Although that effort, when made, failed to achieve decisive results, it did compel the temporary diversion of Allied forces from offensive operations in decisive areas and, in its spoiling effect, prevented full-scale Allied offensive operations in coordination with those of the Red Army in Poland.

This attack exemplifies the German doctrine regarding the function of such fortified zones as the Westwall. In contrast to the "Maginot complex," the Germans intend such a defensive system and its individual strong

Appendix

points to serve as firm bases for tactical counterattack within the system or for strategic counterefforts of an offensive-defensive character, such as the recent thrust into the Ardennes. Consequently, whenever the Germans are able to provide the requisite local reserve strength, the Allies should anticipate an active defense including, according to the circumstances, vigorous attacks in advance of the fixed defenses or strong counteraction to seal off and destroy any penetration. In present circumstances, however, the necessity to reinforce the East will probably result in such a reduction of German strength in the West as to limit Germany's capabilities on that front to a passive defense. The value of the Westwall in either case, together with the vital importance of preventing a closer Allied approach to the Ruhr, will cause the Germans to conduct their defense in the West generally west of the Rhine.

The Germans appreciate the logistical factor in Allied capabilities and the effects of their previous success in denying the use of continental ports. They also attach great importance to the effects of their long-range rockets. For these reasons they may be expected to maintain their hold on Holland and do all in their power to prevent the full use of the ports now in Allied hands, especially Antwerp. They will also do their utmost to deny to Allied shipping the approaches to continental ports.

c. Italy. Allied penetration of the "Gothic Line" did not result in the expulsion of the Germans from the Po Valley. Adroit exploitation of water barriers has enabled them to maintain a front from Lake Comacchio to the Apennines east of Bologna. The Germans are prepared to retire by stages to the Alps if the occasion requires it, but will hold Bologna as long as profitable in order to retain the military, economic, and political advantages of the occupation of northern Italy, to keep their communications through Istria to the Balkans, to continue to contain Allied forces, and to divert Allied shipping and supplies from other vital areas. Their present strong position would permit them, unless vigorously pressed, to release on short notice some three veteran divisions for use elsewhere. Should they retire, comparatively unmolested, to the line of the Adige, they could increase this number to a total of ten to eleven divisions; should they retire to the line of the Alps, the total could be increased to fourteen to sixteen divisions, if the Germans retire in Hungary and Yugoslavia to the Austrian Alps and Bratislava Gap.

d. Southeastern Front (Yugoslavia, Hungary, western Slovakia). The Germans, with some Hungarian support and with considerable reinforcement from the Eastern Front, have offered stubborn resistance to the Soviet advance across Hungary, but have been gradually driven westward. Despite strong efforts, they have been unable to relieve a large force surrounded in

Appendix

Budapest and now almost destroyed. Control of Budapest will materially strengthen Soviet communications. The Germans may attempt to stabilize for the winter on the general line Lake Balaton-Bakony Hills-Hron River. Should the Germans withdraw to the Bratislava Gap, however, they should be able to make a strong stand in prepared positions covering Vienna, with their flanks on the Slovakian mountains and the Austrian Alps. In these circumstances they should be able to transfer some divisions northward.

German forces from the southern Balkans are retreating generally northwestward through Yugoslavia under slight pressure, but subject to considerable Partisan interruption and harassment. Sarajevo will be held as long as necessary as an escape corridor, Vukovar as long as possible in order to block Soviet use of the Danube. An eventual retreat to the general line Fiume-Zagreb-Lake Balaton, or to the Alps, seems probable.

e. Eastern Front (Exclusive of the Southeastern Front). This front was relatively quiet until mid-January. The strength of the German defense based on the fortifications of East Prussia, the Narew, and the Vistula, their own logistical difficulties and to some extent the weather caused the Soviets to transfer their main effort to the Balkans, where they were able to effect easier conquests in an area of great strategic and political importance to Germany. This drive into Hungary caused some diversion of German strength from Poland, thus facilitating a resumption of the offensive there. Nevertheless the Germans, appreciating the decisive character and vulnerability of the Eastern Front north of the Carpathians, kept on that front some 40 percent of their total number of divisions, including a third of their panzer-type divisions and half of their field divisions. Even so, Soviet strength in the Polish and East Prussian sectors is preponderant in a ratio of approximately three to one.

The Narew-Vistula line has now collapsed under the impact of the present Soviet offensive and the Red Army is sweeping across western Poland. The vital industrial area of Upper Silesia is directly threatened. Except for the Eastwall, no strong barrier to the Soviet advance exists between the Vistula and the Oder. As it advances the Red Army must reckon with the necessity to neutralize the potential threat to its flanks. In addition as it approaches Germany it will be confronted with a railway system never adapted for Soviet rolling stock, will meet concrete defenses such as it has probably not encountered before, will enter a hostile country where it can expect no Partisan assistance, and will face the same fanaticism that has been experienced in the West.

The Germans' best hope of checking the Soviet advance would seem to lie in a vigorous counteroffensive undertaken after the Soviet drive had lost its momentum and when the Soviet forces were possibly overextended.

SECRET

There is some indication of a possible German concentration in northwest Poland and East Prussia for this purpose. Such a countereffort to be effective would have to be launched very soon.

In any event, the probable onset of adverse weather in March will presumably slow up operations on the Eastern Front. Although it is unlikely that the Red Army will have accomplished the final defeat of Germany by that time, it will probably have reached positions from which to launch a decisive effort in May or June.

9. *German Hopes and Prospects.* The Germans dread the consequences of unconditional surrender and hope for developments which will enable them to obtain an acceptable peace. They hope that such developments may arise in consequence of cumulative war weariness in one or more of the principal Allied Powers, of dissension among them, and of the impact on them of the employment of new weapons. This dread and these hopes, in conjunction with the continued possession of an unbroken military machine, constitute the basis for continued German resistance.

Although their resources are inadequate for a prolonged defense of the Reich against determined, simultaneous assault on all fronts and in the air, the Germans can postpone the decision by fanatical refusal to accept defeat and by skillful employment of such resources as they have. This factor and the lack of a firm basis for estimating the scale and timing of concerted Allied offensive efforts make any estimate of the probable time of German collapse highly speculative and probably misleading.

Appendix

TOP SECRET

       C.C.S. 746/8
       C.C.S. 746/10
       C.C.S. 746/11

OVER-ALL REVIEW OF CARGO AND TROOP SHIPPING POSITION FOR THE REMAINDER OF 1945

References:

CCS 185th Meeting, Item 3
CCS 187th Meeting, Item 3
CCS 776/3, Paragraph 19

In C.C.S. 746/8, dated 31 January 1945, the United States Chiefs of Staff recommended certain action with regard to the memorandum of agreement signed by Mr. Harry Hopkins and Mr. Richard Law concerning shipping of supplies to liberated countries during the first six months of 1945.

C.C.S. 746/10, dated 2 February, circulated a report submitted on their own initiative by the Combined Military Transportation Committee and the Combined Shipping Adjustment Board presenting the current dry cargo shipping position and certain recommendations to the Combined Chiefs of Staff which, if approved, would serve as a guide for action by the appropriate military and shipping authorities.

The Combined Chiefs of Staff in their 185th Meeting amended and approved the recommendation in C.C.S. 746/8; amended and approved C.C.S. 746/10. C.C.S. 746/8 and C.C.S. 746/10 are published herein as amended and approved.

In accordance with the approved recommendation, paragraph 6 *d.* of C.C.S. 746/10, the report from the Combined Military Transportation Committee and the Combined Shipping Adjustment Board setting forth the over-all review of cargo and troop shipping position for the remainder of 1945 was circulated as C.C.S. 746/11, dated 8 February 1945.

TOP SECRET

The Combined Chiefs of Staff in their 187th Meeting approved C.C.S. 746/11 subject to change of date in sub paragraph (d) of the recommendations, on page 62, from "30 April 1945" to "1 April 1945."

C.C.S. 746/11 is published herein as amended and approved.

TOP SECRET

C.C.S. 746/8   31 January 1945

COMBINED CHIEFS OF STAFF

SHIPPING AGREEMENT

Memorandum by the United States Chiefs of Staff

1. On 14 January 1945 Mr. Harry Hopkins and Mr. Richard Law signed a memorandum of agreement concerning shipping of supplies to liberated European countries during the first six months of 1945 (Enclosure "A").

2. On 14 January 1945 Mr. Law sent a note to Mr. Hopkins in which he gave his interpretation of paragraph 10 of the above agreement as not changing any current procedures and that the clearance called for in no sense gives the power of veto to military authorities on civilian shipping allocations (Enclosure "B").

3. The principal points of the agreement are:

    a. That the French import program and other import programs when received are endorsed for planning purposes, and the U.S. and U.K. agencies concerned should as necessary facilitate through the established procedures, procurement against these programs so that supplies will be readily available for shipment.

    b. That, subject to military necessity, 7 ships are allocated in January, 13 in February, and 13 in March.

    c. That U.S. and U.K. civilian and military authorities should consider what recommendations they can make to heads of governments to reduce the deficit either by downward adjustment programs or more effective use of shipping.

    d. That theater commanders, Allied governments, and combined boards, departments and agencies concerned are to be notified.

4. The United States Chiefs of Staff recommend that the agreement in Enclosure "A" and Enclosure "B" be referred to the Combined Military Transportation Committee for recommendations to the Combined Chiefs of Staff

TOP SECRET

for implementation of those parts of the agreement of primary interest to Combined Chiefs of Staff agencies and that the recommendations of the Combined Military Transportation Committee be coordinated with the Combined Administrative Committee and the Combined Civil Affairs Committee. Coordination should also be effected with the Combined Shipping Adjustment Board.

TOP SECRET

ENCLOSURE "A"

DEPARTMENT OF STATE

WASHINGTON

MEMORANDUM OF AGREEMENT

The following represents the agreed views of the respective United States and United Kingdom authorities concerning the shipment of supplies to liberated European countries during the first six months of 1945:

1. The Supreme Commander, Allied Expeditionary Force has signified his willingness to allocate to the French Provisional Government and to the Belgian Government certain port facilities and inland clearance for national government import programs separate from and additional to military programs.

2. A four-party committee consisting of representatives of the French Provisional Government, the United States and the United Kingdom Governments and Supreme Headquarters, Allied Expeditionary Force has reviewed and recommended an import program put forward by the French Provisional Government. It is expected that the import program of the Belgian Government will be recommended through a similar procedure in the near future.

3. The United Nations Relief and Rehabilitation Administration has submitted a program for Italy. The Supreme Allied Commander, Mediterranean has endorsed it provided that its implementation does not affect his ability to meet his operational and basic civil affairs requirements.

4. It is expected that in due course import programs will be put forward in a similar manner for other liberated European countries by their governments or by the United Nations Relief and Rehabilitation Administration on their behalf.

5. The French import program and the other import programs when received are endorsed for planning purposes and the United States and

Enclosure "A"

TOP SECRET

United Kingdom agencies concerned should as necessary facilitate, through the established procedures, procurement against these programs so that supplies will be readily available for shipment.

6. Subject to military necessity, ships are to be allocated against these programs for January, February and March loading from North America as follows:—

	JANUARY			FEBRUARY			MARCH		
	Total	MWT	WSA	Total	MWT	WSA	Total	MWT	WSA
France	6			10			10		
Belgium	1			2			2		
UNRRA (Italy)	-			1			1		
TOTAL	7			13			13		

7. There is attached a table showing for the period January through June 1945 the over-all shipping deficiency.* The deficit cannot be met by minor adjustments and calls for decision at the coming conference of heads of governments. In the meantime the responsible United States and United Kingdom civilian and military authorities should consider what recommendations they can make to the coming conference of the heads of governments to reduce the deficit either by downward adjustment of programs or more effective use of shipping.

8. Pending the final decision the allocations referred to in paragraph 6 are not to be reduced except in the face of military necessity and not without prior discussion with Mr. Harry Hopkins. The appropriate agencies should be notified accordingly.

9. The theater commander, the Allied governments, the combined boards and the departments and agencies concerned of the United States and United Kingdom Governments are to be notified of the action agreed under paragraphs 5 and 6.

10. Nothing herein contained shall be deemed to alter any present procedures whereby the availability of shipping tonnage shall be determined

---

* Not part of this paper. Identical with table in paragraph 7, page 2, C.C.S. 746/6 (published for convenience on page 53).

Enclosure "A"

TOP SECRET

by the appropriate shipping authorities after clearance with the appropriate Chiefs of Staff. It is also understood that the determination of port and inland clearance capacity shall be certified by the theater commander.

/Initialed/ H.H. by D.A.

R.L.

H.H. (Mr. Harry Hopkins)
D.A. (Mr. Dean Acheson)
R.L. (Mr. Richard Law)

Enclosure "A"

TOP SECRET

ENCLOSURE "B"

14th January 1945

Dear Mr. Hopkins,

Memorandum of Agreement

In initialling this agreement on behalf of His Majesty's Government in the United Kingdom, I must refer to the interpretation of clause 10 which I should have liked to see clarified if time had permitted and if all those concerned had been accessible.

I interpret this clause as a "no prejudice" clause leaving present procedures for the determining of shipping availability as they stand and making it clear that this document in no way compromises any position or claim of anyone as to what those procedures are or should be. I do not interpret it, and I feel sure that it cannot reasonably be interpreted, as introducing any change whatever in current procedures. As you know, my understanding is that these procedures do not provide for "clearance" in the sense of a veto by the military authorities on civilian shipping allocations, but do in practice result in the fullest exchange of information and consultation between the shipping authorities and the Chiefs of Staff.

Yours sincerely,
/s/ Richard Law

Mr. Harry Hopkins,
The White House,
Washington, D.C.

Enclosure "B"

OVER-ALL SHIPPING DEFICIENCY

The combined deficiencies in terms of sailings disclosed by reports*
of the U.S. and British dry cargo shipping positions respectively are:—

	Feb.	March	April	May	June
Atlantic					
British Ministry of War Transport (BMWT)	30	45	50	50	50
War Shipping Administration (WSA)	43	36	40	49	37
Combined	73	81	90	99	87
Pacific					
War Shipping Administration	35	51	45	72	56
Total	108	132	135	171	143

---

* Appendices "A" and "B" to Enclosure "A," C.M.T. 66/3.

TOP SECRET

C.C.S. 746/10   2 February 1945

COMBINED CHIEFS OF STAFF

OVER-ALL REVIEW OF CARGO SHIPPING

Reference:

CCS 746 Series

Note by the Secretaries

    The Combined Military Transportation Committee and the Combined Shipping Adjustment Board on their own initiative submit the enclosed report as a supplement to C.C.S. 746/6* to present the current dry cargo shipping position and to make recommendations to the Combined Chiefs of Staff which will serve as a guide for action by the appropriate military and shipping authorities.

                                     A. J. McFARLAND,

                                     A. T. CORNWALL-JONES,

                                     Combined Secretariat.

---

* Not published herein.

TOP SECRET

ENCLOSURE

OVER-ALL REVIEW OF CARGO SHIPPING

Report by the Combined Military Transportation Committee and the Combined Shipping Adjustment Board

THE PROBLEM

1. To submit changes in the shipping position as given in C.C.S. 746/6, to bring it up to date and to make recommendations for action to be taken by the Combined Chiefs of Staff.

FACTS BEARING ON THE PROBLEM

2. A consideration of the deficits resulting from a restudy of cargo shipping as presented in the following table shows that the shipping position is tight and that deficits approach unmanageable proportions, particularly in the Pacific, to which theater certain diversions from the Atlantic will probably have to be made:—

	March	April	May	June
For U.S.				
Atlantic deficits	31	24	18	35
Pacific deficits	51	38	45	34
For British				
Atlantic deficits	35	35	35	35

3. Military requirements have been severely cut in keeping with recent instructions to theater commanders by the United States Chiefs of Staff and the Combined Chiefs of Staff and provide no factor of safety or provision for new, expanded, or advanced operations.

4. In the event that these deficits materialize some civilian programs will have to contribute by cuts towards the management of present deficits. Increased demands, if accepted, can only make deficits unmanageable.

CONCLUSIONS

5. It is concluded that:

a. In the consideration of basic strategic undertakings supplies to liberated areas should be considered only insofar as they contribute to the over-all war-making capacity of the United Nations.

b. In view of presently foreseen deficits, lack of reserves for stepping up military operations and increasing civilian demands, there is no alternative but to exercise rigid control over all programs and particularly those devoted to rehabilitation rather than to the war effort.

RECOMMENDATIONS

6. It is recommended that:

a. The appropriate Chiefs of Staff require rigid compliance of theater commanders with their orders relative to the control of shipping.

b. The appropriate Chiefs of Staff direct their military transportation committees in conjunction with appropriate shipping authorities to adjust deficits in accord with the following principles:

"In the event of a deficit in shipping resources, first priority should be given to the basic undertakings in support of over-all strategic concepts as agreed in *ARGONAUT*.

"So long as these first priority requirements are not adequately covered, shipping for other requirements will not be allocated without prior consultation with the appropriate Chiefs of Staff."

c. The Combined Chiefs of Staff give careful consideration to the shipping implications of proposed undertakings before their inclusion in the approved basic undertakings in support of the over-all strategic concepts recommended for adoption at *ARGONAUT*.

d. The Combined Chiefs of Staff take note that the over-all shipping position will be reviewed again in determining the shipping position resulting from decisions made at the *ARGONAUT* Conference.

TOP SECRET

C.C.S. 746/11 8 February 1945

COMBINED CHIEFS OF STAFF

OVER-ALL REVIEW OF CARGO AND TROOP SHIPPING
POSITION FOR THE REMAINDER OF 1945

Note by the Secretaries

Pursuant to paragraph 6 *d.* of C.C.S. 746/10, the Combined Military Transportation Committee and the Combined Shipping Adjustment Board have prepared the enclosed report for the consideration of the Combined Chiefs of Staff.

A. J. McFARLAND,
A. T. CORNWALL-JONES,
Combined Secretariat.

TOP SECRET

INDEX to C.C.S. 746/11

OVER-ALL REVIEW OF CARGO AND TROOP SHIPPING POSITION FOR THE REMAINDER OF 1945

		PAGE
Enclosure—*Report by the Combined Military Transportation Committee and the Combined Shipping Adjustment Board*		60
Appendix "A"	Statement by Lord Leathers and Admiral Land of the Combined Shipping Adjustment Board on the Dry Cargo Shipping Position Prior to V-E Day	64
Appendix "B"	Combined Review of Over-all Cargo and Troop Shipping Position for the Remainder of 1945	65
Annex "A"	Combined Shipping Review of Dry Cargo and Troop Shipping Position from March through June, 1945	66
Tab "A"	British Controlled Dry Cargo Shipping Position (March-June, 1945)	67
Tab "B"	U.S. Dry Cargo Shipping Position (March-June, 1945)	74
Exhibit "A"	U.S. Dry Cargo Shipping Position Before V-E Day—Atlantic and Gulf	75
Tab "C"	British Controlled Troop Shipping Position (March-June, 1945)	79
Exhibit "A"	British Operational Commitments	81
Exhibit "B"	Section A — Other British Trooping Commitments	82
	Section B — Miscellaneous Commitments Other Than Trooping to be Carried Out in British Shipping	83

TOP SECRET

		PAGE
Exhibit "C"	British Assistance to Movement of U.S. Forces	84
Tab "D"	U.S. Troop Shipping Position (March-June, 1945)	85
Annex "B"	Provisional Forecast of Combined Dry Cargo and Troop Shipping Position After V-E Day on 1 July 1945	86
Tab "A"	British Dry Cargo Shipping Position (After V-E Day)	87
Tab "B"	U.S. Dry Cargo Shipping Position (After V-E Day)	89
Exhibit "A"	U.S. Military Dry Cargo Requirements After V-E Day of 1 July 1945	91
Tab "C"	British Controlled Troop Shipping Position (After V-E Day)	92
Exhibit "A"	Tentative British Military Requirements for Troopships in Second Half of 1945	93
Tab "D"	U.S. Troop Shipping Position (After V-E Day)	95
Exhibit "A"	U.S. Troop Shipping Position (After V-E Day)	97
Exhibit "B"	U.S. Army Overseas Strengths After V-E Day Required by Assumed Redeployment Plan	99

TOP SECRET

ENCLOSURE

OVER-ALL REVIEW OF CARGO AND TROOP SHIPPING
POSITION FOR THE REMAINDER OF 1945

*Report by the Combined Military Transportation Committee
and the Combined Shipping Adjustment Board*

THE PROBLEM

1. To review the over-all cargo and troop shipping position for the remainder of 1945 under the assumption of defeat of Germany 1 July 1945.

FACTS BEARING ON THE PROBLEM

2. A statement by Lord Leathers and Admiral Land of the Combined Shipping Adjustment Board on the dry cargo shipping position prior to V-E Day* is attached as Appendix "A."

3. This review has been prepared in two parts (see Appendix "B"). The first part (Annex "A" to Appendix "B") summarizes the approved scheme of allocations, U.S. and British, to operate during the months March through June, 1945. The second part (Annex "B" to Appendix "B") is a planning study of some of the problems which will arise on V-E Day and which call for urgent policy decisions in order to ensure that essential preliminary action is taken with the least possible delay.

CONCLUSIONS

4. It is concluded that:

a. With respect to the position up to the defeat of Germany assumed at 1 July 1945:—

---

* Victory Day (Europe).

(1) This review of shipping covering both dry cargo and troop transport shows the following deficits:—

	March	April	May	June
	Dry Cargo (in sailings)			
For U.S.				
Atlantic	-22	-18	-12	-31
Pacific	-44	-38	-45	-34
For British				
Atlantic	-35	-35	-35	-35

	Troop Shipping (in trooplift)
For U.S.	No deficiency
For British	No deficiency

(2) As indicated in C.C.S. 746/10 the cargo shipping position is tight and deficits approach unmanageable proportions until V-E Day. The recommendations given in C.C.S. 746/10 apply and have been approved by the Combined Chiefs of Staff.

b. With respect to the position after the defeat of Germany:—

(1) The indications are that cargo shipping will be easier for the first quarter following V-E Day and will become tight again during the second quarter thereafter. In view of that second, more stringent, quarterly period vigilance will be necessary to ensure meeting military requirements.

(2) It is in the troop shipping position after V-E Day, shown in the following table, that the real problems arise:—

	Troop Shipping Position (in trooplift)	
	3rd Qtr.	4th Qtr.
For U.S.:		
With no British assistance	–88,500	–148,200
If British assistance of 70,000 trans-Atlantic lift monthly is assumed	No deficit	– 59,700
For British	– 3,400	– 60,200

Enclosure

The problem of greatest moment is the use of the combined troop transport pool in the redeployment of our forces to the Pacific and to Malaysia. While sharp definition is not given by figures because of lack of firm redeployment plans, particularly on the British side, the conflicts of interest that will arise are presently apparent. The U.S. position here given, even assuming British monthly assistance of 70,000 trans-Atlantic trooplift shows deficits, as shown in the table above, in meeting the redeployment program as presently planned. On the other hand, present British estimates show that the whole of the British trooping lift will be required for the deployment of British forces for the continuance of the war against Japan concurrently with the inescapable commitments of rotational movement and demobilization of forces already deployed. The problem will become further aggravated by the great pressures that will be exerted to repatriate nationals, both troops and civilians, at the fastest rate possible. Allocations of trooplift cannot be properly and firmly made for redeployment until the operations, the priorities thereof, and the redeployment therefor, are decided on a combined basis.

RECOMMENDATIONS

4. It is therefore recommended that:

   a. With respect to the position prior to the defeat of Germany:
   Action approved in C.C.S. 746/10 be taken.

   b. With respect to the position after the defeat of Germany:

   (1) The Combined Chiefs of Staff direct as a matter of priority:

   (a) The preparation of a combined redeployment plan.

   (b) The fixing of priorities for continuance of the war against Japan.

   (c) The agency or agencies given the task stated in *b.* (1) (a) above to confer with the Combined Military Transportation Committee and the appropriate shipping authorities as to shipping possibilities.

   (d) The combined report of these agencies with accompanying shipping program be submitted to the Combined Chiefs of Staff not later than 1 April 1945. This report will include also the formulation of a shipping program for continuing the war against Germany beyond 1 July 1945 should the occasion require.

Enclosure

TOP SECRET

(2) The combined shipping authorities convert dry cargo shipping after V-E Day on a combined basis to augment personnel lift as may be practicable.

Enclosure

TOP SECRET

APPENDIX "A"

STATEMENT BY LORD LEATHERS AND ADMIRAL LAND OF THE COMBINED SHIPPING ADJUSTMENT BOARD ON THE DRY CARGO SHIPPING POSITION PRIOR TO V-E DAY

The combined dry cargo shipping deficiencies for the remainder of the first half-year are shown in paragraph 4 *a.* (1) of the Enclosure. They have been reduced well below the levels shown in the recent Washington Over-all Review of Cargo Shipping (C.M.T. 66/3, 12 January 1945*). Nevertheless, as indicated in C.C.S. 746/10 the cargo shipping position will be tight and deficits will approach unmanageable proportions until V-E Day. Reliance has been placed upon a substantial relief to the strained shipping situation through economies in the use of tonnage as a result of action by the Combined Chiefs of Staff (C.C.S. 745/1*). On the basis of Combined Chiefs of Staff decision (C.C.S. 184th Meeting, Item 6) loss rates approved in C.C.S. 547/4* have been used and no allowance has been made for the threatened increase of losses through U-boat attacks, although current sinkings are not fully covered by the present loss rate.

The actual deficiencies will be dealt with month by month in accordance with the recommendations given in C.C.S. 746/10.

LEATHERS   E. S. LAND

---

* Not published herein.

TOP SECRET

APPENDIX "B"

COMBINED REVIEW OF OVER-ALL CARGO AND
TROOP SHIPPING POSITION FOR THE REMAINDER OF 1945

TOP SECRET

ANNEX "A" TO APPENDIX "B"

COMBINED SHIPPING REVIEW OF DRY CARGO AND TROOP SHIPPING POSITION FROM MARCH THROUGH JUNE, 1945

TOP SECRET

TAB "A" TO ANNEX "A" TO APPENDIX "B"

BRITISH CONTROLLED DRY CARGO SHIPPING POSITION
(MARCH-JUNE 1945)

1. British military sailings required to all existing theatres of war during March-June 1945, on the basis of known plans and requirements, and including military civil affairs requirements to purely British zones, are as follows:—

FROM	March		April		May		June	
	U.K.	N.A.	U.K.	N.A.	U.K.	N.A.	U.K.	N.A.
India	25	32	28	40	30	40	30	40
Persian Gulf	2	1	2	2	2	1	2	2
Mediterranean—								
C.M.F.	20	16	20	15	18	14	16	14
Malta	1	1	1	1	1	1	1	1
M.E. Maintenance	7	9	6	9	6	9	6	8
M.E. Collier	1	-	1	-	1	-	1	-
Gibraltar	1	-	1	-	1	-	1	-
Total Mediterranean	30	26	29	25	27	24	25	23
Total Mediterranean and Indian Ocean	57	59	59	67	59	65	57	65
Internal Mediterranean Services (Combined requirement, of which the British share is one half) *	120		85		70		60	
Australia	2	-	2	-	2	-	2	-
Russian Aid	4	-	4	-	4	-	4	-
OVERLORD—								
B.L.A. ex N.A.								
Maintenance	-	8	-	8	-	12	-	12
Civil Affairs	-	16	-	12	-	12	-	12
Total	-	24	-	20	-	24	-	24

* Excluding coasters—see paragraph 2 (b).

Tab "A" to Annex "A"
to Appendix "B"

TOP SECRET

N.W. Europe—ex U.K.	40 M.T. ships in service (combined requirement), 24 British and 16 United States.
	50 store ships in service on British account in March and April.
	60 store ships in service on British account in May and June.
	500,000 deadweight tons of coastal shipping allocated as follows:—
	170,000 British stores lift.
	155,000 United States stores lift.
	175,000 Combined coal programme.

From March onwards the coaster allocation for the combined coal programme is likely to increase to 250,000 deadweight tons at the expense of both the British and United States general cargo allocations. Provision has therefore been included to cover this portion of the coaster cargo lift in ocean-going vessels.

2. The statement of the estimated British-controlled dry-cargo ocean-going shipping position during the first six months of 1945 set out in paragraphs 3 and 4 below should be read in conjunction with the following notes:—

(a) *The Fleet Train.* For the supply and maintenance of the British Fleet in the Pacific, British merchant shipping, existing or building, has been allocated or will have been allocated by the end of June 1945 as follows:

	Deadweight tons
(1) Allocated to the Fleet Train while under construction (White Ensign)	330,000
(2) Allocated to the Fleet Train while under construction (Red Ensign)	160,000
(3) Transferred to the Fleet Train from other naval services	225,000
(4) Transferred to the Fleet Train from other employment	120,000
	835,000

Tab "A" to Annex "A"
to Appendix "B"

TOP SECRET

Items (2), (3) and (4) above are allowed for at Serial (5) (b) of the statement in paragraph 4; the tonnage for item (1) has been excluded both from the inventory and from the statement of requirements as it is being transferred direct to the Royal Navy for service under the White Ensign.

The Admiralty have notified further requirements for the Fleet Train which would involve the provision of some 200,000 deadweight tons of additional shipping but these have so far not been agreed, and no provision has therefore been made for them in the statement in paragraph 4.

(b) *The Mediterranean coastal tonnage* combined requirement, assessed at about 350,000 deadweight tons, will continue to be met from British resources. Serial (6) of the statement in paragraph 4 includes 250,000 deadweight tons of these coasters, the remainder being ships of under 1,600 gross registered tonnage (G.R.T.).

(c) *The Northwest Europe coastal tonnage* requirement for British Army Stores, United States Army Stores and coal (combined commitment) will be provided as shown in paragraph 1.

The whole of this requirement (one half of which is included at Serial (7) of the statement in paragraph 4, the other half consisting of shipping of under 1,600 G.R.T.) will be met from British coaster resources.

(d) *The United Kingdom import programme* has been taken as 6.0 million long tons in the first quarter of 1945 and 7.2 million long tons in the second quarter.

(e) *Supplies to liberated areas.* Provision has been made in the estimate for British-controlled shipping sufficient to carry the amounts set out below. These represent the agreed British share of desired import programmes submitted to the Shipping Authorities, phased on the advice of the Combined Staff Planners and screened for limitations likely to be imposed by reception capacity, or by supply or financial considerations, and after making allowance for cargoes carried in tonnage not under W.S.A. or B.M.W.T. control or as flatting in ships allocated for military cargoes.

	First quarter of 1945	*Second quarter of 1945*
	(million long tons)	
Civil Affairs	0.6	0.7
National Government	0.4	0.75

Tab "A" to Annex "A"
to Appendix "B"

TOP SECRET

The estimated shipping cost set out at Serial (10) of the statement in paragraph 4 excludes provision for:—

(1) Supplies within the Mediterranean (which are carried in the tonnage referred to in paragraph 2 (b)).

(2) Civil Affairs supplies from the United Kingdom to Northwest Europe (which are carried in the tonnage referred to in paragraph 2 (c)).

(f) *The termination of the war in Europe* has been assumed as July 1, 1945.

(g) *Future shipping losses* have been estimated at the rates previously approved for planning purposes, and now reaffirmed, by the Combined Chiefs of Staff.

3. Total shipping available (ships of 1,600 G.R.T. and over) is estimated to be as follows:—

Date	Estimated losses during preceding quarter-year	Estimated new construction during preceding quarter-year	Estimated inventory at date
	(million deadweight tons)		
31st December, 1944	...	...	22.09
31st March, 1945	0.16	0.36	22.29
30th June, 1945	0.12	0.45	22.62

Average for the first quarter of 1945: 22.20

Average for the second quarter of 1945: 22.45

Tab "A" to Annex "A"
to Appendix "B"

TOP SECRET

4. The estimated requirements against this shipping are as follows:—

	First quarter of 1945		Second quarter of 1945	
Serial	(million deadweight tons)			
(1) Estimated tonnage available	22.20		22.45	
(2) Deduct average allowance for tonnage awaiting or undergoing repair	2.30		2.30	
Net amount of tonnage available	19.90		20.15	
(3) Tonnage for United Kingdom coastal services	0.60		0.60	
(4) Tonnage engaged permanently abroad in maintenance of the war-making capacity of areas of British responsibility (see also Serial (11))	2.20		2.20	
(5) Non-importing Naval and Military tonnage:—				
(a) Naval Commissioned vessels	0.50		0.50	
(b) Vessels for the Fleet Train (see para. 2 (a))	0.40		0.45	
(c) Other Naval, Military and R.A.F. Auxiliaries	0.25		0.25	
(d) Troopships	1.20		1.20	
(e) Vessels permanently in the Indian Ocean area carrying military cargoes	0.25	5.40	0.25	5.45
Tonnage available for voyage-by-voyage allocation		14.50		14.70

(*Table Continued on Following Page*)

Tab "A" to Annex "A"
to Appendix "B"

TOP SECRET

(Continued)

	First quarter of 1945	Second quarter of 1945
(6) Tonnage for Mediterranean internal shipments (including coasters)	0.80	0.55
(7) Tonnage for shipments from the United Kingdom to N.W. Europe (including coasters)	1.00	1.05
(8) Tonnage for military maintenance from the United Kingdom and N. America to the Indian Ocean area and the Mediterranean, from the United Kingdom to N. Russia and from N. America to N.W. Europe	5.00	5.30
(9) Tonnage for United Kingdom imports (after allowing for imports brought in tonnage at Serial (8)) (see para. 2 (d))	6.95	7.35
(10) Tonnage for carrying supplies to liberated areas other than locally (see para. 2 (e)):—		
(a) Civil Affairs	0.60	0.75
(b) National Government	0.25	0.65
(11) Tonnage engaged temporarily abroad in maintenance of the war-making capacity of areas of British responsibility (see also Serial (4))	1.90	1.85
Total tonnage required for allocation	16.50	17.50
(12) *Deficiency*	2.00	2.80

Tab "A" to Annex "A"
to Appendix "B"

TOP SECRET

5. In the W.S.A. shipping statement (Tab "B" to Annex "A") provision is made for the following sailings from North America:—

		March	April	May	June
(a) to the Indian Ocean area)	Eastern				
(b) to the Mediterarnean)	customaries	24	24	24	24
(c) to South and East Africa and the Anzac area)))	Southern customaries	9	8	9	8
(d) on the North Atlantic*		26	36	38	38

6. These sailings are insufficient to eliminate the whole of the deficiencies shown at Serial (12) of paragraph 4, and there remains an apparent deficit in the British-controlled shipping situation equivalent to the following North Atlantic sailings*:—

March	April	May	June
35	35	35	35

---

* The use of North Atlantic sailings as a convenient yardstick does not imply that their number is a measure of a deficiency arising exclusively from programmes on that route. They, and all the other sailings mentioned, are associated jointly with the British deficiency as a whole, which it is impracticable to analyze according to cause.

Tab "A" to Annex "A"
to Appendix "B"

TOP SECRET

TAB "B" TO ANNEX "A" TO APPENDIX "B"

U.S. DRY CARGO SHIPPING POSITION
(March-June, 1945)

1. The estimated United States dry cargo shipping is given through June of 1945 in Exhibit "A" on the assumption that hostilities will be terminated in Europe July 1st. In the event of the termination of hostilities at any earlier date, the position set forth would apply until that date.

2. United States military requirements, as stated in Exhibit "A," include provision for maintenance of all deployed forces and for all presently planned operations and have been adjusted by the United States Army and Navy as far as possible, so as to be within the limits of the availability of cargo and of estimated reception capacity in all theaters. Other requirements listed include regular W.S.A. allocations to British services, obligations under the Russian Protocol, and the programs for liberated areas accepted for planning purposes. The latter have been modified downward from the figures included in C.M.T. 66/3 as a result of a re-examination by the appropriate civilian agencies of the United States and British Governments.

3. Allowance has been made in estimating the availability of shipping for authorized retentions in all theaters. It has been assumed that any presently existing shipping congestion will be immediately cleared and that vessels are turned around promptly and used in accordance with directions issued by the Joint Chiefs of Staff to theater commanders.

Tab "B" to Annex "A"
to Appendix "B"

TOP SECRET

EXHIBIT "A" TO TAB "B" TO ANNEX "A" TO APPENDIX "B"

U.S. DRY CARGO SHIPPING POSITION BEFORE V-E DAY

ATLANTIC AND GULF

	1945			
	March	*April*	*May*	*June*
1. U.S. ARMY				
ETO				
U.K. Military	30	30	30	30
Continent — Military	185	185	185	185
Civil Affairs	1	1	1	1
Sub-Total	186	186	186	186
S. France — U.S. & French Military	65	65	67	65
Civil Affairs	6	7	6	6
Sub-Total	71	72	73	71
TOTAL—ETO	287	288	289	287
ETO & Azores				
Military	47	45	45	45
Civil Affairs	43	42	42	42
TOTAL	90	87	87	87
Persian Gulf	1	1	1	1
India-Burma & China	1	1	1	1
Pacific Areas incl. SWPA	20	20	20	20
2. U.S. NAVY				
Pacific Areas	34	34	34	34
Sub-Total Military	433	431	432	430

(Table Continued on Following Page)

Exhibit "A" to Tab "B" to
Annex "A" to Appendix "B"

TOP SECRET

(Continued)

	1945			
	March	April	May	June
3. WAR-MAKING CAPACITY OF WESTERN HEMISPHERE	12	20	20	20
4. BRITISH PROGRAMS				
North Atlantic Sailings(2)	26	36	38	38
Other British Programs				
Military(1)	24	24	24	24
Civilian	6	5	6	5
TOTAL BRITISH LEND-LEASE	56	65	68	67
5. RUSSIAN LEND-LEASE(3)	38	36	28	28
6. DESIRED NATIONAL GOVT. IMPORT PROGRAMS FOR LIBERATED AREAS	28	38	41	44
Sub-Total Lend-Lease and Civilian	134	159	157	159
7. *TOTAL REQUIREMENTS*	567	590	589	589
8. *TOTAL AVAILABLE*	545	572	577	558
9. *BALANCE*	−22	−18	−12	−31

(1) Includes 1 India-China Defense sailing each month.

(2) Sailings for Liberated Areas included in sailings entered for North Atlantic sailings.

(3) Does not provide for 275,000 short tons per month now under consideration for trans-Atlantic delivery of Protocol cargo.

Exhibit "A" to Tab "B" to
Annex "A" to Appendix "B"

TOP SECRET

EXHIBIT "A" TO TAB "B" TO ANNEX "A" TO APPENDIX "B" (Continued)

U.S. DRY CARGO SHIPPING POSITION BEFORE V-E DAY

PACIFIC

	1945			
	March	*April*	*May*	*June*
1. U.S. ARMY				
Pacific Ocean Areas				
CPBC	21	24	26	18
SPBC	10	10	10	10
Southwest Pacific Area	50	55	60	65
India-Burma and China	23	24	22	21
2. U.S. NAVY				
Pacific Ocean Areas	129	132	151	154
Southwest Pacific Area	32	20	20	20
3. RUSSIAN	8	7	0	0
4. BRITISH EMPIRE PROGRAM	3	3	3	3
5. NON-MILITARY	9	9	9	9
6. *TOTAL REQUIREMENTS*	285	284	301	300
7. *TOTAL AVAILABLE*	241	246	256	266
8. *BALANCE*	−44	−38	−45	−34

Exhibit "A" to Tab "B" to
Annex "A" to Appendix "B"

TOP SECRET

EXHIBIT "A" TO TAB "B" TO ANNEX "A" TO APPENDIX "B" (Continued)

RETENTIONS OF U.S. DRY CARGO SHIPS ALLOWED FOR

(All retentions are as of first day of month)

	1945			
	March	*April*	*May*	*June*
UNITED KINGDOM				
WSA M.T.	16	16	16	16
WSA Stores	12	12	12	12
WSA Other	0	0	0	0
Total Ocean	28	28	28	28
WSA Coasters (DWT)	70,000	70,000	70,000	70,000
MEDITERRANEAN				
Inside U.S. Sailings	(60)	(43)	(35)	(30)
WSA Retentions required for above sailings	40	29	24	20
SOUTH PACIFIC	8	8	8	8
SOUTHWEST PACIFIC	135	122	120	120
CENTRAL PACIFIC	30	36	45	48

Exhibit "A" to Tab "B" to
Annex "A" to Appendix "B"

TOP SECRET

TAB "C" TO ANNEX "A" TO APPENDIX "B"

BRITISH CONTROLLED TROOP SHIPPING POSITION

(March-June, 1945)

1. In our consideration of the British personnel shipping position the following assumptions have been made:—

(a) That British personnel shipping commitments for operational requirements will be as shown in Exhibit "A."

(b) That British personnel shipping will be required to carry out troop movements (other than operational) and miscellaneous movements as detailed in Exhibit "B," Sections A and B, respectively.

(c) That British personnel shipping of the "Indian Ocean" type will be capable of meeting all local requirements (both normal trooping and operational commitments) in the Indian Ocean.

(d) That the frequency of the convoy cycle for normal trooping between UK/ITALY/MIDDLE EAST/INDIA, will be maintained at 20 days, as at present, and that no developments occur which would alter the conditions and areas in which fast ships are at present allowed to sail free of escort.

(e) That the Chiefs of Staff proposal to develop an overland route for trooping via France (*MEDLOC*) will not result in any material benefits to long sea voyage troop movements before 1 July 1945.

(f) That internal personnel movements in the Mediterranean (other than operational) can be met by allocation of a trooplift of 15,000 during the period under consideration.

(g) That any losses to the troopship fleet, whether by enemy action, marine risk or transfer to other service (e.g., hospital ships) cannot be made good by new construction or conversion prior to 1 July 1945. The most serious effect on British estimates would result from any such loss in the unescorted class.

(h) That the normal capacity of troopships proceeding from the United Kingdom to India will be reduced by at least 10% when east of Suez, in the interests of the health and morale of the troops, and the capacity of ships proceeding to the Antipodes (which have in the past been employed on the short Atlantic trip) will have to be reduced by some 20%.

Tab "C" to Annex "A"
to Appendix "B"

TOP SECRET

2. On the above assumptions, it is estimated that existing British personnel shipping will be sufficient to provide for the whole of the British commitments, shown in Exhibits "A" and "B," and that it will also be possible to meet the assistance as requested by the U.S. authorities as indicated in Exhibit "C."

Tab "C" to Annex "A"
to Appendix "B"

TOP SECRET

EXHIBIT "A" TO TAB "C" TO ANNEX "A" TO APPENDIX "B"

BRITISH OPERATIONAL COMMITMENTS

1. Move of five divisions from Mediterranean area to N.W. Europe between mid-February and early May 1945 requiring a total lift of the order of 200,000.

2. Any operational commitments in SEAC.

TOP SECRET

EXHIBIT "B" TO TAB "C" TO ANNEX "A" TO APPENDIX "B"

Section A. OTHER BRITISH TROOPING COMMITMENTS

	Area	*Estimated Numbers*	*Remarks*
(i)	Canada & North America to U.K.	10,000 per month	Covers RAF, Cdn. & misc. requirements.
(ii)	U.K. to Gibraltar, W. Africa, Italy, PAIC, India and S. Africa	50,000 per month	Includes Army & RAF rotational movement and reinforcements from W. Africa to India.
(iii)	Internal Mediterranean movement, N. Africa & M.E. to Italy, etc.	—	Covered by 15,000 lift retained locally.
(iv)	Naval forces to Australia	4,000 per month	
(v)	N. Zealand to M.E.	(3,000 mid-Apr.) (3,000 mid-Jun.)	Rotational moves of New Zealand forces.
(vi)	M.E. to N. Zealand	(5,800 mid-Mar.)	
(vii)	W. Indies to U.K.	6,000 RAF recruits	
(viii)	E. Africa to Ceylon	4,500 in March	Rfts for 11th) E.A. Div.)
(ix)	Italy to India) India to Italy)	2,000 a month	Rotational) Indian moves of) Ocean Indian troops.) shipping
(x)	PAIC to India) India to PAIC)	1,200 a month	Rotational) moves of) Indian troops.)

(Table Continued on Following Page)

Exhibit "B" to Tab "C" to Annex "A" to Appendix "B"

TOP SECRET

(Continued)

Section B. MISCELLANEOUS COMMITMENTS OTHER THAN TROOPING TO BE CARRIED OUT IN BRITISH SHIPPING

	Area	Estimated Numbers	Remarks
(i)	U.K. to M.E.	8,000)	German P.W.) To be
	U.K. to Malta	2,000)	) fitted in
(ii)	U.K.)	26,000	Repatriation) as and
	SE Europe) to	21,000	of Soviets.) when
	Italy) USSR	4,000	The figures) shipping
	M.E.)	2,500	for UK and SE) available.
			Europe are) US ship-
			likely to) ping may
			increase.) be able to
			) assist.

Exhibit "B" to Tab "C" to
Annex "A" to Appendix "B"

TOP SECRET

EXHIBIT "C" TO TAB "C" TO ANNEX "A" TO APPENDIX "B"

BRITISH ASSISTANCE TO MOVEMENT OF U.S. FORCES

(i) *NORTH ATLANTIC*　　　Feb/May incl.　48,000 per month
　　　　　　　　　　　　　　June　　　　　　36,000 per month

NOTE: This will be effected in the main by 20-knot class ships, in order to allow of the continuance of assistance to westbound evacuation of U.S. casualties as agreed. It will result in the necessity of such U.S. troop movement as is destined for N.W. Europe being oncarried from U.K.

(ii) *CROSS CHANNEL*

A lift of 10,000 has been allowed for in the estimates which should provide for a daily flow of some 3,000.

(iii) *OTHER AREAS*

Mutual assistance to troop movement in other areas will continue to be agreed between the authorities concerned, in order to achieve an overall economy of shipping.

TOP SECRET

U.S. TROOP SHIPPING POSITION
(March-June, 1945)

U.S. personnel shipping supplemented by British assistance in the Atlantic, which is estimated at 48,000 spaces per month February through May and 36,000 spaces in June, is adequate to meet presently estimated deployment requirements up to the defeat of Germany which is assumed at 1 July 1945. Allowance has been made for the probable U.S. troopship assistance to the movement of five divisions from the Mediterranean to southern France between mid-February and early May 1945.

Tab "D" to Annex "A"
to Appendix "B"

TOP SECRET

ANNEX "B" TO APPENDIX "B"

PROVISIONAL FORECAST OF COMBINED DRY CARGO AND
TROOP SHIPPING POSITION AFTER V-E DAY ON 1 JULY 1945

Annex "B" to Appendix "B"

TOP SECRET

TAB "A" TO ANNEX "B" TO APPENDIX "B"

BRITISH DRY CARGO SHIPPING POSITION

(After V-E Day)

1. For the first few months after the conclusion of hostilities in Europe, maintenance requirements for the theatre as a whole will drop very considerably. On the other hand there will be additional demands of which the principal will be:—

   a. The rapid occupation of certain European areas, e.g., Norway.

   b. The redeployment of forces from Europe to India and Southeast Asia.

   c. The redeployment of air forces to the Australian area.

In the absence of any detailed plan for these contingencies it is clearly impossible to give a firm table of the monthly sailings required, but the table following paragraph 2 gives an indication of the way in which current levels are likely to vary during the first two quarters after V-E Day.

2. Tonnage required for military programmes would accordingly show a substantial reduction in the first month following V-E Day, and a smaller reduction in the second and subsequent months. Other factors, the scale of some of which cannot at present be estimated, would tend to improve the British-controlled shipping situation. These include the reduction in sinkings, the increase in Allied and Neutral tonnage willing to trade to European liberated areas, the tonnage that may be recovered from enemy hands, the additional tonnage provided by the continuance of shipbuilding, and the substantial gain in performance resulting from the abolition of much of the convoying system. On the other hand, it is expected that there will be some increase in ship repairing, the Fleet Train may require additional tonnage, turn-round time in ports may suffer some deterioration, and there will be a substantial increase in the import requirements of the United Kingdom and European liberated areas. It is expected that, on balance, the British-controlled shipping situation will show an improvement during a temporary period of up to perhaps two months, but that thereafter a stringent situation will again develop.

Tab "A" to Annex "B"
to Appendix "B"

TOP SECRET

Theater	VE 1 mth		VE 2 mths		VE 3 mths		4th Qtr.		Remarks
	UK	NA	UK	NA	UK	NA	UK	NA	Some U.K. sailings will in fact originate from the Med.
India	30	45	50	45	65	45	180	135	
P.G.	1	1	1	1	1	1	3	3	
Mediterranean Mtce.	12	12	12	12	15	15	45	45	
Australia	2	-	12	-	12	2	26	6	
B.L.A. Maint.	-	3	-	3	-	3	-	10	
Civil Affairs	-	12	-	15	-	18	-	60	
Russia	4		4	-	4	-	12	-	
Med. Retentions Combined	40		35		30		20		
N.W. Europe RETENTIONS M.T. (Combined)	50		40		20		20		
Stores	40		35		25		25		

NOTE: If the Coaster fleet is partially withdrawn, the ocean tonnage retained for stores movement will have to be correspondingly increased.

Tab "A" to Annex "B"
to Appendix "B"

TOP SECRET

TAB "B" TO ANNEX "B" TO APPENDIX "B"

U.S. DRY CARGO SHIPPING POSITION
(After V-E Day)

1. United States military requirements for the first and second quarters following the cessation of hostilities in Europe are set forth in Exhibit "A." On the assumption of July 1st as the date for the termination of the European war Exhibit "A" reflects the military requirements for the third and fourth quarters of 1945. On the assumption of any earlier date the requirements for months in the last half of 1945 would apply for the appropriate months succeeding V-E Day with only minor adjustments. These requirements are based upon present redeployment plans.

2. No authoritative advice has been forthcoming at *ARGONAUT* on the magnitude of requirements for U.S. shipping other than those of the United States Army and Navy after termination of hostilities in Europe. It is noted that some of these requirements are subject to a substantial increase as a result of the occupation of numerous additional Continental ports, the opening of access to large Allied populations now inaccessible or under enemy control, and the occupation of enemy territories, which demands, if accepted, would require more shipping.

3. The shipping situation during the first quarter following V-E Day will be eased by the reduction of military requirements to Europe incident to the cessation of hostilities against Germany and improvement in turn-rounds in the Atlantic trades.

4. Consideration of the United States troopship position indicates the desirability of further conversions of approximately 200 dry cargo ships to lift 500 personnel each. These conversions should be initiated immediately upon V-E Day subject to the urgency of other shipyard activity. For planning purposes, it is estimated that conversions should be accomplished at a rate of 50 the first month following V-E Day and 75 each of the following two months. The effect of these conversions has been taken into account in the estimation of available sailings.

Tab "B" to Annex "B"
to Appendix "B"

TOP SECRET

5. Estimated military requirements show a large increase beginning in the second quarter after the end of hostilities in Europe, as a result of which it is expected that a renewed shipping stringency will develop. Non-military commitments which would extend into this period should, therefore, be assumed only with the greatest caution, and should be subject to the principles enunciated in C.C.S. 746/10.

Tab "B" to Annex "B"
to Appendix "B"

TOP SECRET

EXHIBIT "A" to TAB "B" TO ANNEX "B" TO APPENDIX "B"

U.S. MILITARY DRY CARGO REQUIREMENTS
AFTER V-E DAY OF 1 JULY 1945

	1945				
PACIFIC	*July*	*Aug.*	*Sept.*	*3rd Qtr.*	*4th Qtr.*
POA (Army and Navy)	225	233	235	693	812
SWPA (Army and Navy)	97	116	129	342	355
India-Burma & China	10	6	6	22	18
Less Army Atlantic Sailings	−50	−65	−75	−190	−220
Less Navy Atlantic Sailings	−45	−50	−55	−150	−240
TOTAL PACIFIC	237	240	240	717	725
ATLANTIC					
Army — ETO & MTO	170	160	155	485	406
CBI	15	19	19	53	63
Minor Areas	2	2	2	6	6
Pacific Areas	50	65	75	190	220
Navy — Pacific Areas	45	50	55	150	240
TOTAL ATLANTIC	282	296	306	884	935
Conversions*	50	0	−50	0	0
Europe — Pacific Sailings	(40)	(55)	(65)	(160)	(254)
Europe — Pacific Sailings Effect		40	55	95	232
TOTAL ATLANTIC ADJUSTED	332	336	311	979	1167
Retentions in Overseas Theaters	250	250	250	250	250

* Effect of 50 ships continuously under conversion during first quarter after V-E Day to provide a total of 200.

TOP SECRET

TAB "C" TO ANNEX "B" TO APPENDIX "B"

BRITISH CONTROLLED TROOP SHIPPING POSITION
(After V-E Day)

1. Exhibit "A" indicates availability of British trooping lift in the second half of 1945 with an estimate of military requirements as presently known. These are no more than tentative estimates. They include, as presently directed, certain allowances for inescapable commitments such as Class A demobilisation and rotational leave schemes. They do not, however, include any allowance for essential movement of a non-military nature for which it is considered certain provision will have to be made.

2. Apart from variation in the estimated British military requirements which have been used as a basis for Exhibit "A," the following factors may affect the problem:

   (a) Conversion of cargo shipping, which is already under investigation by M.W.T.

   (b) The achievement in practice of the planning figures assumed for air trooping.

   (c) No credit has been assumed for any captured shipping.

   (d) No allowance has been made for losses.

   (e) It has been assumed that convoys will be required east of Aden, and between Aden and Bombay these will be every 3 days.

   (f) No allowance has been made for any savings resulting from the opening of *MEDLOC*, but on the other hand no requirement has been included for ocean-going shipping for movement between the United Kingdom and Northwest Europe.

3. The balance between military requirements and total availabilities as shown in Exhibit "A" indicates no surplus in the third quarter and an appreciable deficit in the fourth quarter. To the extent that the requirements of any operations in SEAC during the period exceed the capacity of the available Indian Ocean shipping, a further deficit will occur.

Tab "C" to Annex "B"
to Appendix "B"

TOP SECRET

EXHIBIT "A" TO TAB "C" TO ANNEX "B" TO APPENDIX "B"

TENTATIVE BRITISH MILITARY REQUIREMENTS FOR TROOPSHIPS IN SECOND HALF OF 1945

	Personnel to be moved		Troop lift	
	3rd Qtr.	4th Qtr.	3rd Qtr.	4th Qtr.
1. TROOPSHIP POSITION			*Availability*	
(a) Average number of spaces available			376,000	380,000
(b) Estimate for repairs and conversions (12-½%)		47,000		
(c) Less Indian Ocean (local)		49,000		
(d) Less retentions in Mediterranean		5,000	101,000	101,000
(e) *Available for long sea voyage*			275,000	279,000
			Turn-round in days	*Requirements*
2. ARMY FORCES TO BE MOVED				
(a) U.K. to India	146,500	153,000	60	97,700	102,000
(b) U.K. to Mediterranean	40,000	40,000	30	13,000	13,000
(c) Mediterranean to New Zealand	17,000	17,000	120	22,600	22,600
(d) U.K. to Canada	—	20,000	20	—	4,400
(e) U.K. to Pacific	—	8,000	120	—	10,700
(f) W. Africa to India	6,000	6,000	60	4,000	4,000
	209,500	244,000		137,300	156,700
3. R.N. FORCES TO BE MOVED					
(a) U.K. to India (incl. M.N.)	28,500	25,500	60	19,000	17,000
(b) U.K. to Mediterranean	1,000	1,000	30	300	300
(c) U.K. to Australia	22,500	15,700	120	30,000	20,900
	52,000	42,200		49,300	38,200

(Table continued on next page)

Exhibit "A" to Tab "C" to
Annex "B" to Appendix "B"

TOP SECRET

(Continued)	Personnel to be moved		Turn-round in days	Troop lift	
	3rd Qtr.	4th Qtr.		3rd Qtr.	4th Qtr.
				Requirements	
4. R.A.F. FORCES TO BE MOVED					
(a) U.K. to India	30,500	40,000	60	20,300	26,700
(b) U.K. to Mediterranean	17,000	17,000	30	5,600	5,600
(c) U.K. to Pacific	10,000	20,000	120	13,300	26,700
(d) U.K. to Canada	52,000	—	20	11,600	—
(e) Canada to Pacific	—	30,000	120	—	40,000
(f) India to Pacific	10,000	20,000	90	10,000	20,000
	119,500	127,000		60,800	119,000
Total to be moved to India 2(a), 3(a) & 4(a)	205,500	218,500		137,000	145,700
Less estimated air lift	17,000	30,000			
Net to be moved by sea	188,500	188,500			
Add 10% additional spaces	18,800	18,800			
	207,300	207,300		138,200	138,200
5. *Net + or — in troop lift*				+1,200	—7,500
6. Excess of 20% required to Australia on 2(c), (e), 3(c) & 4(c)				13,200	16,200
7. REPATRIATION OF VARIOUS COMMONWEALTH ex Ps.W.	25,000	25,000	60	16,600	16,600
8. TOTAL LONG SEA VOYAGE REQUIREMENT Items 2 to 7 incl.				278,400	339,200
9. OVER-ALL DEFICIT 8 less 1(e)				3,400	60,200

Exhibit "A" to Tab "C" to
Annex "B" to Appendix "B"

TOP SECRET

TAB "D" TO ANNEX "B" TO APPENDIX "B"

U. S. TROOP SHIPPING POSITION

(After V-E Day)

1. Exhibit "A" indicates for the last half of 1945 the U.S. troop shipping requirements compared to availability. The requirements are based upon V-E Day of 1 July 1945, with the same troop movement following the beginning of redeployment as presently planned for a 31 March 1945 V-E Day and do not permit of any repatriation for demobilization during this period. Resulting United States Army overseas strengths are shown in Exhibit "B." Trooplift capabilities that were considered in determining the trooplift position were based on the following assumptions:

a. Additions to United States troopship inventory resulting from construction now scheduled by the U.S. Maritime Commission after allowance for a six percent repair rate and approved C.C.S. loss rates.

b. Scheduled use in the Pacific of APA's not assigned to operations.

c. Full use of accommodations on cargo ships already converted for return of troops from Europe.

d. Restoration to use of captured enemy shipping.

2. The balance between requirements and availability indicates an appreciable deficit during the third quarter increasing to a substantial deficit in the fourth quarter based on no British troopship assistance. To the extent that these deficits cannot be overcome by various expedients the rate of redeployment to the Pacific, both direct and through the United States will have to be slowed down. Acceptance of a reduced rate of troop movement will deny Pacific theater commanders desired forces with which to initiate the presently projected large-scale operations against Japan during the period September through December 1945 and would probably result in postponement of these operations.

3. Some of the possibilities which exist for reducing the deficit in troopship availability to meet requirements are:

a. Double loading of ships during the summer and fall.

Tab "D" to Annex "B"
to Appendix "B"

b. Conversion of approximately 200 additional cargo ships to lift 500 troops each involving the acceptance of the attendant inconveniences to personnel. These conversions could probably be accomplished at a rate of 50 the first month following V-E Day and 75 each of the following two months. This action would result in having practically all of the cargo ships employed between United States and Europe equipped to carry troops.

c. Greater assistance from British and captured enemy shipping.

d. Use of landing craft being transferred from Europe to the Pacific.

e. Full utilization of all available facilities of the Air Transport Command as well as movement by combat and troop carrier planes being transferred from Europe to the Pacific.

f. Scheduling of greater assistance from APA's in the Pacific and such other naval vessels as can be made available.

g. Integration of United Nations transport fleet to eliminate cross hauling and maximum use of troopships when returning from their outbound trips.

h. Careful scheduling of the return of sick and wounded so that the least interference is made with the quickest turn-round possible.

Tab "D" to Annex "B"
to Appendix "B"

TOP SECRET

EXHIBIT "A" TO TAB "D" TO ANNEX "B" TO APPENDIX "B"

U.S. TROOP SHIPPING POSITION

(After V-E Day)

	Personnel to be moved 1945		Turn-round (in days)	Troopship spaces 1945	
	3rd Qtr.	4th Qtr.		3rd Qtr.	4th Qtr.
1. TROOPSHIP POSITION					
a. Average number of spaces available during quarter				620,700	685,800
b. Est. spaces in repair (6%)				37,200	41,100
c. Net troopship spaces available				583,500	644,700
d. Less local retentions				62,000	62,000
e. Troopship availability				521,500	582,700
				Requirements	
2. ARMY TROOPS TO BE DEPLOYED*					
a. Europe to the Pacific	287,800	267,900	90	287,800	267,900
b. Europe to C.B.I.	32,600	23,300	60	21,800	15,600
c. U.S. to Pacific (troops)	147,800	236,800	60	98,000	157,600
d. U.S. to Pacific (replacements)	123,600	171,700	60	82,400	114,000
e. U.S. to C.B.I. (troops)	0	0	90		
f. U.S. to C.B.I. (replacements)	20,200	21,800	90	20,200	21,800
g. Minor Areas to U.S.	16,750	13,050	45	8,400	6,500
h. Total	628,750	734,550		518,600	583,400
3. NAVY TROOPS TO BE DEPLOYED					
a. U.S. to Pacific	191,000	220,100	60	127,300	146,700
b. Other Areas to U.S.	17,400	9,400	38	7,300	3,900
c. Total	208,400	229,500		134,600	150,600

(*Table continued on next page*)

---

* Deployment to North Pacific to be accomplished in tonnage frozen in the Alaskan pool.

Exhibit "A" to Tab "D" to
Annex "B" to Appendix "B"

(Continued)

	Personnel to be moved 1945		Turn-round (in days)	Troopship spaces 1945	
	3rd Qtr.	4th Qtr.		3rd Qtr.	4th Qtr.
				Requirements	
4. TOTAL TROOPSHIP REQUIREMENT FOR ABOVE MOVEMENT				653,200	734,000
a. Less APA assistance[a]				116,000[b]	33,300
b. Net requirement				537,200	700,700
c. Troop spaces available for use between Europe and U.S. (1 e. minus 4 b.)				–15,700	–118,000
5. TROOP FLOW FROM EUROPE TO U.S. FOR REDEPLOYMENT TO PACIFIC	217,300	237,000			
a. Less cargo ship assistance	45,000	90,000			
b. Less use of captured enemy shipping	0	75,000			
c. Net troopship requirement	172,300	72,000	38	72,800	30,200
d. Troopship availability (4 c.)				–15,700	–118,000
e. Over-all deficiency in troopship spaces (non-cumulative)				–88,500	–148,200
f. If British monthly assistance of 70,000 in terms of trans-Atlantic lift is assumed, over-all deficiency will be				0	–59,700

---

[a] These figures represent the theoretical number of troopship spaces which, during a given quarter, would accomplish the same personnel movement as the APA facilities which will be available during the quarter.

[b] Based on scheduled use of APA's not assigned to operations.

Exhibit "A" to Tab "D" to Annex "B" to Appendix "B"

TOP SECRET

EXHIBIT "B" TO TAB "D" TO ANNEX "B" TO APPENDIX "B"

U.S. ARMY OVERSEAS STRENGTHS AFTER V-E DAY
Required by Assumed Redeployment Plan

	1945 3rd Qtr.	4th Qtr.
EUROPE		
Strength 1 July 1945	3,500,000	
Cumulative Strength at end of quarter	2,960,000	2,430,000
PACIFIC		
Pacific Ocean Areas		
Strength 1 July 1945	600,000	
Cumulative Strength at end of quarter	860,000	1,545,000
Southwest Pacific Area		
Strength 1 July 1945	845,000	
Cumulative Strength at end of quarter	1,035,000	865,000
India-Burma and China		
Strength 1 July 1945	240,000	
Cumulative Strength at end of quarter	265,000	280,000
North Pacific		
Strength 1 July 1945	70,000	
Cumulative Strength at end of quarter	75,000	75,000
Total Pacific		
Strength 1 July 1945	1,755,000	
Cumulative Strength at end of quarter	2,235,000	2,765,000

Exhibit "B" to Tab "D" to Annex "B" to Appendix "B"

TOP SECRET

C.C.S. 747/7 (ARGONAUT)

ALLOCATION OF RESOURCES BETWEEN INDIA-BURMA
AND CHINA THEATERS

References:

CCS 183d Meeting, Item 5
CCS 184th Meeting, Item 4

C.C.S. 747/7 (ARGONAUT), a memorandum by the British Chiefs of Staff, dated 31 January 1945, was considered by the Combined Chiefs of Staff in their 184th Meeting together with C.C.S. 452/35 and C.C.S. 452/36.

In view of their agreement on the policy set out in C.C.S. 452/37, the Combined Chiefs of Staff took note that the British Chiefs of Staff withdraw C.C.S. 747 (ARGONAUT).

TOP SECRET

C.C.S. 747/7 (ARGONAUT)　　　　　　　　　　　　　31 January 1945

COMBINED CHIEFS OF STAFF

ALLOCATION OF RESOURCES BETWEEN INDIA-BURMA AND CHINA THEATERS

Memorandum by the British Chiefs of Staff

1. The British Chiefs of Staff fully recognise the importance and magnitude of the United States commitments to China, both political and military.

2. They trust that the United States Chiefs of Staff will also recognise the political and military importance of the British stake in operations in Burma.

3. The circumstances in which the British Chiefs of Staff accepted without discussion in conference the United States reservation stated in C.C.S. 308 no longer apply. A year ago, British land forces were not committed to operations in which their security was dependent to the same extent upon air transportation as it is now. Moreover, the situation in China was not such as to demand such urgent increase of the Fourteenth Air Force as to preclude prior discussion. It was more a question of taking advantage of opportunities in China rather than of warding off dangers.

4. In present circumstances, the British Chiefs of Staff feel bound to reopen the question and to ask that no transfer of forces to the China Theatre from the India-Burma Theatre which is not acceptable to Supreme Allied Commander, Southeast Asia Command should be made without the agreement of the Combined Chiefs of Staff.

　　The British Chiefs of Staff are very ready to discuss means of reducing to an absolute minimum the time occupied in discussion of projected moves.

TOP SECRET

C.C.S. 755/3

C.C.S. 755/4

PROVISION OF LVT'S FOR THE MEDITERRANEAN

References:

CCS 185th Meeting, Item 6
CCS 186th Meeting, Item 4

C.C.S. 755/3, a memorandum by the United States Chiefs of Staff, dated 2 February 1945, and C.C.S. 755/4, a memorandum by the British Chiefs of Staff, dated 5 February, were considered by the Combined Chiefs of Staff in their 185th and 186th Meetings respectively. The Combined Chiefs of Staff approved the recommendations in C.C.S. 755/4.

TOP SECRET

C.C.S. 755/3   2 February 1945

COMBINED CHIEFS OF STAFF

PROVISION OF LVT'S FOR THE MEDITERRANEAN

Memorandum by the United States Chiefs of Staff

1. In MEDCOS 238 Field Marshal Alexander expresses concern over the delay in shipment of 600 LVT's recently assigned to his theater, which he states are vital to his spring offensive. In view of the change in strategy in the Mediterranean as agreed at the present conference and the tight shipping situation it would appear that a review of these requirements is now warranted.

2. The United States Chiefs of Staff therefore recommend that the Combined Chiefs of Staff obtain Field Marshal Alexander's views on this matter.

TOP SECRET

C.C.S. 755/4   5 February 1945

COMBINED CHIEFS OF STAFF

PROVISION OF LVT'S FOR THE MEDITERRANEAN

Memorandum by the British Chiefs of Staff

1. In accordance with the recommendation in C.C.S. 755/3, we have asked Field Marshal Alexander for his views on the requirement of 600 LVT's for the Italian Theatre. The situation is as follows:

    a. SACMED's original requirement was 400 for British, and 200 for United States forces, making a total of 600. These have been assigned.

    b. 95, and possibly more, have already been shipped to the Mediterranean for the British.

    c. 100 have been diverted towards the urgent requirement of 21st Army Group.

    d. 21st Army Group require a further 100 for future operations, which include 7 river crossings, 4 of which will be assault crossings involving at least one division. These LVT's are required to be available in the theatre by mid-February.

2. Field Marshal Alexander states that in view of the urgent requirements of the Western Front he is prepared to surrender 200 LVT's forthwith.

3. It is recommended that the Combined Chiefs of Staff should:

    a. Approve as an immediate measure the reduction of the assignment to the Mediterranean Theatre of LVT's from 600 to 400.

    b. Approve the diversion to 21st Army Group of the 200 LVT's surrendered by Field Marshal Alexander.

    c. Agree that consideration of the final requirements of the Mediterranean Theatre should await the result of detailed study of the position by AFHQ in the light of the new directive.

TOP SECRET

C.C.S. 761/3
C.C.S. 761/6

STRATEGY IN NORTHWEST EUROPE

References:

CCS 182d Meeting, Item 4
CCS 183d Meeting, Item 3
CCS 184th Meeting, Item 7
1st U.S.-U.K. Plenary Meeting, Item c.
Tripartite Plenary Meeting
CCS 776/3, Paragraph 9

In C.C.S. 761/3, dated 29 January 1945, the report of the Supreme Commander, Allied Expeditionary Force on progress of operations in Northwest Europe and his appreciation and plan of operations for the winter and spring of 1945 were circulated for the information of the Combined Chiefs of Staff.

C.C.S. 761/4, dated 30 January, and C.C.S. 761/5, dated 31 January, circulated proposals by the United States and British Chiefs of Staff respectively.

C.C.S. 761/6, dated 31 January, circulated SCAEF's plan of operations in Northwest Europe as reworded by General W. B. Smith and agreed to by General Eisenhower.

The Combined Chiefs of Staff in their 184th Meeting took note of SCAF 180 (Enclosure "B" to C.C.S. 761/3) as amended by SCAF 194 (paragraphs (A) and (B) of Appendix "A" to C.C.S. 761/6) and as amplified by Appendix "B" to C.C.S. 761/6.

TOP SECRET

C.C.S. 761/3   29 January 1945

COMBINED CHIEFS OF STAFF

SCAEF REPORT ON STRATEGY IN NORTHWEST EUROPE

Note by the Secretaries

1. The report of the Supreme Commander, Allied Expeditionary Force, requested by FACS 123 (C.C.S. 761/2) is circulated for information.

2. SCAF 179 (Enclosure "A") gives an account of the development of operations. SCAF 180 (Enclosure "B") contains an appreciation and plan of operations.

                                                     A. J. McFARLAND,

                                                     A. T. CORNWALL-JONES,

                                                     Combined Secretariat.

TOP SECRET

ENCLOSURE "A"

SCAF 179

DEVELOPMENT OF OPERATIONS 28 OCTOBER 1944 - 20 JANUARY 1945

From: Supreme Headquarters, Allied Expeditionary Forces, Main, Versailles, France

To: War Department

Nr: S-75872   SCAF 179   20 January 1945

S-75872 to AGWAR for Combined Chiefs of Staff repeat for information to AMSSO for British Chiefs of Staff from SHAEF Main signed Eisenhower cite SHSC TOPSEC this is SCAF 179

Distribution of this message will be held to the absolute minimum.

1. In accordance with the instructions of the Combined Chiefs of Staff (FACS 123) I submit herewith an account (supplementary to SCAF 141) showing the progress of operations carried out as a result of my directive of 28 October and the effect of the recent counteroffensive. Development of Operations 28 October 1944 to 20 January 1945.

2. In SCAF 114 I gave first priority to the early opening of Antwerp as it was abundantly clear that major operations east of the Rhine could not be supported without this port.

Convinced as I was of the advantages of the northern line of approach into Germany I directed my main effort against the Ruhr to the protection of which major enemy forces were committed. The closing of the Rhine by the Northern and Central Groups of Armies north of the Ardennes was an essential prerequisite to the latter phases of crossing the river and deploying to the east. These attacks were to begin on about 10 November.

Prior to the opening of the Port of Antwerp, logistical considerations limited the scale of the offensive which could be supported north of the

Enclosure "A"

TOP SECRET

Ardennes. However, Third Army could be supported offensively by the line of communications extending east of Paris. Therefore, concurrently with the main attack in the North, I decided to press forward with my secondary effort towards the Saar hoping to destroy important German forces and as the advance progressed to divert further enemy divisions which would otherwise oppose my thrust in the North. The Southern Group of Armies astride the Vosges was similarly to divert enemy forces.

OPERATIONS

Capture of Antwerp.

3. By 9 November operations by the Northern Group of Armies and Second Tactical Air Force, particularly the capture of Walcheren Island in which RAF Bomber Command played a large part, had rendered the approaches to Antwerp secure from land attack and by 28 November the port was open.

Advance Toward the Rhine.

4. The eastwards drive by the Northern Group of Armies began on 15 November, progress was slow over ground made extremely difficult by unseasonable weather and it was 4 December before the last enemy pocket on the west bank of the Maas was cleared. A direct advance across the Maas to the Rhine was judged impracticable and extensive regrouping was required for a drive southeast from the Nijmegen area along the relatively dry watershed separating the Rhine from the Maas. This would have involved reducing the frontage of the Northern Group of Armies at the expense of weakening the concentration of my forces in the Aachen sector, a course which was not acceptable. It was therefore necessary to postpone further major operations by the Northern Group of Armies until the drive toward Cologne had made adequate progress.

5. In the Aachen sector the offensive by First and Ninth Armies began on 16 November. Fourteen and eventually seventeen divisions were employed in this sector and at the height of the offensive no fewer than 10 divisions were in line on a 24 mile front, this being the maximum number which it was practicable to deploy. In spite of this concentration, and in spite of very large scale strategic and tactical air effort, progress was slow and fighting bitter. During these operations very heavy casualties were inflicted on the enemy. Throughout this time the relatively static situation on the Russian Front

Enclosure "A"

TOP SECRET

enabled the enemy to divert the majority of his replacements of men and equipment against our front and thus preserve intact his reserves of armor. By 3 December Ninth Army had reached the Roer River with First Army conforming more slowly, but it was considered imprudent to cross the river while the Schmidt dams, which control the flooding of the Roer valley, remained intact in enemy hands especially since the Sixth Panzer Army had moved west of the Rhine. Efforts to breach the dams by air attack having failed, First Army on 13 December launched a new attack to capture them. This attack was still in progress when the German counteroffensive began. All our operations during November and early December were attended by worse weather than has been known in these parts for very many years.

Advance to the Saar.

6. Meanwhile south of the Ardennes the Third Army offensive towards the Saar which started on 8 November had made excellent progress. Metz fell on 22 November and by 2 December a substantial stretch of the Saar River had been closed. Three bridgeheads were secured in the Saar-Lautern area and contact was made with the main Siegfried defenses. While I had hoped that Third Army would be able to achieve victory in the Saar I had nevertheless set a time limit for these operations. Third Army's final attack was to begin on 19 December after which, regardless of results, divisions were to be transferred to the North.

7. Further south the Southern Group of Armies assumed the offensive on 13 November and within a week the First French Army had breached the Belfort Gap and reached the Rhine, while north of the high Vosges the Seventh Army had broken through the Saverne Gap and by 27 November had cleared Strasbourg using French armor. After rapid regrouping Seventh Army was directed north to breach the Siegfried Line west of the Rhine (SCAF 136). Its advance in the West afforded direct assistance to Third Army's operations against the Saar while to the east our troops by 19 December had crossed the German frontier on a 22 mile front and penetrated well into the Siegfried defenses northeast of Wissembourg. I believe that our progress in the Saar and Wissembourg sectors contained 14 enemy divisions and had we been able to continue it, must soon have compelled the enemy to divert forces from the North and thus have indirectly assisted our main effort. Meantime enemy forces driven from the Vosges maintained a bridgehead west of the Rhine in the Colmar area which the First French Army, weakened by their offensive operations and short of infantry replacements, have so far been unable to liquidate.

Enclosure "A"

TOP SECRET

8. As a result of deploying my maximum effort in the Aachen sector and sustaining the successful progress of the Saar-Wissembourg operations with the balance of my available forces other stretches of my front were weakly held. In particular the Eifel sector of some 75 miles between Trier and Monschau was entrusted to no more than four divisions. This was a calculated risk based on the absence of strategic objectives or large depots in the area, the relatively difficult terrain and my current estimate of the enemy's intentions.

The December German Counteroffensive.

9. The counteroffensive opened by the enemy in the Eifel sector on 16 December was prepared in very great secrecy and launched in greater strength than we had believed likely on this sector at the time although evidence of build-up was received. The enemy's immediate intention was to seize the Meuse crossings between Namur and Liege. The Fifth and Sixth Panzer Armies supported by the Seventh German Army, in all about 14 infantry and 10 Panzer and Panzer Grenadier divisions were employed.

10. The brunt of the assault was met by three infantry and one armored divisions in the line which in spite of being by-passed and divided by the enemy penetration denied him the important area of St. Vith during a critical period. The momentum of the thrust was further reduced by the arrival of two airborne divisions moved from reserve in the Reims area on 18 December. One of these (reinforced by armor) although under constant attack and completely surrounded for five days, held the important road center at Bastogne. This was made possible by concentrated fighter-bomber effort and a determined and hazardous feat of resupply by air, troop-carrying aircraft achieving 911 sorties in spite of most unfavorable weather and air opposition. The shoulders of the penetration at Monschau and Echtermach were held and the salient gradually stabilized by divisions moved both from the North and from the South. Immediate steps were taken to maintain a reserve by hastening forward divisions from the United Kingdom, one of these being moved by air.

11. On 19 December as soon as the magnitude of the enemy's effort and its effect on communications within the Central Group of Armies became known, I realized that it would be impracticable for one commander to handle the American forces both north and south of the large salient which was being created. Moreover it was essential to divert our maximum resources, including those of the Northern Group of Armies, to counter the threat which appeared greatest on that flank. I therefore fixed a boundary running east and west through the breach in our lines and placed all forces north of it, including the

Enclosure "A"

major part of the First and Ninth U.S. Armies and part of the Ninth Air Force under operational command of Commander in Chief, Northern Group of Armies and Air Officer Commanding in Chief, Second Tactical Air Force, respectively, leaving the Commanding Generals, Central Group of Armies and Ninth Air Force free and suitably located to command the forces south of the salient mainly comprising Third U.S. Army and the XIX Tactical Air Command considerably reinforced.

12. Meanwhile precautionary measures had been taken to ensure that the enemy could not cross the Meuse if he reached it, especially in the Liege-Namur sector where protection of our lines of communication and installations was of vital importance. Extensive regrouping was rapidly effected both north and south of the salient to provide forces to check the enemy's thrust and for our subsequent counterattacks. At the same time the main weight of German armor thrusting against the northern flank of the salient was held and headed away from vital sectors of the Meuse. During this period, fog temporarily deprived us of the greater part of our air effort, including air reconnaissance, giving the enemy an important advantage in the initial stages.

13. On 22 December, Third Army, largely relieved from the Saar by the Seventh Army, launched an attack on the Arlon-Luxembourg area northeastwards into the gap. On this date the weather began to improve and our air action had a paralyzing effect on movement in and into the battle area. Throughout the period the strategical air forces battered marshalling yards east of the Rhine and blocked centers of movement such as St. Vith, while the medium and light bombers of the tactical air forces backed up the efforts of the heavies, destroyed bridges, headquarters, dumps and other targets in the battle area. The fighter-bombers ranged far and wide in and beyond the battle area creating havoc among enemy rail and road movement, the efficacy of which in starving the enemy of fuel, food and ammunition has been amply testified by enemy prisoners. A concerted attack on the German Air Force airfields on 24 December helped to reduce the activity of the enemy fighters and thus afforded our fighter-bombers still greater opportunity for concentration on ground targets rather than on air fighting. By 26 December, Third Army had firmly linked up with the garrisons in Bastogne and finally checked the enemy's advance on that flank. This attack also drew strong enemy forces away from the north of the salient. By the time the enemy's drive was halted, he had breached a 45-mile gap in our front through which elements had penetrated to within four miles of the Meuse near Celles. But by 26 December additional reserves were so disposed as to relieve anxiety in this area and it was then clear that the enemy had failed in his main intention.

Enclosure "A"

TOP SECRET

Reduction of the German Salient.

14. As soon as the enemy's advance had been checked, my intention, as outlined in SCAF 151, was to cut the enemy's lines of communication into the salient and if possible to destroy him by launching coordinated ground attacks from both North and South in close coordination with continued heavy air attacks concentrated on enemy communication targets to extend paralysis of movement over a large area. Simultaneously, the strategic air effort employed so effectively in the battle area was released. The attack from the North aimed at Houffalize was launched by First Army on 3 January on a two corps front, with a corps of Second British Army confronting on the west flank. On 9 January, Third Army launched a fresh attack from the South also directed towards the Houffalize road net. Both these attacks were hampered by adverse weather with snow covered minefield and met by stubborn enemy resistance. Slow progress was however made and the gap between the attacking armies had by 10 January been narrowed to some ten miles. By this time the enemy had begun to withdraw from the western end of his salient while still stoutly opposing our pressure against his northern and southern flanks.

Enemy Operations in the South.

15. Commanding General, Southern Group of Armies has orders to regard the eastern slopes of the Vosges as his main position but, because of its political and moral importance, to defend the Strasbourg area as strongly as possible consistent with the overriding necessity of maintaining the integrity of his forces. Since 20 December the Southern Group of Armies has taken over an additional 20 miles of front westwards to Saarlautern in order to set free the bulk of Third Army for offensive operations. The enemy has not failed to take advantage of this by attacking our lines at many points and is likely to continue to do so.

Effect of German Counteroffensive.

16. The counteroffensive immediately succeeded in stopping our attacks against the Ruhr and the Saar. Operations to deal with it have already occupied a month and are not yet concluded: some regrouping will be necessary before offensive operations can be resumed and my present estimate is that the enemy's attack has delayed our offensive operations by at least six weeks. The strategic air forces were of necessity drawn into the immediate battle area thus leaving oil, jet aircraft and communication targets deeper in Germany free of attack for nearly a month. The counteroffensive, however, has not been

Enclosure "A"

TOP SECRET

without its effect on the enemy. Land and air forces were built up for months and supplies, particularly of fuel, were carefully hoarded for this all-out effort. At a general estimate, during the month ended 16 January, he has suffered 120,000 serious casualties and lost 600 tanks and assault guns; his air losses have been severe, about 620 planes, and his fuel stocks after nearly a month of large-scale effort must now be reduced to the bare minimum. Possibly more serious in the final analysis is the widespread disillusionment likely to ensue from the failure to seize any really important objective and the realization that this offensive for which every effort had been brought to bear and on which such great hopes were pinned, has in no sense achieved anything decisive. Furthermore the fighting state of his reserve withdrawn from the Ardennes salient is likely to preclude offensive action on a comparable scale but undoubtedly he will make all efforts to accelerate the refitting of the divisions engaged in the Ardennes offensive in the hope of maintaining the initiative in the West.

    Please acknowledge.

End

CM-IN-19747   (21 Jan 45)

Enclosure "A"

TOP SECRET

ENCLOSURE "B"

APPRECIATION AND PLAN OF OPERATIONS
FOR THE WINTER AND SPRING, 1945

From: Supreme Headquarters, Allied Expeditionary Forces, Main, Versailles, France

To: War Department

Nr: S-75871   SCAF 180   20 January 1945

S-75871 to AGWAR for Combined Chiefs of Staff repeated to AMSSO for information for British Chiefs of Staff from SHAEF Main signed Eisenhower cite SHSC TOP SECRET this is SCAF 180.

Distribution of this message will be held to the absolute minimum.

1. In accordance with the instructions of the C.C.S. (FACS 123) I submit herewith my appreciation and plan of operations for the winter and spring of 1945.

2. My object remains, as in my original directive from the C.C.S., to undertake operations aimed at the heart of Germany and the destruction of her armed forces.

3. These operations fall into three phases:—

Phase I. The destruction of the enemy forces west of the Rhine and the closing of the Rhine.

Phase II. The seizing of bridgeheads over the Rhine from which to develop operations into Germany.

Phase III. The destruction of enemy forces east of the Rhine and advance into Germany.

Enclosure "B"

TOP SECRET

4. These three phases form three distinct operations. The destruction of the bulk of the enemy forces west of the Rhine is my immediate aim. If this can be effected the remaining phases will be immeasurably simplified. Such destruction, however, cannot be guaranteed and operations in Phase I must thus, to some extent, be designed to facilitate subsequent operations in Phases II and III. I therefore propose in this appreciation to examine possible courses of action in Phases II and III before discussing Phase I. Before proceeding to this examination I wish to emphasize that by all odds the attack north of the Ruhr is the one that we must hold in front of us as our principal purpose. In all this discussion it is to be understood that other areas are analyzed from two standpoints:

(A) For staging a supporting effort for the northern attack with such means as may be left over after concentrating in the North all the power that can be sustained and,

(B) To have the flexibility to switch the main effort if the northern attack encounters an impossible situation.

PHASE III

5. To consider first Phase III. On the assumption that serious opposition is still to be met east of the Rhine, there are two main avenues of approach into Germany by which we can advance and defeat enemy forces. These run from the Mainz-Karlsruhe area to Frankfurt and Kassel, and from the lower Rhine north of the Ruhr into the plains of North Germany. (I omit the possible axis of advance into southern Germany in view of FACS 119.)

6. (A) An advance on the Frankfurt-Kassel axis would secure early the important industrial area around Frankfurt. The Germans in the West are likely to give priority to the defense of this area second only to the Ruhr, and therefore there should be an opportunity of destroying considerable German forces although we should have less opposition to our advance than would be the case in the North. In addition, the occupation of the Frankfurt-Giessen area offers very suitable airfield sites both to support a further advance and to assist in the support of operations north of the Ruhr.

(B) The advance from Frankfurt on Kassel would be over terrain less suitable for armored operations than the area north of the Ruhr. But once we reached the Kassel area there would be several possibilities of further

Enclosure "B"

TOP SECRET

developments — a thrust northward to cut some of the communications from the Ruhr, a thrust northeast towards Berlin or a thrust eastward towards Leipzig.

7. (A) An advance north of the Ruhr offers the quickest means of denying the enemy the Ruhr industries. The eastern exits from the industrial area could be cut by enveloping the area on the north and east, and the southern exits by air action. The area north of the Ruhr offers the most suitable terrain east of the Rhine for mobile operations and it is this type of warfare which we want to force upon the enemy because of our superior mobility.

(B) In view of the importance of the Ruhr to German economy, and the fact that this route offers the most direct and obvious approach to the center of Germany, this area is likely to receive first priority from the defense point of view. While I should be glad of an opportunity of defeating on favorable terrain the bulk of the German forces, I would have to deploy a superior force rapidly across the Rhine to ensure success. It will not, however, be possible to maintain more than some 35 divisions across the Rhine in this sector until the railway has been extended over the river.

8. The country between the Ruhr and Frankfurt is very defensible and is not suited for offensive operations.

9. To sum up. An examination of Phase III indicates that operations across the Rhine north of the Ruhr offer the greatest strategic rewards within a short distance, but this area will be most strongly held by the enemy. An advance in the Frankfurt area offers less favorable terrain and a longer route to vital strategic objectives. Depending on the degree of enemy resistance it may be necessary to use either or both of these two avenues.

PHASE II

10. To examine next the most favorable areas in which to seize bridgeheads across the Rhine. Bearing in mind the possible routes of subsequent development of operations into Germany there are two areas in which both bridging and tactical conditions facilitate the seizure of bridgeheads. These are the sector north of the Ruhr, and the sector between Mainz and Karlsruhe.

Enclosure "B"

TOP SECRET

11. North of the Ruhr there are suitable sites for three divisional assaults on a 20-mile front; strong defense works already exist in the area. There is, in addition, one further possible though difficult site which might be used. Flooding conditions west of Emmerich preclude an extension of this front unless operations are delayed till about June, in which case sites for an additional two assault crossings might possibly be available.

12. In the Mainz-Karlsruhe sector there are sites for five divisional assault crossings, with the possibility of a further one south of Karlsruhe. If the whole of this sector is taken into use it should be possible to maintain across the Rhine some 50 divisions, until railways have been extended over the river.

13. In addition to these main crossings there is one site on each side of Cologne suitable for a divisional assault crossing, but a crossing in this area would be tactically difficult, and after the seizure of a bridgehead, the hinterland is unsuitable for the development of operations against opposition. There are two isolated sites between Coblenz and Bonn, but owing to the nature of the terrain operations would not be practicable except against very light opposition.

14. Weighing all the climatic conditions, assault operations could be carried out in all sectors after early March when the ice menace is over. In the sectors south of Mainz, however, where floods occur in summer, there is a risk of incurring great difficulties if we do not complete the permanent bridges and their approaches before the onset of the flood season in May.

15. To sum up.

(A) There are two main areas suitable for forming bridgeheads, namely between Emmerich and Wesel and between Mainz and Karlsruhe.

(B) An assault crossing in the North would be on a very narrow frontage, and would be opposed by the heaviest available enemy concentrations. To effect a crossing in the North it may, therefore, be necessary to divert enemy forces by closing and perhaps crossing the Rhine in the Frankfurt sector — operations in the Saar would not have a comparable effect.

(C) An assault in the southern sector would be on a wider front and would not meet such heavy opposition. It would be desirable to carry it out in time to have our permanent bridges completed by May.

Enclosure "B"

TOP SECRET

Other Factors Affecting Phase I.

16. The comparative strength of my own and the enemy forces is a factor of the greatest importance in the development of my operations. The enemy has now some 80 divisions on the Western Front, not all of them at full strength. Provided the Russian offensive is continued with vigor and the enemy maintains his front in Italy, this number is likely to dwindle. Should, however, the Russian offensive weaken and the Germans carry out a partial withdrawal from the Italian Front there might be a diversion to my front of some ten or more divisions from Russia, and a dozen divisions from Italy. Thus I may be faced in the spring with about 80 divisions, some understrength, at the best and a hundred or more divisions with adequate replacements at the worst.

17. Moreover, by reasons of the suitability of the terrain for defense and his Siegfried fortifications, the enemy will be able to get the maximum value even out of his weaker divisions in a defensive role. Only when we too have closed the Rhine shall we share with the enemy a strong defensive barrier giving us the ability to hold defensive sectors with security and economy of effort.

18. To drive the German forces from their strong positions I have 71 divisions immediately available, including many below strength. In May I should have 85 divisions (including six airborne) with a possibility of five to eight more French divisions becoming available during the summer.

19. My superiority on land on present reckoning is not therefore so very great. Before we advance east of the Rhine I must be assured of security in other sectors, and as explained above it will probably be essential to close the Rhine along its length, leaving only minor bridgeheads in enemy hands from which he cannot stage a major counterstroke. In this way only shall I be able to concentrate in great strength east of the River.

CONCLUSIONS

20. Bearing in mind the above factors and the probable development of further operations, it is clear that my operations to destroy the enemy forces west of the Rhine must be so designed as to enable me to close the Rhine throughout its length. In view of the present relative strengths I am not in a position to carry out more than one offensive at a time. I am therefore concentrating at the moment on a series of offensives designed to destroy the enemy and close the Rhine in the North.

Enclosure "B"

TOP SECRET

PLAN

21. My plan is as follows:—

(A) To carry out immediately a series of operations north of the Moselle with a view to destroying the enemy and closing the Rhine north of Dusseldorf. South of the Moselle we shall remain on the defensive.

(B) After closing the Rhine in the North, to direct our main effort to destroying any enemy remaining west of the Rhine, both in the North and in the South.

(C) To seize bridgeheads over the Rhine in the North and the South.

(D) To deploy east of the Rhine and north of the Ruhr the maximum number of divisions which can be maintained (estimated at some 35 divisions). The initial task of this force, assisted by air action, will be to deny to the enemy the industries of the Ruhr.

(E) To deploy east of the Rhine, on the axis Frankfurt-Kassel, such forces, if adequate, as may be available after providing 35 divisions for the North and essential security elsewhere. The task of this force will be to draw enemy forces away from the North by capturing Frankfurt and advancing on Kassel.

22. It will be realized that a crossing of the Rhine, particularly on the narrow frontages in which such crossings are possible, will be a tactical and engineering operation of the greatest magnitude. I propose to spare no efforts in allotting such operations the maximum possible support. For this purpose I envisage the use of airborne forces and strategic air support on a large scale. In addition I foresee the necessity for the employment on a very large scale of amphibious vehicles of all types. The possibility of failure to secure bridgeheads in the North or in the South cannot, however, be overlooked. I am, therefore, making logistical preparations which will enable me to switch my main effort from the North to the South should this be forced upon me. Please acknowledge.

End

Footnote: Receipt of this message has been acknowledged by WD CMC

CM-IN-19766   (21 Jan 45)   DTG   201500A   es

Enclosure "B"

TOP SECRET

C.C.S. 761/6   31 January 1945

COMBINED CHIEFS OF STAFF

STRATEGY IN NORTHWEST EUROPE

Note by the Secretaries

1. Appendix "A" is a copy of General Eisenhower's plan of operations in Northwest Europe, incorporating amendments proposed by General W. B. Smith as a result of the discussion of Item 4, C.C.S. 182d Meeting, 30 January 1945.

2. Appendix "B" is a copy of a telegram from General Eisenhower to General Smith, accepting the amendments proposed by the latter and incorporated in Appendix "A."

A. J. McFARLAND,
A. T. CORNWALL-JONES,
Combined Secretariat.

TOP SECRET

APPENDIX "A"

My plan is as follows:—

(A) To carry out immediately a series of operations north of the Moselle with a view to destroying the enemy and closing the Rhine north of Dusseldorf.

(B) To direct our efforts to eliminating other enemy forces west of the Rhine which still constitute an obstacle or a potential threat to our subsequent Rhine-crossing operations.

(C) To seize bridgeheads over the Rhine in the North and the South.

(D) To deploy east of the Rhine and north of the Ruhr the maximum number of divisions which can be maintained (estimated at some 35 divisions). The initial task of this force, assisted by air action, will be to deny to the enemy the industries of the Ruhr.

(E) To deploy east of the Rhine, on the axis Frankfurt-Kassel, such forces, if adequate, as may be available after providing 35 divisions for the North and essential security elsewhere. The task of this force will be to draw enemy forces away from the North by capturing Frankfurt and advancing on Kassel.

Appendix "A"

TOP SECRET

APPENDIX "B"

From: Supreme Headquarters, Allied Expeditionary Forces, Main, Versailles, France

To: *ARGONAUT*

Nr: S-77211   31 January 1945

To Lieutenant General Walter Bedell Smith signed Eisenhower.

    I agree with the rewording of the directive as suggested in your CRICKET 18* and will issue the necessary amendment. You may assure the Combined Chiefs of Staff in my name that I will seize the Rhine crossings in the North just as soon as this is a feasible operation and without waiting to close the Rhine throughout its length. Further, I will advance across the Rhine in the North with maximum strength and complete determination immediately the situation in the South allows me to collect necessary forces and do this without incurring unreasonable risks.

CM-IN-99

---

* Appendix "A" to this paper.

TOP SECRET

C.C.S. 765/1
C.C.S. 765/4
C.C.S. 765/8

SUBJECTS FOR CONSIDERATION AT THE NEXT U.S.-BRITISH-
U.S.S.R. STAFF CONFERENCE

Reference:

CCS 182d Meeting, Item 2

In C.C.S. 765/1, dated 17 January 1945, the United States Chiefs of Staff proposed subjects for consideration at the next U.S.-British-U.S.S.R. staff conference. The British Chiefs of Staff replied in C.C.S. 765/4, dated 20 January, accepting the subjects as proposed.

In C.C.S. 765/8, dated 25 January, the British Chiefs of Staff suggested the agenda for discussion at *CRICKET*.*

The Combined Chiefs of Staff in their 182d Meeting agreed upon the program for business to be transacted by the Combined Chiefs of Staff on each day at *CRICKET*, as outlined in Annex "A" to the minutes of that Meeting.

---

* Staff Conferences in Malta.

TOP SECRET

C.C.S. 765/1   17 January 1945

COMBINED CHIEFS OF STAFF

SUBJECTS FOR CONSIDERATION AT THE NEXT U.S.-BRITISH-U.S.S.R. STAFF CONFERENCE

Memorandum by the United States Chiefs of Staff

1. The United States Chiefs of Staff suggest that the following subjects be considered at the next U.S.-British-U.S.S.R. staff conference:—

a. The War Against Germany

(1) Enemy dispositions, capabilities and intentions.

(A discussion and exchange of information.)

(2) Coordination of operations in western Europe and Italy with operations in eastern Europe.

(a) Timing and scope of offensives on the various fronts.

(b) Establishment of effective liaison at Chiefs of Staff level and between Anglo-American-U.S.S.R. field commanders.

(c) A determination of policy on bombline and air liaison parties if not resolved prior to a tripartite conference.

(3) Shuttle bombing and arrangements for staging and/or basing units of Fifteenth Air Force in Vienna-Budapest area.

(4) Military aspects of Zones of Occupation in Germany and Austria.

(Discussion of the necessity that the areas allotted each nation, particularly in Berlin and Vienna, contain adequate military administrative facilities and access by rail, road and air, with a view to recommending adoption by the Heads of State of a policy for guidance of the European Advisory Commission.)

TOP SECRET

    b. War Against Japan

        (1) Japanese dispositions, capabilities and intentions in the Far East.

        (A discussion and exchange of information.)

        (2) Russian participation in the war against Japan.

2. In this connection General Deane has been asked to present the above proposed agenda to the Chief of the Soviet General Staff requesting that he indicate any other military subjects the U.S.S.R. may consider desirable for discussion by the staff conference.

3. Aside from discussion at the conference concerning broad strategic objectives of the U.S.S.R. in the Pacific war, the Russians may wish to discuss with the U.S. staff representatives the operational details such as the supply project now under way for stockpiles in Siberia and other operational details.

TOP SECRET

C.C.S. 765/4   20 January 1945

COMBINED CHIEFS OF STAFF

SUBJECTS FOR CONSIDERATION AT THE NEXT U.S.-BRITISH-U.S.S.R. STAFF CONFERENCE

*Memorandum by the Representatives
of the British Chiefs of Staff*

1. The British Chiefs of Staff agree with the subjects proposed by the United States Chiefs of Staff for discussion at the next U.S.-British-U.S.S.R. staff conference, as set out in C.C.S. 765/1.

2. With reference to Item *a.* (4) in paragraph 1 of C.C.S. 765/1, the British Chiefs of Staff point out that the French are now represented on the European Advisory Commission and have already expressed their views on French participation in control of Germany and Austria. Thus it would seem to the British Chiefs of Staff that any conclusions reached at the conference on the military aspects of the Zones of Occupation in these countries, should either take into account French aspirations or else be subject to discussion with the French after the conference.

TOP SECRET

C.C.S. 765/8　　　　　　　　　　　　　　　　　　　　　　25 January 1945

COMBINED CHIEFS OF STAFF

AGENDA FOR THE NEXT U.S.-BRITISH STAFF CONFERENCE

Memorandum by the Representatives
of the British Chiefs of Staff

The British Chiefs of Staff suggest the following agenda for the discussions at CRICKET and further suggest that it would save time in starting the discussions when we assemble if this agenda could be agreed before the United States Chiefs of Staff leave Washington.

1. *The War Against Germany*

    (A) *Strategy in Northwest Europe*

    (i) Discussion with General Eisenhower.

    (ii) Draft directive to the Supreme Commander, Allied Expeditionary Force will be tabled by the British Chiefs of Staff.

    (B) *Strategy in the Mediterranean*

    (i) Discussion with Field Marshal Alexander.

    (ii) Draft directive to the Supreme Allied Commander, Mediterranean will be tabled by the British Chiefs of Staff.

    (C) *Coordination of Operations on the Three European Fronts*

    Bomblines and air liaison with the Russians.

    (D) *The U-Boat Threat*

    Memorandum may be tabled by the British Chiefs of Staff.

    (E) *The Combined Bomber Offensive* (Unless disposed of separately)

    (F) *Planning Date for the End of the German War*

TOP SECRET

2. *The War Against Japan*

(A) *Strategy in Southeast Asia Command (SEAC)*

Draft directive to Supreme Allied Commander, Southeast Asia Command will be tabled by the British Chiefs of Staff.

(B) *Allocation of Resources between SEAC and China*

(C) *Pacific Operations*

Proposals tabled by the United States Chiefs of Staff.

(D) *Planning Date for the End of the Japanese War*

3. *Review of Cargo Shipping*

Consideration of report in the light of discussions on strategy.

4. *Basic Undertakings in Support of Over-All Strategic Concept*

TOP SECRET

C.C.S. 768/1 (ARGONAUT)
C.C.S. 768/2

EQUIPMENT FOR ALLIED AND LIBERATED FORCES

References:

CCS 184th Meeting, Item 3
CCS 185th Meeting, Item 2
CCS 187th Meeting, Item 5
CCS 776/3, Paragraph 22

C.C.S. 768/1 (ARGONAUT), dated 1 February 1945, circulated a memorandum by the United States Chiefs of Staff.

The Combined Chiefs of Staff considered C.C.S. 768/1 (ARGONAUT) in their 185th Meeting and agreed to the implementation of NAF 841* subject to certain assurances by the British Chiefs of Staff. In their 187th Meeting the Combined Chiefs of Staff took note of certain assurances given by the British Chiefs of Staff which are set forth in the minutes of that meeting and subsequently circulated as C.C.S. 768/2 on 8 February.

---

* See page 188.

TOP SECRET

C.C.S. 768/1 (ARGONAUT)   1 February 1945

COMBINED CHIEFS OF STAFF

EQUIPMENT FOR ALLIED AND LIBERATED FORCES

Memorandum by the United States Chiefs of Staff

1. In the 183d Meeting of the Combined Chiefs of Staff on 31 January 1945 the British Chiefs of Staff indicated the urgency for implementing action during the current conference covering the forming of a Greek Army to take over responsibility for internal security within Greece as set forth in NAF 841, 25 January 1945.

2. It is noted that no difficulty is anticipated in meeting the phased requirements for the bulk of the items from British resources in or "due in" the Mediterranean Theater of Operations, but that all issues made for this purpose will require replacement.

3. The categories of supply required for either initial issue or replacement purposes involve many classes of equipment presently in or approaching a short supply position in the United States.

4. The Combined Administrative Committee is presently studying the problem of equipping Allied and liberated manpower in northwestern Europe. This program involves the provision of necessary matériel for:—

   a. The French Metropolitan Rearmament Program of eight divisions and supporting troops.

   b. The Polish 2d Division.

   c. Six Belgium infantry brigades.

   d. Internal security, mobile military labor, and miscellaneous units (Liberated Manpower Program) aggregating 460,000 troops.

5. The United States have assumed responsibility for supplying those requirements requested from United States resources for the French Metropolitan Rearmament Program, and initial shipments thereon are now in

progress. It has been tentatively agreed that the British will accept responsibility for supplying the 2d Polish Division and the six Belgium brigades. It has been proposed on the United States side that necessary equipment for liberated manpower program be also a British responsibility with the understanding that special equipment required for labor units to perform designated projects will be provided by the United Kingdom or the United States for those projects in the sphere of their respective armies. No finalized action on this latter program has been possible on the subcommittee level because of the inability of the British members to secure advice from London.

6. Until the program covering equipment for Allied and liberated manpower in northwestern Europe is resolved, it is impracticable to make a determination of availability of United States equipment to meet any commitments necessary to implement the Greek Army proposal.

7. The subject of providing equipment for additional liberated manpower has been under study since early November. In view of the desirability of making maximum use of liberated manpower in northwestern Europe at the earliest practicable date, as emphasized by General Eisenhower in SCAF 193, dated 30 January 1945, the United States Chiefs of Staff request that the British Chiefs of Staff take such action as is necessary to insure an early solution to this problem.

8. Pending a satisfactory resolution of the program covering the equipping of Allied and liberated forces in northwestern Europe, the United States Chiefs of Staff can make no commitments of United States resources towards implementing the proposed Greek Army. They have no objection, however, to the implementation of this program provided that the British Chiefs of Staff can give assurances that such implementation will not interfere with the provision already approved in principle of equipment for Allied and liberated forces in northwestern Europe and without subsequent direct or indirect charges against United States resources.

9. Upon resolution of the problem of equipment for Allied and liberated forces of northwestern Europe, the United States Chiefs of Staff will be glad to review NAF 841 again.

TOP SECRET

C.C.S. 768/2　　　　　　　　　　　　　　　　　　　　　8 February 1945

COMBINED CHIEFS OF STAFF

EQUIPMENT FOR ALLIED AND LIBERATED FORCES

Memorandum by the British Chiefs of Staff

1. At their 185th Meeting the Combined Chiefs of Staff agreed to the implementation of the proposals put forward by the Supreme Allied Commander, Mediterranean, in NAF 841 in regard to equipping Greek forces upon certain assurances by the British Chiefs of Staff, confirmation of which would be obtained from London.

2. The British Chiefs of Staff are now in a position to assure the United States Chiefs of Staff that the implementation of the proposals contained in NAF 841,

　　(a) will not interfere with the equipment for Allied and liberated forces in Northwest Europe;

　　(b) will not result in subsequent direct or indirect charges against United States resources.

3. With regard to the scale of equipment for the Allied and liberated forces in Northwest Europe, this will, in general, be British scales but modified in some respects in the light of shortages which exist in certain types of equipment.

TOP SECRET

C.C.S. 772

PLANNING DATE FOR THE END OF THE WAR WITH GERMANY

References:

CCS 182d Meeting, Item 7
CCS 183d Meeting, Item 4
CCS 186th Meeting, Item 3
1st Tripartite Military Meeting, Item 6
CCS 776/3, Paragraph 18

In C.C.S. 772, dated 3 January 1945, the British Chiefs of Staff submitted certain conclusions with regard to a planning date for the end of the war with Germany.

The Combined Chiefs of Staff in their 186th Meeting agreed to accept for planning purposes the following dates for the end of the war with Germany:

a. Earliest date, 1 July 1945.

b. Date beyond which war is unlikely to continue, 31 December 1945.

TOP SECRET

C.C.S. 772   30 January 1945

COMBINED CHIEFS OF STAFF

PLANNING DATE FOR THE END OF THE WAR WITH GERMANY

Memorandum by the British Chiefs of Staff

We have reviewed the planning date for the end of the war against Germany as follows:—

1. In considering German capacity to resist we have been guided by the latest study by the Joint Intelligence Subcommittee on this subject. Their conclusions are:—

   a. If, as seems just possible, the Russians succeed in overrunning the eastern defences of Germany before the Germans can consolidate there, the effect might be to force the Germans so to denude the West as to make an Allied advance comparatively easy. As the result of such advances in the East and in the West, a German collapse might occur before mid-April, 1945.

   b. On balance, however, we conclude that distance combined with stiffening German resistance is likely to bring the Russians to a halt on approximately the line Landsberg-Giant Mountains. This will involve the loss of industrial Silesia.

   c. As the result of the loss of industrial Silesia, production of finished armaments, mainly land armaments, would fall over a period of about six months by a quarter or more.

   d. If, as now appears improbable, the Germans succeed in stopping the Russian advance forward of Upper Silesia, thus retaining their two main industrial areas, in Silesia and in the Ruhr, we nevertheless consider that the over-all decline in Germany's capacity to resist will be such that an Allied offensive in the West followed by a further Russian offensive in the summer should lead to the collapse of German resistance before November.

   e. The need for forces to stem the Russian advance may cause a German withdrawal in Italy, at least to the line of the River Adige.

TOP SECRET

f. Germany, at any rate until the summer of 1945 when the U-boat campaign is expected to be at its height, is likely to retain sufficient forces to hold at least southern Norway.

2. Based on the above, we have considered three cases:

   a. The best case.

   b. A reasonably favourable case.

   c. An unfavourable case.

THE BEST CASE

3. It is clear from paragraph 1 *a.* above that there is a possibility that the result of the present Russian offensive may lead to a German collapse by mid-April. We do not consider, however, that there is sufficient likelihood of this timing being realised to justify its acceptance, for planning purposes, as the earliest date for the defeat of Germany.

THE REASONABLY FAVOURABLE CASE

4. *Eastern Front.* Distance and stiffening German resistance may well bring the Russians to a halt on approximately the line Landsberg-Giant Mountains. Thereafter, the Russians will have to re-establish their communications and prepare for a further major offensive as soon as weather conditions and their logistics allow. This might be in mid-May or early June.

5. *Western Front.* Preliminary operations to reach the Rhine should be completed before the end of March. An all-out Allied offensive could then be launched in the latter part of April or early May, with the object of isolating the Ruhr and advancing deep into Germany.

6. The result of these two offensives, if successful, should bring the end of organised German resistance by the end of June.

THE UNFAVOURABLE CASE

7. *Eastern Front.* In this case, we assume that the Russian advance is stopped short of Upper Silesia. Thereafter, if all factors are unfavourable, the combination of German resistance and Russian logistic difficulties may prevent a further major Russian offensive from being launched until the late summer.

TOP SECRET

8. *Western Front.* The Allied offensive in the spring may fail to achieve any decisive result. This might be caused by too great a dispersion of effort along the whole front, together with the qualitative superiority of the German heavy tanks and jet-propelled aircraft. It would then be necessary to re-group with a view to launching another offensive. This offensive could be launched in the summer, but it might well suffer in weight and momentum as the result of a successful U-boat campaign of which the effects are likely to be felt in the third quarter of the year.

9. In these circumstances we consider that the results of these two offensives, particularly the Russian, should bring about the end of German organised resistance by the beginning of November.

CONCLUSION

10. There is a possibility that, as a result of the present Russian offensive, Germany may be defeated by the middle of April. This, however, should be regarded as a bonus and should not influence our production or manpower planning.

For planning purposes, we consider that:—

a. The earliest date on which the war is likely to end is the 30th June, 1945.

b. The date beyond which the war is unlikely to continue is the 1st November, 1945.

TOP SECRET

C.C.S. 773/2

C.C.S. 773/3

OPERATIONS IN THE MEDITERRANEAN

References:

CCS 183d Meeting, Item 2
CCS 184th Meeting, Item 2
CCS 185th Meeting, Item 5
1st U.S.-U.K. Plenary Meeting, Item *d.*
CCS 776/3, Paragraph 11

In C.C.S. 773, dated 31 January 1945, the British Chiefs of Staff submitted for approval a draft directive to the Supreme Allied Commander, Mediterranean.

The United States Chiefs of Staff circulated C.C.S. 773/1 on 1 February suggesting certain amendments to C.C.S. 773.

In C.C.S. 773/2, dated 1 February 1945, the British Chiefs of Staff asked agreement to certain decisions in principle with regard to withdrawal of tactical air forces from the Mediterranean to the Western Front.

The Combined Chiefs of Staff, after consideration of C.C.S. 773/1 and 773/2, amended and approved the directive to the Supreme Allied Commander, Mediterranean proposed in C.C.S. 773/1. The agreed directive was subsequently circulated as C.C.S. 773/3.

TOP SECRET

C.C.S. 773/2 1 February 1945

COMBINED CHIEFS OF STAFF

TRANSFER OF TACTICAL AIR FORCES FROM SACMED TO SCAEF

Memorandum by the British Chiefs of Staff

1. It is recommended that the following decisions in principle should be made by the Combined Chiefs of Staff and implemented by the Supreme Commanders in accordance with the development of the situation in the Mediterranean Theatre.

2. In view of the intention stated in paragraph 5 of the directive to SACMED (Enclosure to C.C.S. 773), no substantial reduction should be made in the tactical air forces now available for the support of the 15th Group of Armies so long as the enemy maintains approximately his present position in Italy.

3. Should the enemy retire from his present positions in Italy, the tactical air forces now in the Mediterranean Theatre should be employed to the full for the purpose of achieving the object stated in paragraph 6 (c) of the directive to SACMED (Enclosure to C.C.S. 773).

4. If, after retiring, the enemy succeeds in stabilising his position on a line such as the Adige, a substantial withdrawal of tactical air forces from the Mediterranean to the Western Front will be desirable and should be proposed by the Supreme Commanders to the Combined Chiefs of Staff.

TOP SECRET

C.C.S. 773/3   17 February 1945

COMBINED CHIEFS OF STAFF

OPERATIONS IN THE MEDITERRANEAN

Note by the Secretaries

1. In their 185th Meeting, the Combined Chiefs of Staff approved the directive to the Supreme Allied Commander, Mediterranean, contained in C.C.S. 773/1 subject to the substitution of the following for the existing paragraph 5:—

"5. Two fighter groups of the Twelfth Air Force will be moved to France at once. The Combined Chiefs of Staff intend to move to France in the near future as much of the Twelfth Air Force as can be released without hazard to your mission. You should consult with SCAEF and submit agreed proposals for confirmation by the Combined Chiefs of Staff."

2. The directive to the Supreme Allied Commander, Mediterranean as approved and dispatched (FAN 501 — FACS 151) is attached.

                                                                       A. J. McFARLAND,
                                                                       A. T. CORNWALL-JONES,
                                                                       Combined Secretariat.

TOP SECRET

ENCLOSURE

DIRECTIVE TO SUPREME ALLIED COMMANDER, MEDITERRANEAN

1. It is our primary intention in the war against Germany to build up the maximum possible strength on the Western Front and to seek a decision in that theatre. We have, therefore, reviewed your directive and decided as follows.

GREECE

2. The earliest possible discharge of British obligations in Greece must be your constant aim.

The object of British presence and operations in Greece is to secure that part of Greece which is necessary for the establishment of the authority of a free Greek Government.

3. This object must always be regarded in the light of the paramount need for releasing troops from Greece for use against the Germans. You should, therefore, concentrate on building up a Greek force on a national basis as soon as possible.

ITALY

4. In pursuance of the policy given in paragraph 1, it has been decided to withdraw from your theatre to the Western Front up to five divisions (of which not more than two should be armoured) as follows:—

(a) At the earliest possible date three Allied divisions drawn from the Allied Armies in Italy.

(b) Further complete formations equivalent to the forces now in Greece as the latter are released from that country.

(c) It is intended to withdraw Canadian and British divisions. The nomination of ground formations to be withdrawn and the arrangements for their transfer will form the subject of a separate instruction. The programme will be agreed between you and Supreme Commander, Allied Expeditionary Force and approved by the Combined Chiefs of Staff before any moves take place.

TOP SECRET

5. Two fighter groups of the Twelfth Air Force will be moved to France at once. The Combined Chiefs of Staff intend to move to France in the near future as much of the Twelfth Air Force as can be released without hazard to your mission. You should consult with SCAEF and submit agreed proposals for confirmation by the Combined Chiefs of Staff.

6. There will be no significant withdrawal of amphibious assault forces.

7. We recognise that these withdrawals will affect the scope of your operations in the Italian Theatre. We, therefore, redefine your objects as follows:—

(a) Your first object should be to ensure that, subject to any minor adjustments you may find necessary, the front already reached in Italy is solidly held.

(b) Within the limits of the forces remaining available to you after the withdrawals in paragraph 4 above have been effected, you should do your utmost, by means of such limited offensive action as may be possible and by the skillful use of cover and deception plans, to contain the German forces now in Italy and prevent their withdrawal to other fronts.

(c) You should, in any case, remain prepared to take immediate advantage of any weakening or withdrawal of the German forces.

ADRIATIC

8. Subject to the requirements of the Italian Theatre, you should continue to give all possible support to the Yugoslav Army of National Liberation, until the territory of Yugoslavia has been completely cleared. You will carry out such minor operations on the eastern shores of the Adriatic as your resources allow.

TOP SECRET

C.C.S. 774/1
C.C.S. 774/3

U-BOAT THREAT DURING 1945

References:

CCS 182d Meeting, Item 9
CCS 183d Meeting, Item 7
CCS 184th Meeting, Item 6
CCS 185th Meeting, Item 7
1st U.S.-U.K. Plenary Meeting, Item *b*.
Tripartite Plenary Meeting
CCS 776/3, Paragraph 7

In C.C.S. 774, dated 31 January 1945, the United States Chiefs of Staff submitted a proposal for combatting the German U-boat threat.

In C.C.S. 774/1, dated 31 January, the British Chiefs of Staff summarized the present situation with regard to the U-boat threat during 1945.

In C.C.S. 774/2, dated 1 February, the British Chiefs of Staff submitted a reply to C.C.S. 774 and suggested alternate proposals to combat the German U-boat menace.

In their 184th Meeting the Combined Chiefs of Staff took note of C.C.S. 774/1 and in their 185th Meeting they approved a draft directive prepared by the Secretaries, based upon C.C.S. 774 and C.C.S. 774/2. The approved directive was subsequently circulated as C.C.S. 774/3.

TOP SECRET

C.C.S. 774/1   31 January 1945

COMBINED CHIEFS OF STAFF

U-BOAT THREAT DURING 1945

Memorandum by the British Chiefs of Staff

1. By the introduction of the Schnorkel and other technical developments, the lack of mobility of U-boats when diving, and the necessity of surfacing for recharging batteries, have been overcome. U-boats now remain dived for long periods and are enabled to work in inshore waters where detection is most difficult and targets are numerous. These methods of operating submarines have produced new problems in countering the submarine threat.

2. The problem of the U-boat threat during 1945 is discussed below under two headings:—

   (a) A forecast of future developments in the U-boat campaign.

   (b) An assessment of the effect of increased losses.

PRESENT SITUATION

3. After the failure of the U-boats to interrupt *OVERLORD* a comparative lull ensued. The enemy has used this lull to work up his new submarines, refit the older types, and to give his commanders and crews experience, during working-up patrols, in operating in inshore waters.

4. The number of U-boats on patrol around the British Isles is now increasing slowly but steadily, and there are 8 to 12 in inshore waters, some of which have penetrated into the Irish Sea and Clyde Approaches. Altogether about 25 U-boats are patrolling in U.K. waters or are on passage.

COUNTERMEASURES

5. Both surface forces and aircraft are greatly handicapped by the Schnorkel, together with G.S.R., which makes radar detection extremely difficult. Aircraft also find that even if detection is achieved, the U-boat will dive below periscope depth and thus leave no visible target for attack.

TOP SECRET

6. By making use of the tactics of bottoming in the presence of escorts, the U-boats are extremely difficult to detect by ASDIC's, due to the number of wrecks and other "non-sub echoes" in coastal waters, and to the reduced efficiency of ASDIC's caused by density layers and bottom reverberations.

7. An additional complication is the gnat torpedo. Tactical or mechanical countermeasures to this further reduce the efficiency of ASDIC's or the speed with which an attack can be delivered.

8. As a result it has been necessary to examine other methods for countering U-boats. Intensified training has been undertaken, but training at sea in the Irish Sea has been interfered with temporarily due to the presence of the U-boats.

9. Other countermeasures in hand include improvement in radar for detection of Schnorkel, laying of deep minefields in areas of U-boat operation, laying of obstructions and methods of indicating the presence of U-boats. In addition Bomber Command continue mining of the approaches to German bases and working-up areas. Bombing has been carried out with success on the U-boat assembly yards by Bomber Command and United States Strategic Air Force.

10. In view of the reduced effectiveness of the ASDIC to detect U-boats in inshore waters, a plan for extensive patrolling of the focal points on convoy routes by day, and of probable schnorkelling areas by night, is being put into force in the inshore waters in the Western Approaches with the object of harassing the U-boats and reporting incidents with the least possible delay.

11. In addition the close approach of the Russian forces to Danzig and Gdynia must have a considerable effect on the German U-boat building and working-up programme. A third of their U-boat assembly capacity is situated in this area.

FUTURE DEVELOPMENTS

12. Two new types of U-boats will shortly come into operation.

Type 21: 1,600 tons, 26 torpedoes, 15 knots surfaced and submerged, with greatly increased submerged endurance.

Type 23: 180 tons, 2 torpedoes, about 13 knots submerged, and low endurance.

TOP SECRET

About 30 Type 21 and 15 Type 23 could be ready for operations during February. It is probable that these numbers will be considered sufficient to start the campaign in strength.

13. It is considered that the old and new types will be used simultaneously, and an estimation of their likely operational areas has been made as follows:—

(a) *Type 21*. Possibly in Western Approaches to the United Kingdom initially, but mainly in operations against ocean convoys.

(b) *Type 23*. On the coastal convoy routes on the east and southeast coasts of England.

(c) *740 tonners and U-kreuzers*. On the Indian Ocean, Caribbean, West African and N. and S. American coasts.

(d) *500 tonners*. In United Kingdom coastal waters and between the United Kingdom and Gibraltar.

ESTIMATION OF THE SHIPPING LOSSES WHICH MAY BE EXPECTED

14. Given good morale of the U-boat commanders, on whom success depends, sinkings by U-boats may rise to the order of 150 ships a quarter. These figures are, however, estimates and the figures may vary greatly, but are on the assumption that each U-boat will sink one ship per month.

15. These figures are exclusive of the casualties that may be caused by midget U-boats, to the destruction of which a proportion of our anti-submarine forces are diverted, and other marine losses.

CONCLUSIONS

16. The main U-boat offensive in strength could begin to take shape about mid-February.

Although the Russian threat to the Danzig area will seriously reduce the enemy's constructional and training facilities, he should be able to maintain a total of 50 boats on patrol, compared with an average of about 60 during the height of the U-boat campaign in the spring of 1943.

The Schnorkel and other new technical developments have increased the U-boat's potential for offensive action and have considerably reduced the effectiveness of our present naval and air countermeasures.

TOP SECRET

17. The success of the U-boat is so largely dependent on the morale and offensive spirit of its crew that it is impossible to give any firm figures for the shipping losses to be expected. If, however, morale is good, and the enemy is able to maintain the optimum number of U-boats on patrol, merchant shipping losses of the order of 150 ships a quarter may possibly be expected, compared with 183 ships a quarter during the spring of 1943. The majority of these losses are likely to occur in the inshore waters of the British Isles and in the North Atlantic. Account must also be taken of losses which may occur from mines, E-boats, air attack and small battle units. The above figures take no account of the possible effect of additional countermeasures which may be practicable.

ASSESSMENT OF EFFECT OF ESTIMATED INCREASED LOSSES

18. We have been unable accurately to assess the effects of the estimated sinkings on the world shipping situation, owing to the many implications and complexity of the problem. We have, therefore, attempted to give a broad indication of the potential gravity of the threat with which we may be confronted should the U-boat campaign materialise on the scale indicated above.

ASSUMPTIONS

19. We have taken, as a basis for calculation, that:—

(a) The sinkings from U-boats alone will be 50 ships a month from March onwards.

(b) In addition, damaged ships will increase the effect of these losses by some 20%.

(c) Two-thirds of the ships lost will be loaded.

(d) One-fifth of the ships sunk will be tankers.

(e) The merchant ship construction programme in 1945 will remain unchanged.

DRY CARGO SHIPS

20. The Over-all Review of Cargo Shipping* forecasts that between February and June, 1945, both inclusive, there will be a total deficiency of 689 sailings on the main ocean routes including the Pacific. In assessing this deficiency

---

* C.M.T. 66/3.

it was assumed that the ships "locked up" in essential military assignments in various theatres, or permanently abroad (amounting to some 33% of the total Allied Nations' tonnage available) are kept up to strength, and that if losses occur among these ships they are replaced by ships from the main ocean pool. The resulting deficiency amounts to some 8% of the remaining combined requirements.

21. This deficiency figure was based on a low "loss rate" of some 100,000 gross tons per month from all causes, including marine (this may be taken as some 13-15 ships per month, of which only 6 are attributed to U-boats).

22. The additional losses from U-boats, together with an allowance for damaged ships, produce an additional 3% deficiency on combined requirements, making a total deficiency of sailings for the first half of 1945 of 11%.

23. We understand that, while a portion of the deficit revealed in the "Overall Review of Cargo Shipping" would be manageable, an apparent deficit of 8% must entail some reduction in commitments.

It is clear that an extra 3% deficiency caused by U-boat sinkings would entail yet further and more serious reductions.

It has not been possible to assess the direct effect on the fighting fronts caused by the material sunk and by delays in replacing military shipping.

TANKERS AND OIL

24. In the first half of 1945, it is possible that the increased submarine activity might result in the loss of oil cargoes amounting to 320,000 tons and that up to 35 tankers in the United Kingdom service might be sunk or damaged.

It would, therefore, be essential to transfer tankers from other theatres at an early date to replace the lost cargoes and tankers, if the fall of stocks to a dangerous level is to be prevented.

PERSONNEL SHIPS

25. It is not possible to forecast sinkings of personnel ships and no account, therefore, has been taken of the possible loss of these ships, which, as opposed

TOP SECRET

to dry cargo ships and tankers, are irreplaceable. The loss of or damage to a Monster, for instance, would have most serious consequences on the trooping programme.

CONCLUSION

26. We therefore conclude that, while it is not possible to translate the effect of the assumed losses due to U-boats into terms of supplies and reinforcements for individual theatres, the additional over-all deficiency in sailings may bring the 8% already forecast up to some 11% for the first half of the year. For planning purposes, however, we propose that a figure of 10% should be taken.

TOP SECRET

C.C.S. 774/3 2 February 1945

COMBINED CHIEFS OF STAFF

U-BOAT THREAT DURING 1945

Note by the Secretaries

In their 185th Meeting, the Combined Chiefs of Staff approved the enclosed directive and invited the United States and British Chiefs of Staff to dispatch it to all appropriate commanders.

A. J. McFARLAND,
A. T. CORNWALL-JONES,
Combined Secretariat.

TOP SECRET

ENCLOSURE

DIRECTIVE

The Combined Chiefs of Staff consider that the current German U-boat program, if not countered, will present a serious threat to our North Atlantic shipping lanes.

It is therefore directed that the following countermeasures be taken by all appropriate commanders:—

a. Build up as much as is practicable the strength of surface hunting groups and anti-U-boat air squadrons.

b. Maintain, and if possible increase "marginal" bomber effort on assembly yards, concentrating as far as is practicable against Hamburg and Bremen.

c. Maintain "marginal" effort against operating bases, being ready to increase this when bases become crowded beyond the capacity of concrete pens.

d. Increase, by 100% if possible, the air mining effort against U-boats, including the training areas.

e. Mine waters beyond range of *d.* above by using surface minelayers and carrier-borne aircraft.

f. Intensify operations against enemy minesweepers.

g. Maintain and intensify operations against the enemy shipping used to supply U-boat bases.

TOP SECRET

C.C.S. 775

BASIC UNDERTAKINGS IN SUPPORT OF OVER-ALL
STRATEGIC CONCEPT

References:

CCS 185th Meeting, Item 8
CCS 186th Meeting, Item 6
CCS 776/3, Paragraph 6

In C.C.S. 775, dated 1 February 1945, the British Chiefs of Staff proposed a substitute for paragraph *h.* of the basic undertakings in support of over-all strategic concept as shown in Part III of the *OCTAGON* report to the President and Prime Minister.

The Combined Chiefs of Staff considered the proposed substitute in their 185th and 186th Meetings and agreed upon the wording recorded in the *ARGONAUT* report to the President and Prime Minister, C.C.S. 776/3, paragraph 6.

TOP SECRET

C.C.S. 775   1 February 1945

COMBINED CHIEFS OF STAFF

BASIC UNDERTAKINGS IN SUPPORT OF OVER-ALL STRATEGIC CONCEPT

Memorandum by the British Chiefs of Staff

The British Chiefs of Staff recommend that the basic undertakings agreed upon at *OCTAGON* and set out in C.C.S. 680/2, paragraph 6,* be reaffirmed, subject to the following amendment.

For existing *h.* substitute the following:—

"*h.* Continue assistance to the forces of the liberated areas in Europe to enable them to fulfill an active role in the war against Germany and/or Japan. Within the limits of our available resources to assist other co-belligerents to the extent they are able to employ this assistance against the Enemy Powers in the present war. Within the limits of our available resources to provide such supplies to the liberated areas as will effectively contribute to the war-making capacity of the United Nations."

---

* *OCTAGON* Conference book, page 131.

TOP SECRET

C.C.S. 776/3

REPORT TO THE PRESIDENT AND PRIME MINISTER

References:

CCS 185th Meeting, Item 9
CCS 187th Meeting, Item 6
CCS 188th Meeting, Item 2
1st U.S.-U.K. Plenary Meeting, Item *a*.
2d U.S.-U.K. Plenary Meeting

C.C.S. 776, dated 2 February 1945, the first interim draft report to the President and Prime Minister was amended and approved by the Combined Chiefs of Staff in their 185th Meeting and circulated as C.C.S. 776/1.

The final draft report to the President and Prime Minister, C.C.S. 776/2, dated 8 February, was approved by the Combined Chiefs of Staff in their 188th Meeting. Following its acceptance by the President and Prime Minister in their Second Plenary Meeting, the final *ARGONAUT* report was recirculated as C.C.S. 776/3.

TOP SECRET

C.C.S. 776/3 9 February 1945

COMBINED CHIEFS OF STAFF

REPORT TO THE PRESIDENT AND PRIME MINISTER

Note by the Secretaries

The final report of the Combined Chiefs of Staff on the *ARGONAUT* Conference as approved by the President and the Prime Minister is enclosed.

> A. J. McFARLAND,
> A. T. CORNWALL-JONES,
> Combined Secretariat.

TOP SECRET

ENCLOSURE

REPORT TO THE PRESIDENT AND PRIME MINISTER OF
THE AGREED SUMMARY OF CONCLUSIONS REACHED BY THE
COMBINED CHIEFS OF STAFF AT THE "ARGONAUT" CONFERENCE

1. The agreed summary of the conclusions reached at *ARGONAUT* Conference is submitted herewith:—

I. *OVER-ALL OBJECTIVE*

2. In conjunction with Russia and other Allies, to bring about at the earliest possible date the unconditional surrender of Germany and Japan.

II. *OVER-ALL STRATEGIC CONCEPT FOR THE PROSECUTION OF THE WAR*

3. In cooperation with Russia and other Allies, to bring about at the earliest possible date the unconditional surrender of Germany.

4. Simultaneously, in cooperation with other Pacific Powers concerned, to maintain and extend unremitting pressure against Japan with the purpose of continually reducing her military power and attaining positions from which her ultimate surrender can be forced. The effect of any such extension on the over-all objective to be given consideration by the Combined Chiefs of Staff before action is taken.

5. Upon the defeat of Germany, in cooperation with other Pacific Powers and with Russia, to direct the full resources of the United States and Great Britain to bring about at the earliest possible date the unconditional surrender of Japan.

III. *BASIC UNDERTAKINGS IN SUPPORT OF OVER-ALL STRATEGIC CONCEPT*

6. Whatever operations are decided on in support of the over-all strategic concept, the following established undertakings will be a first charge against our resources; subject to review by the Combined Chiefs of Staff in keeping with the changing situation:—

a. Maintain the security and war-making capacity of the Western Hemisphere and the British Isles.

b. Support the war-making capacity of our forces in all areas.

c. Maintain vital overseas lines of communication.

d. Continue the disruption of enemy sea communications.

e. Continue the offensive against Germany.

f. Undertake such measures as may be necessary and practicable to aid the war effort of Russia to include coordinating the action of forces.

g. Undertake such measures as may be necessary and practicable in order to aid the war effort of China as an effective ally and as a base for operations against Japan.

h. Provide assistance to such of the forces of the liberated areas in Europe as can fulfill an active and effective role in the war against Germany and/or Japan. Within the limits of our available resources to assist other co-belligerents to the extent they are able to employ this assistance against the Enemy Powers in the present war. Having regard to the successful accomplishment of the other basic undertakings, to provide such supplies to the liberated areas as will effectively contribute to the war-making capacity of the United Nations against Germany and/or Japan.

i. Reorient forces from the European Theater to the Pacific and Far East as a matter of highest priority having regard to other agreed and/or inescapable commitments as soon as the German situation allows.

j. Continue operations leading to the earliest practicable invasion of Japan.

IV. *EXECUTION OF THE OVER-ALL STRATEGIC CONCEPT*

DEFEAT OF GERMANY

THE U-BOAT WAR

7. We are concerned with the possibility that German U-boats may again constitute a serious threat to our North Atlantic shipping lanes. It is too early yet to assess the extent to which such an offensive could achieve success, and we propose to review the matter again on 1 April 1945.

Enclosure

TOP SECRET

8. Meanwhile, we have agreed on the following countermeasures:—

a. To build up as much as is practicable the strength of surface hunting groups and anti-U-boat air squadrons.

b. To maintain and, if possible, increase "marginal" bomber effort on assembly yards, concentrating as far as is practicable against Hamburg and Bremen.

c. To maintain "marginal" effort against operating bases, being ready to increase this when bases become crowded beyond the capacity of concrete pens.

d. To increase, by 100% if possible, the air mining effort against U-boats, including the training areas.

e. To mine waters beyond range of *d.* above by using surface minelayers and carrier-borne aircraft.

f. To intensify operations against enemy minesweepers.

g. To maintain and intensify operations against the enemy shipping used to supply U-boat bases.

OPERATIONS IN NORTHWEST EUROPE

9. In two telegrams, SCAF 180 as amended by SCAF 194, the Supreme Commander, Allied Expeditionary Force, has presented his appreciation and his plan of operations for Northwest Europe. His plan is as follows:—

a. To carry out immediately a series of operations north of the Moselle with a view to destroying the enemy and closing the Rhine north of Dusseldorf.

b. To direct our efforts to eliminating other enemy forces west of the Rhine, which still constitute an obstacle or a potential threat to our subsequent Rhine crossing operations.

c. To seize bridgeheads over the Rhine in the North and the South.

d. To deploy east of the Rhine and north of the Ruhr the maximum number of divisions which can be maintained (estimated at some 35 divisions). The initial task of this force, assisted by air action, will be to deny to the enemy the industries of the Ruhr.

Enclosure

TOP SECRET

    e. To deploy east of the Rhine, on the axis Frankfurt-Kassel, such forces, if adequate, as may be available after providing 35 divisions for the North and essential security elsewhere. The task of this force will be to draw enemy forces away from the North by capturing Frankfurt and advancing on Kassel.

10. We have taken note of SCAF 180 as amended by SCAF 194 and of the Supreme Commander's assurance that he will seize the Rhine crossings in the North just as soon as this is a feasible operation and without waiting to close the Rhine throughout its length. Further, that he will advance across the Rhine in the North with maximum strength and complete determination, immediately the situation in the South allows him to collect the necessary forces and do this without incurring unreasonable risks.

STRATEGY IN THE MEDITERRANEAN

11. We have reviewed our strategy in the Mediterranean in the light of the development of the situation in Europe and of the fact that the enemy is at liberty at any time to make a voluntary withdrawal in Italy. We have agreed that our primary object in the war against Germany should be to build up the maximum possible strength on the Western Front and to seek a decision in that theater.

12. In accordance with this concept we have agreed to withdraw certain forces from the Mediterranean Theater and to place them at the disposal of the Supreme Commander, Allied Expeditionary Force, and to redefine the tasks of the Supreme Allied Commander, Mediterranean.

13. Our proposals are contained in the directive to the Supreme Allied Commander, Mediterranean, attached as Appendix "A."

THE WAR AGAINST JAPAN

OVER-ALL OBJECTIVE IN THE WAR AGAINST JAPAN

14. We have agreed that the over-all objective in the war against Japan should be expressed as follows:

    To force the unconditional surrender of Japan by:—

Enclosure

TOP SECRET

a. Lowering Japanese ability and will to resist by establishing sea and air blockades, conducting intensive air bombardment, and destroying Japanese air and naval strength.

b. Invading and seizing objectives in the industrial heart of Japan.

OPERATIONS IN THE PACIFIC AREA

15. We have taken note of the plans and operations proposed by the United States Chiefs of Staff in C.C.S. 417/11 (Appendix "B").

OPERATIONS IN SOUTHEAST ASIA COMMAND

16. We have agreed to the following policy in respect of employment in Southeast Asia Command of United States resources deployed in the India-Burma Theater:—

a. The primary military object of the United States in the China and India-Burma Theaters is the continuance of aid to China on a scale that will permit the fullest utilization of the area and resources of China for operations against the Japanese. United States resources are deployed in India-Burma to provide direct or indirect support for China. These forces and resources participate not only in operating the base and the line of communications for United States and Chinese forces in China, but also constitute a reserve immediately available to China without permanently increasing the requirements for transport of supplies to China.

b. The United States Chiefs of Staff contemplate no change in their agreement to SACSEA's use of resources of the U.S. India-Burma Theater in Burma when this use does not prevent the fulfillment of their primary object of rendering support to China including protection of the line of communications. Any transfer of forces engaged in approved operations in progress in Burma which is contemplated by the United States Chiefs of Staff and which, in the opinion of the British Chiefs of Staff, would jeopardize those operations, will be subject to discussion by the Combined Chiefs of Staff.

17. We have reviewed the progress of the campaign in Burma and agreed upon the terms of a directive to the Supreme Allied Commander, Southeast Asia. This directive is attached as Appendix "C."

Enclosure

TOP SECRET

PLANNING DATES FOR THE END OF THE WAR AGAINST GERMANY AND JAPAN

18. We feel that it is important to agree and promulgate planning dates for the end of the war against Germany and Japan. These dates are necessary for the purpose of planning production and the allocation of manpower.

We recommend that the planning dates for the end of the war against Germany should be as follows:—

a. Earliest date — 1 July 1945.

b. Date beyond which the war is unlikely to continue — 31 December 1945.

We recommend that the planning date for the end of the war against Japan should be set at 18 months after the defeat of Germany.

All the above dates to be adjusted periodically to conform to the course of the war.

SHIPPING

19. We have reviewed the over-all cargo and troop shipping position for the remainder of 1945 under the assumption that Germany is defeated on 1 July 1945.

For the first half of 1945 the principal difficulty will be with cargo shipping, which will be tight and in which deficits will approach unmanageable proportions until V-E Day. We have issued instructions to theater commanders to exercise strict control of shipping and have agreed that deficits should be adjusted in accordance with the following principles:—

In the event of a deficit in shipping resources, first priority should be given to the basic undertakings in support of the over-all strategic concepts as agreed in *ARGONAUT*.

So long as these first priority requirements are not adequately covered, shipping for other requirements will not be allocated without prior consultation with the appropriate Chiefs of Staff.

Enclosure

TOP SECRET

20. For the second half of 1945 the principal difficulty will be troop shipping, which will become particularly acute in the last quarter of the year. We have agreed that the matter should be reviewed and a report submitted to the Combined Chiefs of Staff not later than 1 April 1945. This report will take account, from the shipping point of view, of the possibility that the war against Germany may continue beyond 1 July 1945.

OIL

21. We have reviewed and agreed upon the levels of stocks of all petroleum products that should be maintained in all theaters. The text of our agreement is attached as Appendix "D."

EQUIPMENT FOR ALLIED AND LIBERATED FORCES

22. The Supreme Allied Commander, Mediterranean, has submitted proposals (NAF 841*) designed to assist the Greek Government in forming their own army and so releasing British forces for employment elsewhere.

We have agreed that the British Chiefs of Staff should proceed to implement the Supreme Commander's proposals, on the understanding that this will not interfere with the provision of equipment for Allied and liberated forces in Northwest Europe, nor result in subsequent direct or indirect charges against United States resources.

---

* See page 188.

Enclosure

TOP SECRET

APPENDIX "A"

DIRECTIVE TO SUPREME ALLIED COMMANDER, MEDITERRANEAN, REPEATED TO SCAEF

1. It is our primary intention in the war against Germany to build up the maximum possible strength on the Western Front and to seek a decision in that theater. We have, therefore, reviewed your directive and decided as follows:—

GREECE

2. The earliest possible discharge of British obligations in Greece must be your constant aim.

The object of British presence and operations in Greece is to secure that part of Greece which is necessary for the establishment of the authority of a free Greek Government.

3. This object must always be regarded in the light of the paramount need for releasing troops from Greece for use against the Germans. You should, therefore, concentrate on building up a Greek force on a national basis as soon as possible.

ITALY

4. In pursuance of the policy given in paragraph 1, it has been decided to withdraw from your theater to the Western Front up to five divisions (of which not more than two should be armored) as follows:—

a. At the earliest possible date three Allied divisions drawn from the Allied Armies in Italy.

b. Further complete formations as the forces now in Greece are released from that country.

Appendix "A"

TOP SECRET

    c. It is intended to withdraw Canadian and British divisions. The nomination of ground formations to be withdrawn and the arrangements for their transfer will form the subject of a separate instruction. The program will be agreed between you and Supreme Commander, Allied Expeditionary Force, and approved by the Combined Chiefs of Staff before any moves take place.

AIR FORCES

5. Two fighter groups of Twelfth Air Force will be moved to France at once. Combined Chiefs of Staff intend to move to France in the near future as much of the Twelfth Air Force as can be released without hazard to the accomplishment of your mission. You should consult with SCAEF and submit agreed proposals for confirmation by the Combined Chiefs of Staff.

6. There will be no significant withdrawal of amphibious assault forces.

7. We recognize that these withdrawals will affect the scope of your operations in the Italian Theater. We, therefore, redefine your objects as follows:—

    a. Your first object should be to ensure that, subject to any minor adjustments you may find necessary, the front already reached in Italy is solidly held.

    b. Within the limits of the forces remaining available to you after the withdrawals in paragraph 4 above have been effected, you should do your utmost, by means of such limited offensive action as may be possible and by the skillful use of cover and deception plans, to contain the German forces now in Italy and prevent their withdrawal to other fronts.

    c. You should, in any case, remain prepared to take immediate advantage of any weakening or withdrawal of the German forces.

ADRIATIC

8. Subject to the requirements of the Italian Theater, you should continue to give all possible support to the Yugoslav Army of National Liberation, until the territory of Yugoslavia has been completely cleared. You will carry out such minor operations on the eastern shores of the Adriatic as your resources allow.

Appendix "A"

TOP SECRET

APPENDIX "B"

OPERATIONS FOR THE DEFEAT OF JAPAN

References:

a. CCS 417/9
b. CCS 417/10

Memorandum by the United States Chiefs of Staff

(See paragraph 1 (3) (f), CCS 765)

1. The agreed over-all objective in the war against Japan has been expressed as follows (C.C.S. 417/9):—

   To force the unconditional surrender of Japan by:—

   (1) Lowering Japanese ability and will to resist by establishing sea and air blockades, conducting intensive air bombardment, and destroying Japanese air and naval strength.

   (2) Invading and seizing objectives in the industrial heart of Japan.

2. The United States Chiefs of Staff have adopted the following as a basis for planning in the war against Japan:

   The concept of operations for the main effort in the Pacific is (C.C.S. 417/10):—

   a. Following the Okinawa operation, to seize additional positions to intensify the blockade and air bombardment of Japan in order to create a situation favorable to:

   b. An assault on Kyushu for the purpose of further reducing Japanese capabilities by containing and destroying major enemy forces and further intensifying the blockade and air bombardment in order to establish a tactical condition favorable to:

   c. The decisive invasion of the industrial heart of Japan through the Tokyo Plain.

Appendix "B"

TOP SECRET

3. The following sequence and timing of operations have been directed by the United States Chiefs of Staff and plans prepared by theater commanders:—

Objectives	Target Date
Continuation of operations in the Philippines (Luzon, Mindoro, Leyte)	—
Iwo Jima	19 February 1945
Okinawa and extension therefrom in the Ryukyus	1 April-August 1945

4. Until a firm date can be established when redeployment from Europe can begin, planning will be continued for an operation to seize a position in the Chusan-Ningpo area and for invasion of Kyushu-Honshu in the winter of 1945-1946.

5. Examination is being conducted of the necessity for and cost of operations to maintain and defend a sea route to the Sea of Okhotsk when the entry of Russia into the war against Japan becomes imminent. Examination so far has shown that the possibility of seizing a position in the Kuriles for that purpose during the favorable weather period of 1945 is remote due to lack of sufficient resources. The possibility of maintaining and defending such a sea route from bases in Kamchatka alone is being further examined.

6. The United States Chiefs of Staff have also directed examination and preparation of a plan of campaign against Japan in the event that prolongation of the European war requires postponement of the invasion of Japan until well into 1946.

Appendix "B"

TOP SECRET

APPENDIX "C"

DIRECTIVE TO THE SUPREME ALLIED COMMANDER, SOUTHEAST ASIA

1. Your first object is to liberate Burma at the earliest date. (To be known as operation *LOYALIST*.)

2. Subject to the accomplishment of this object, your next main task will be the liberation of Malaya and the opening of the Straits of Malacca. (To be known as operation *BROADSWORD*.)

3. In view of your recent success in Burma, and of the uncertainty of the date of the final defeat of Germany, you must aim at the accomplishment of your first object with the forces at present at your disposal. This does not preclude the dispatch of further reinforcements from the European Theater should circumstances make this possible.

4. You will prepare a program of operations for the approval of the Combined Chiefs of Staff.

5. In transmitting the foregoing directive the Combined Chiefs of Staff direct your attention to the agreed policy in respect of the use in your theater of United States resources deployed in the India-Burma Theater (see paragraph 16 of the Report).

TOP SECRET

APPENDIX "D"

AGREEMENT ON LEVELS OF SUPPLY OF ALL
PETROLEUM PRODUCTS IN ALL THEATERS

1. The theater level should equal operating level plus emergency reserve level.

2. Each level shall be expressed in days of forward consumption. The rate of forward consumption used takes into account the size and degree of activity of the consuming forces as estimated by the theater commanders or other appropriate authorities.

3. The operating level provides the working stock required to be in the theater to provide for planned operations. It represents the number of days of supply to sustain the theater at the expected rate of consumption during the maximum interval which may exist between sustaining shipments. Experience has shown that all theaters (except icebound ports for which special levels must be established) can be assured of such a shipment at least every 30 days.

4. The emergency reserve level is intended to provide for unexpectedly high rates of consumption, destruction of stocks and handling facilities, and interruption of supply due to enemy action. It is based on the number of days or average number of days necessary to make emergency replacements from the principal port or ports of embarkation to the points of consumption in a theater of operation, and it includes loading time, voyage time, unloading time, and theater distribution time. Theater distribution time provides for the products which are necessarily absorbed and immobilized in the internal theater distribution system and takes account of variations in the different theaters.

It is considered that an emergency reserve level based on emergency replacement time in each theater is adequate to meet any contingency that might arise until special provision can be made for additional supplies.

5. The theater level of petroleum products shall include all bulk and packed stocks in the theater except those products which are (a) en route to the theater prior to discharge ashore, unless held as stock afloat, (b) issued to civilian garages, retailers and other small consumers, (c) issued to actual

Appendix "D"

TOP SECRET

consuming units (aircraft, vehicles, ships, craft, and so forth) or issued to dumps forward of Army rear boundary in combat zone.

6. The following theater levels expressed in days of forward consumption have been agreed upon for the supply of all petroleum products for military services and essential civilian use:—

THEATER	Operation Level	Emergency Reserve Level	Theater Level	
Northwest Europe and U.K.*				
Admiralty				
Fuels	30	60	90	
War Office and European Theater of Operations, U.S. Army				
Motor Transport Fuels	30	30	60	
Air Ministry				
100 Octane	30	35	65	
Other Grades	30	35	65	
Others				
Motor Spirit	30	45	75	
Other White	30	60	90	
Gas/Diesel	30	60	90	
Fuel Oil	30	60	90	
Lubricants	30	150	180	
Central Mediterranean	30	40	70	
Middle East	30	30	60	) see para-
Persia and Iraq	30	30	60	) graph 6 a.
South & East & West Africa	30	30	60	)
Southeast Asia Command (Including India-Burma)	30	55	85	
China Theater	30	55	85	
Southwest Pacific	30	55	85	
South Pacific	30	45	75	
Central Pacific	30	50	80	
Alaska	30	30	60	) see para-
North America	30	25	55	) graph 6 b.
Latin America	30	30	60	

* Emergency level for this theater takes special cognizance of the complexity of the distribution systems.

Appendix "D"

a. In these theaters the theater level for aviation spirit will be 75 days instead of 60.

b. Within the Alaskan, North American, and other applicable theaters special levels over and above the theater level will be necessary for icebound areas.

c. It is agreed that the above theater levels except as noted for Northwest Europe and U.K. will not apply to stocks of lubricating oils and greases which are subject to special considerations, particularly in areas where blending or packing takes place. The stocks required consequently vary considerably between theaters but normally approximate to 180 days consumption needs.

7. As some theaters have insufficient tankage to accommodate stocks at theater level, consideration will be given to the holding of a proportion of the reserves for these theaters in other areas which have surplus storage capacity available and are suitably placed strategically for this purpose.

8. Priority for providing supplies and allocating tankers shall be accorded to the maintenance of the emergency reserve levels in all theaters with the balance of all theater levels to be accumulated as rapidly as practicable thereafter, each theater taking its proportionate share of any shortage in supplies and tankers.

After all theater levels have been attained, any surplus supplies should be stored, under the control of the owner or as otherwise agreed upon, in available tankage nearest to the source of supply or where it appears most desirable strategically.

Theater stocks in excess of the theater level, unless permitted by specific agreement of the Combined Chiefs of Staff, shall be reduced promptly to authorized levels by appropriate allocations of supplies and/or tankers.

9. If priorities among theaters become necessary they will be determined by the Combined Chiefs of Staff.

10. The Army-Navy Petroleum Board and appropriate British authorities will be the agencies of the Combined Chiefs of Staff primarily charged with the proposal to the Combined Chiefs of Staff of any required revision of the levels of supply of petroleum products in any or all theaters and the principles governing these levels.

Appendix "D"

TOP SECRET

C.C.S. 777/2

RECIPROCAL AGREEMENT ON PRISONERS OF WAR

Reference:

CCS 187th Meeting, Item 4

In C.C.S. 777, dated 4 February 1945, the British Chiefs of Staff expressed their concurrence with a draft agreement proposed by the United States Secretary of State and the British Foreign Secretary which was submitted for the consideration of the Combined Chiefs of Staff before pursuing further negotiations with the Russians.

The United States Chiefs of Staff proposed in C.C.S. 777/1, dated 7 February, certain modifications to the draft agreement.

The Combined Chiefs of Staff in their 187th Meeting amended and approved C.C.S. 777/1. The draft agreement as amended and approved by the Combined Chiefs of Staff was circulated as C.C.S. 777/2.

TOP SECRET

C.C.S. 777/2   8 February 1945

COMBINED CHIEFS OF STAFF

RECIPROCAL AGREEMENT ON PRISONERS OF WAR

Note by the Secretaries

In their 187th Meeting the Combined Chiefs of Staff amended the agreement set forth in the Enclosure to C.C.S. 777/1. The agreement as amended and approved by the Combined Chiefs of Staff is enclosed herewith.

                                                      A. J. McFARLAND,
                                                      A. T. CORNWALL-JONES,
                                                      Combined Secretariat.

TOP SECRET

ENCLOSURE

AGREEMENT RELATING TO PRISONERS OF WAR AND CIVILIANS LIBERATED BY THE SOVIET ARMIES AND U.S. (BRITISH) ARMIES

Preamble.

The Government of the U.S.S.R. and the Government of the United States of America (the Government of His Britannic Majesty) wishing to conclude an agreement on arranging for the care and repatriation of Soviet citizens freed by Allied troops, and for American citizens (British subjects) freed by the Red Army, through their appointed representatives, acting mutually in the authority duly and fully invested in them, have agreed as follows:—

Article 1.

All Soviet citizens liberated by forces operating under U.S. (British) command and American citizens (British subjects) liberated by the forces operating under Soviet command will, without delay after their liberation, be separated from enemy prisoners of war and will be maintained separately from them in camps or points of concentration until they have been handed over to the Soviet or U.S. (British) authorities, as the case may be, at places agreed upon between those authorities.

U.S. (British) and Soviet military authorities will respectively take necessary measures for protection of camps, and points of concentration from enemy bombing, artillery fire, etc.

Article 2.

The contracting parties shall ensure that their military authorities shall without delay inform the competent authorities of the other party regarding citizens (or subjects) of the other contracting party found by them, and will undertake to follow all the provisions of this agreement. Soviet and U.S. (British) repatriation representatives will have the right of immediate access into the camps and points of concentration where their citizens (or subjects) are located and they will have the right to appoint the internal administration and set up the internal discipline and management in accordance with the military procedure and laws of their country.

TOP SECRET

Facilities will be given for the despatch or transfer of officers of their own nationality to camps or points of concentration where liberated members of the respective forces are located and there are insufficient officers. The outside protection of and access to and from the camps or points of concentration will be established in accordance with the instructions of the military commander in whose zone they are located, and the military commander shall also appoint a commandant, who shall have the final responsibility for the over-all administration and discipline of the camp or point concerned.

The relocation of camps as well as the transfer from one camp to another of liberated citizens will be notified to the competent Soviet or U.S. (British) authorities. Hostile propaganda directed against the contracting parties or against any of the United Nations will not be permitted.

Article 3.

Except in so far as the obligations set out in this article may be affected by obligations undertaken in connection with the use of UNRRA (or other agreed relief agencies) the competent U.S. (British) and Soviet authorities will do their utmost in the circumstances obtaining in any area, and from time to time, to supply liberated citizens (or subjects) of the contracting parties with adequate food, clothing, housing and medical attention both in camps or at points of concentration and en route, and with transport until they are handed over to the Soviet or U.S. (British) authorities at places agreed upon between those authorities. The standards of such food, clothing, housing and medical attention shall so far as possible be consistent with the normal practice relating to military rank.

The contracting parties will not demand compensation for these or other similar services which their authorities may supply respectively to liberated citizens (or subjects) of the other contracting party.

Article 4.

Either of the contracting parties shall be at liberty to use such of its own means of transport as may be available for the repatriation of its citizens (or subjects) held by the other contracting party. Similarly each of the contracting parties shall be at liberty to use its own facilities for the delivery of supplies to its citizens (or subjects) held by the other contracting party.

Article 5.

Soviet and U.S. (British) military authorities shall make such advances on behalf of their respective governments to liberated citizens (and subjects) of the other contracting party as the competent Soviet and U.S. (British) authorities shall agree upon beforehand.

Advances made in currency of any enemy territory or in currency of their occupation authorities shall not be liable to compensation.

In the case of advances made in currency of liberated non-enemy territory, the Soviet and U.S. (British) Governments will effect, each for advances made to their citizens (or subjects) necessary settlements with the governments of the territory concerned, who will be informed of the amount of their currency paid out for this purpose.

Article 6.

Ex-prisoners of war (with the exception of officers) and civilians of each of the contracting parties may, until their repatriation, be employed in the management, maintenance and administration of the camps or billets in which they are situated. They may also be employed on a voluntary basis on other work in the vicinity of their camps in furtherance of the common war effort in accordance with agreements to be reached between the competent Soviet and U.S. (British) authorities. The question of payment and conditions of labor shall be determined by agreement between those authorities. It is understood that liberated members of the respective forces will be employed in accordance with military standards and procedure.

Article 7.

The contracting parties shall, wherever necessary, use all practicable means to ensure the evacuation to the rear of these liberated citizens (and subjects). They also undertake to use all practicable means to transport liberated citizens (and subjects) to places to be agreed upon where they can be handed over to the Soviet or U.S. (British) authorities respectively. The handing over of these liberated citizens (and subjects) shall in no way be delayed or impeded by the requirements of their temporary employment.

TOP SECRET

Article 8.

The contracting parties will give the fullest possible effect to the foregoing provisions of this Agreement, subject only to the limitations in detail and from time to time of operational, supply and transport conditions in the several theatres.

TOP SECRET

C.C.S. 778/1

LIAISON WITH THE SOVIET HIGH COMMAND OVER ANGLO-AMERICAN STRATEGIC BOMBING IN EASTERN GERMANY

References:

CCS 182d Meeting, Item 5
CCS 186th Meeting, Item 7
CCS 188th Meeting, Item 3
1st Tripartite Military Meeting, Item 4
2d Tripartite Military Meeting, Item 1

In their 186th Meeting the Combined Chiefs of Staff considered C.C.S. 778, a memorandum by the British Chiefs of Staff dated 5 February 1945, and amended and approved the views expressed therein. C.C.S. 778 as amended and approved was circulated as C.C.S. 778/1.

TOP SECRET

C.C.S. 778/1　　　　　　　　　　　　　　　　　　　21 February 1945

COMBINED CHIEFS OF STAFF

LIAISON WITH THE SOVIET HIGH COMMAND OVER ANGLO-AMERICAN STRATEGIC BOMBING IN EASTERN GERMANY

Note by the Secretaries

C.C.S. 778, as amended in the C.C.S. 186th Meeting, 6 February 1945, is enclosed for information.

A. J. McFARLAND,
R. D. COLERIDGE,
Combined Secretariat.

TOP SECRET

ENCLOSURE

LIAISON WITH THE SOVIET HIGH COMMAND OVER ANGLO-AMERICAN STRATEGIC BOMBING IN EASTERN GERMANY

1. Our wishes are:—

   a. To continue to do the greatest possible damage to the German military and economic system.

   b. To avoid interference with or danger to the Soviet forces advancing from the East.

   c. To do what is possible to assist the advance of the Soviet Army.

2. To achieve the first wish, that is, maximum damage to the Germans, it is essential to avoid as far as possible any restriction of strategic bomber action. It is not our wish to draw a line on the map which would exclude our bombers from attacking any targets which are important to the war-making power of the enemy, whether against the Soviet or the British and American forces.

3. To achieve the second wish, that is, avoidance of interference with Soviet land operations, we must rely upon the Soviet High Command to inform the British and United States Missions in Moscow of the positions of the Red Army from day to day. We also invite the Soviet High Command to inform the British and United States Missions if there are any particular objectives, for example, railway centers or centers of road communication close in front of their armies which they wish us *not* to attack. We should require at least 24, and preferably 48 hours' notice for action upon such requests.

4. A regular daily meeting between the British and United States Missions in Moscow and a responsible officer of the Soviet General Staff seems to us to be essential.

5. To achieve the third wish, that is, assistance to the Russian advance, we should be glad to receive through the British and American Missions in Moscow any suggestions from the Soviet High Command. This suggestion would have to be considered in the light of other commitments and such factors as the distance and the weather.

TOP SECRET

6. To summarize, we suggest:—

   a. That there should be no rigid division of Eastern Germany into spheres of action of the Soviet and British and American strategic bombers respectively;

   b. That day-to-day liaison should be established between a responsible officer of the Russian High Command and representatives of the British and American Missions in Moscow, in order to exchange information upon which we can regulate the action of the Anglo-U.S. strategic bombers in accordance with the development of Soviet operations on land.

7. When the Soviet Air Force is ready to undertake strategic bombing deep into Germany from the East, the coordination of policy should be discussed by Soviet, American and British Staff representatives in London or in Moscow. Some further machinery for the closer coordination of operations would appear to be necessary at that time.

MESSAGES

FAN 477 and NAF 841 are reproduced in this volume for convenience of reference.

TOP SECRET

Combined Chiefs of Staff
15 January 1945

Commanding General
Allied Force Headquarters
Caserta, Italy

U.S. Military Mission
Moscow, Russia

Commanding General
Mediterranean Allied Air Force
Caserta, Italy

British Joint Staff Mission
Washington, D. C.

Commanding General
U.S. Strategic Air Forces in Europe
St. Germain, France

Number: WARX 21167

TOPSEC book message from the Combined Chiefs of Staff to Deane, Archer, Alexander and Spaatz for action; to McNarney and Eaker for information; to British Joint Staff Mission pass to British Chiefs of Staff and Bottomley for information. This message is FAN 477 to Alexander.

1. Combined Chiefs of Staff have reviewed the dispatches concerning the bombline in eastern Europe and the Balkan area between the Allied and Soviet Armies.

2. Existing procedure for Anglo-U.S. designation of a bombline in advance of Soviet armies is contrary to our accepted operational principles under which any army field commander designates his own bombline. The Combined Chiefs of Staff therefore recognize the Soviet right to establish bomblines to protect their own forces in the Balkans and in eastern Europe, subject to agreement on the following:—

a. Acceptance by the Soviets of the following definition of a bombline: "A bombline may be defined as an imaginary line on the ground established by army field commanders setting forth the forward boundary of an area in front of their ground forces in which the attack of ground targets by friendly aircraft is prohibited. This line must be delineated by terrain features easily recognizable to pilots in the air at all altitudes. It should be close enough to advancing troops to permit the attack of all vital strategic air objectives and tactical targets, air attacks on which will materially assist in the advance of ground troops or are necessary to the success of a strategic bomber offensive in carrying the war to the enemy. It should not be construed as a boundary for restricting movement of friendly aircraft."

b. Establishment of effective liaison parties with the Russian forces in the field. Any bombline is subject to frequent and rapid changes in accordance with the moving military situation of the ground forces concerned. Such timely changes, in the opinion of the Combined Chiefs of Staff, can be effectively disseminated only by the establishment of direct liaison between the Russian forces in the field and the U.S.-British forces concerned.

c. Acceptance of the right of the Allied air forces to fly over areas occupied by the Soviet ground forces in order to reach target objectives in front of any established bombline. (This would be necessary if the current Russian drive in western Hungary should continue westward.)

3. You should inform the Soviet General Staff that the Combined Chiefs of Staff feel that in the absence of agreement on the above, including the arrangements in paragraph 2 *b.* and *c.*, the Soviets share responsibility for any incidents of air attacks on their troops which occur as the result of their troops over-running a bombline which must be established on the basis of the poor liaison which presently exists with the Russian field armies.

4. Until such time as agreement is reached with the Soviet General Staff on the above,

a. The Supreme Allied Commander, Mediterranean is authorized to make changes in the bombline south of the latitude of Vienna, transmitting the information to the Commanding General, U.S. Strategic Air Forces and Deputy Chief of Air Staff, and the Heads of the U.S. and British Missions in Moscow for transmittal to the Red Army Staff, with copies of such communications to the Combined Chiefs of Staff for information.

b. The Commanding General, United States Strategic Air Forces and the Deputy Chief of Air Staff are authorized jointly to establish and make changes in the bombline north of the latitude of Vienna; the Commanding

TOP SECRET

General, U.S. Strategic Air Forces, to transmit such information to the Supreme Allied Commander, Mediterranean and to the Heads of the U.S. and British Military Missions in Moscow for transmittal to the Red Army Staff, with copies of such communications to the Combined Chiefs of Staff for information.

5. This is Combined Chiefs of Staff action on MX-21926, MX-22201 and MX-21984 from Deane and Archer and NAF 827 from Wilson.

End

ORIGINATOR: Gen. McFarland (C.C./S)

CM-OUT-21167   (Jan 45)   DTG 152334Z   ef

TOP SECRET

From: Allied Force Headquarters, Caserta, Italy

To: War Department
        Supreme Headquarters, Allied Expeditionary Forces, Main, Versailles, France

Nr: FX 91225   NAF 841   25 January 1945

    Signed Alexander cite FHGCT. FX 91225 addsd AGWAR for Combined Chiefs of Staff, rptd AMSSO for British Chiefs of Staff, SHAEF. This is NAF 841.

    1. If the withdrawal of British armed forces from Greece is to take place expeditiously it is essential to render assistance to the Greek Government in forming their army so that they may take over responsibility for internal security within Greece without delay.

    2. Proposals for the organization of the Greek National Forces have been examined with great care; and set out in paragraphs 3 to 13 below are the recommendations which it is considered are the minimum which will allow the British armed forces now in Greece to be withdrawn.

    3. Final organization will be an army of three field service divisions plus garrison troops on National Guard battalion basis.

    4. Role of field divisions is to provide Greek Government with mobile reserve for internal security with National Guard battalions as garrison troops for internal security duties in cities and towns.

    5. Recommend that field divisions should be developed from cadres drawn from Greek Mountain Brigade and Sacred Regiment and other units which have already been formed and have operated in Mideast and Italy. Divisions would then be brought up to strength by transfer of best material from Greek National Guard battalions which would be replaced in the latter by further call-up.

    6. Field force divisions to be organized armed and equipped on simplest possible lines to carry out their role. Each division would consist of approx. 10,000 all ranks, 30 armored cars, 24 field guns and 770 vehicles. Infantry battalions to be armed on small arms basis plus 3-inch mortars and small number

TOP SECRET

of Piats. Technical vehicles and equipment to be kept to a minimum. Animal transport considered most desirable in lieu proportion motor transport but resources non-existent after meeting present commitments.

7. National Guard battalions to be under command static headquarters set up at appropriate centers and woven into eventual general military administrative organization of country which will probably be on a territorial basis. Anticipate 15 static headquarters will be required each of which will command 3 to 7 battalions according to territorial area under their control. Minimum number of National Guard battalions required is 60. Each battalion will be some 550 all ranks strong equipped with 3 armored cars and armed on a small arms basis. Total National Guard commitment will be approx. 40,000 all ranks, 180 armored cars and 500 vehicles. Vehicles to latter number essential owing to complete absence of local resources.

8. Base and training units will require approx. 200 vehicles.

9. To summarize the total commitment for divisions and National Guard organization and to cover base and reinforcement and training establishments will be about 100,000 all ranks, 300 armored cars, 80 field guns and 3,000 vehicles. Against this existing Greek units have some 900 vehicles and 24 field guns.

10. Propose implementing this in 3 phases.

First phase. Build up of National Guard to ceiling of 80,000 on battalion basis. Formation of cadres for 3 field divisions from Greek Mountain Brigade, Sacred Regiment and existing artillery units. Organization of country into military districts and setting up static headquarters in each district.

Second phase. Progressive build up and training of 3 field divisions by transfer of personnel from National Guard. Replacement these personnel in National Guard units by further call-up. Completion military district organization aid final allocation National Guard units.

Third phase. Completion organization and training 3 field divisions.

11. If you approve proposals difficulty not anticipated in meeting phased requirements clothing arms equipment and vehicles from British resources in Mediterranean and dues in over next 3 months except in 3-inch

TOP SECRET

mortars, rifles and "B" vehicles* for which extra provision by you will be necessary. Must stress necessity replacement of all issues from Mediterranean stocks and dues in. Your instructions re rations for Greek Army will also be required on which commitment separate signal is being sent.

12. In early stages of formation of Greek Army British assistance in shape of liaison personnel must be on a generous scale if Greek forces are to replace British troops in Greece at early date, but such liaison should be scaled down rapidly as soon as Greek Army can stand on its own feet. Initial estimate approximately 300 officers and 1,000 other ranks.

13. Emphasize that keynote of organization will be simplicity and directly related to tasks, terrain and Greek way of life.

14. Request your earliest approval to these proposals as rapid relief of British troops in Greece is essential for success of future operations in Italy.

15. Cable regarding Greek policy being despatched separately today.

End

CM-IN-25346   (26 Jan 45)   DTG 251817A   da

---

* Non-combatant vehicles.

ARGONAUT CONFERENCE

MINUTES OF MEETINGS

OF THE

COMBINED CHIEFS OF STAFF

TOP SECRET

COMBINED CHIEFS OF STAFF

C.C.S. 182d Meeting

ARGONAUT CONFERENCE

MINUTES OF MEETING HELD IN
THE MAIN CONFERENCE ROOM, MONTGOMERY HOUSE, MALTA,
ON TUESDAY, 30 JANUARY 1945, AT 1200.

PRESENT

United States

General of the Army
  G. C. Marshall, USA
Fleet Admiral E. J. King, USN
Maj. Gen. L. S. Kuter, USA
  (Representing General of the
  Army H. H. Arnold)

British

Field Marshal Sir Alan F. Brooke
Marshal of the Royal Air Force
  Sir Charles F. A. Portal
Admiral of the Fleet
  Sir Andrew B. Cunningham

ALSO PRESENT

Lt. Gen. B. B. Somervell, USA
Lt. Gen. W. B. Smith, USA
Vice Adm. C. M. Cooke, Jr., USN
Maj. Gen. H. R. Bull, USA
Maj. Gen. F. L. Anderson, USA
Maj. Gen. J. E. Hull, USA
Rear Adm. L. D. McCormick, USN
Brig. Gen. J. L. Loutzenheiser, USA
Colonel H. A. Twitchell, USA

Field Marshal Sir H. M. Wilson
General Sir Hastings L. Ismay
Admiral Sir James Somerville
General Sir Thomas Riddell-Webster
  (For items 4 to 8 only)
Air Marshal Sir James M. Robb
Maj. Gen. R. E. Laycock

SECRETARIAT

Maj. Gen. E. I. C. Jacob
Brig. Gen. A. J. McFarland, USA
Brigadier A. T. Cornwall-Jones
Captain E. D. Graves, Jr., USN
Commander R. D. Coleridge, RN

TOP SECRET

1. *PROCEDURE FOR THE CONFERENCE*

SIR ALAN BROOKE said that it had been suggested by the United States Chiefs of Staff that he should take the chair at the Combined Chiefs of Staff meetings in Malta and he was glad to do so. He hoped, however, that a member of the United States Chiefs of Staff would take the chair at the meeting of the Combined Chiefs of Staff at *MAGNETO*.

GENERAL MARSHALL agreed to this proposal.

SIR ALAN BROOKE suggested that the meetings of the Combined Chiefs of Staff should normally take place at 1430 daily.

ADMIRAL KING, in agreeing to this proposal, stated that alterations in the timing might have to be made in the light of circumstances.

THE COMBINED CHIEFS OF STAFF:—

Agreed to meet daily at 1430, circumstances permitting.

2. *AGENDA FOR THE CONFERENCE*
(C.C.S. 765/8)

SIR ALAN BROOKE tabled a note setting out proposals for the business to be transacted by the Combined Chiefs of Staff on each day. (Annex to these Minutes, page 204.)

GENERAL MARSHALL said that the United States Chiefs of Staff agreed to these proposals. He felt, however, that one or two items should be earmarked as susceptible of earlier consideration if time allowed.

It was agreed that the U-boat threat and the planning date for the end of the Japanese war should be so earmarked.

3. *GERMAN FLYING BOMB AND ROCKET ATTACKS*

GENERAL MARSHALL referred to the data made available by the British Chiefs of Staff to enable him to show the Congress the scale of rocket and flying bomb attacks on London. He explained that in the course of his

TOP SECRET

talk to the Congress he had stressed the importance of a common understanding in order to assist the formation of combined decisions and policies. He had stressed the necessity for teamwork and the importance of understanding the other man's point of view and difficulties. The data with regard to flying bomb and rocket attacks on London had been of great value in this connection and had made a very strong impression on his audience.

SIR ALAN BROOKE said that on behalf of the British Chiefs of Staff he would like to thank General Marshall for the action he had taken in this connection. Sir Alan Brooke outlined the suggestions which had been made to mitigate the German rocket attacks and the views of the British Chiefs of Staff on this matter.

SIR CHARLES PORTAL then explained the proposals for air action against the rocket attacks and the course of action which it had been decided to follow.

SIR CHARLES PORTAL then explained the difficulties which had arisen with regard to the United States proposal to use war-weary bombers against industrial targets. The possibility of retaliation against the unique target of London had been felt to outweigh the advantages of the employment of this weapon.

GENERAL MARSHALL then outlined certain discussions he had had at Allied Force Headquarters with regard to the possibility of employing small formations of fighter-bombers to attack communications and particularly for attacks against the entrances to tunnels, possibly by skip bombing. He felt that skip bombing might also be used against the entrances to the underground production plant where the rockets were assembled.

SIR CHARLES PORTAL said that he was not accurately informed as to the topography of the terrain above the underground factory concerned and thought it likely that baffles had been erected before the entrances. It was probably also extremely well defended by guns; however, the possibility of skip bombing the entrances to this factory was very well worth investigating. With regard to attacks on communications, he had recently discussed the possibility of further attacks on communications with General Spaatz, who was arranging that the long-range fighters of the Eighth Air Force should, as a matter of course, attack communications on their return from escorting daylight bombers.

GENERAL MARSHALL then referred to the possibility of the Germans instigating suicide attacks on vital targets, particularly in the Antwerp area in which the lock gates were a vital and vulnerable target.

Some doubt was expressed as to the suitability of the German temperament to such a form of attack.

In reply to a question, *ADMIRAL KING* said that the Japanese suicide attacks were, on the whole, slightly less numerous than they had been, but they were still difficult to meet and there was apparently no panacea for it. The Commander of the Pacific Fleet had recently issued explicit instructions as to the method of employing anti-aircraft gunnery against these attacks.

THE COMBINED CHIEFS OF STAFF:—

Took note with interest of the above statements.

THE COMBINED CHIEFS OF STAFF adjourned until 1430.

4. *STRATEGY IN NORTHWEST EUROPE*
   (C.C.S. 761/3 and 761/4)

At General Bedell Smith's suggestion *GENERAL BULL* outlined the projected operations in Northwest Europe. The first phase entailed a closing up to the Rhine and the destruction of the enemy forces to the west of that river; the second phase consisted of obtaining bridgeheads across the Rhine; the third phase, of advancing into the heart of Germany and defeating her armed forces. The first phase was now going on. General Bradley was endeavoring to advance on the Prüm-Bonn axis. Divisions were now being released from the southern front, and were already being moved up to the North to be available for the offensive operations *VERITABLE* and *GRENADE*, the latter of which was an alternative in the event that General Bradley's present attack did not proceed with sufficient rapidity.

GENERAL BULL then outlined these two operations. Field Marshal Montgomery's forces would strike down in a southeasterly direction parallel to the Rhine while the Ninth United States Army would strike from its present position north of Aachen in the direction of Dusseldorf. A decision would shortly have to be taken as to whether it was worthwhile to continue General Bradley's operations in the Ardennes. Operations were also in progress to clear

TOP SECRET

the Colmar pocket and were being undertaken by French forces to be assisted by three United States divisions. It was obviously desirable, if it proved possible, to clear the entire west bank of the Rhine since by so doing security would be improved and additional divisions released for the offensive.

Turning to the second phase — the seizure of bridgeheads across the Rhine — *GENERAL BULL* explained that in the North between Emmerick and Wesel there were three good and two possible positions for bridging points. In the South, in the Mainz area, there were four good bridging points and in addition two possible ones. In the center, in the Cologne-Bonn area, there were three possible bridging sites.

Field Marshal Montgomery's operation *VERITABLE* would be launched between the eighth and tenth of February and operation *GRENADE* approximately a week later if the decision was taken to mount the latter. There was therefore a reasonable chance that the area west of the Rhine from Dusseldorf northwards would be clear of the enemy by the end of February. Field Marshal Montgomery would be instructed to grasp any possibility which presented itself of seizing bridgeheads on the lower Rhine during the southerly drive.

GENERAL BULL explained that the Supreme Commander was strongly of the opinion that a second line of advance into Germany must be available. It was for this reason that the bridgeheads in the Mainz-Mannheim area were to be seized. The line of advance of this army would be on Frankfurt and Kassel and would assist in isolating the Ruhr. In the North, Field Marshal Montgomery's drive would be directed on Munster and would swing down toward Hamm. It had been estimated that logistically it would not be possible to maintain more than 35 divisions in the northern thrust until rail bridgeheads had been established across the Rhine. In the South there were no serious logistic limitations and up to 50 divisions could be maintained before rail bridgeheads had been established.

The Supreme Commander had emphasized throughout the importance of flexibility in his planning. All forces which could be maintained would be employed in the northern thrust but the short length of the river available for the crossings, together with other limiting factors, made it essential to have an alternative thrust available should the northern thrust be held up. The forces not employed in the two thrusts would be used to secure the remainder of the line and to stage diversions and threats.

TOP SECRET

GENERAL BEDELL SMITH explained that the only factor which had altered since General Eisenhower's appreciations and intentions had been communicated to the Combined Chiefs of Staff in SCAF 179 and SCAF 180 (C.C.S. 761/3), was the factor of time which had now become of great importance in view of the Russian advance. It was felt that on the Western Front freedom of movement could be counted on until the 15th of March. The Sixth Panzer Army was thought to be in process of withdrawal. There was no longer believed to be any serious threat to Strasbourg and there was a good chance of clearing up the Colmar pocket quickly, thus releasing four divisions. In view of the present diminution of German offensive capabilities in the West, it was essential to get to the Rhine in the North as soon as possible and it was hoped that Field Marshal Montgomery's attack would start on 8 February.

Turning to the question of the distribution of forces, *GENERAL SMITH* explained that initially the Staff of 21st Army Group had said that only about 21 divisions could be maintained in the northern thrust; this strength was obviously too small a proportion to use in the main thrust out of a total of some 85 divisions available. The Supreme Commander, however, had directed that logistic arrangements be made to support initially 30 divisions in the main effort and later a total of 36 divisions. These arrangements were under way. Grave thought had been given to the area in which the secondary effort should be staged. The neighborhood of Cologne presented certain advantages in that there could be no question of an Allied dispersal of forces. On the other hand this area was so close to the area of the main effort that the Germans could quickly reinforce between these two threatened areas and little diversion of enemy strength would be achieved. To sum up, in General Eisenhower's view the thrust in the North was absolutely essential, that in the South necessary and desirable and to be undertaken if at all possible.

In reply to a question, *GENERAL SMITH* explained that it was obviously desirable to close the Rhine throughout its whole length but that the Supreme Commander did not intend to do this if resistance was such that the operation would delay the main attack until midsummer or would militate against an opportunity to seize a bridgehead and effect a crossing in strength on the northern front. A discussion then ensued as to the effect of the spring thaws on the possibilities of crossing the Rhine. *GENERAL SMITH* and *GENERAL BULL* explained that the lower Rhine could, it was believed, be crossed at any date after the first of March, though certain risks were entailed. The spring thaws affected the upper Rhine but had no effect on the lower Rhine.

SIR ALAN BROOKE explained that the British Chiefs of Staff felt that there was not sufficient strength available for two major operations, and that

TOP SECRET

therefore it would be necessary to decide on one of those proposed. Of the two, the northern appeared the most promising. The base port of Antwerp was nearer, the armies were already closer to the Rhine in that area, and the advance into Germany immediately threatened the vital Ruhr area whose importance had been even further increased by the fall of Silesia to the advancing Russian Army. In the South, though the actual crossings might prove easier, our armies had further to go before being in a position to cross the Rhine and, after crossing, the country was less favorable for operations and our forces would be further from the Ruhr or the lines of communications thereto. It was therefore felt that the plan should be based on the whole effort being made in the North if this was to be certain of succeeding and that every other operation must be regarded as subsidiary to this main thrust. There was, it was felt, a danger of putting too much into the southern effort and thereby weakening the main northern attack.

Another doubt which had been felt by the British Chiefs of Staff was in regard to the closing up to the Rhine on its whole length, which it was felt would slow up the advance into Germany. This point had already been cleared up by the explanations given by General Smith and General Bull. The general impression gained from SCAF 180 was that the southern thrust was regarded to be almost as important as the northern and that it diverted too much strength from the latter, both in forces and in the available facilities such as bridging material. The present situation on the Eastern Front obviously necessitated the speeding up of operations in the West in order to engage as many Germans as soon as possible, both to prevent the withdrawal of forces to the East and to take advantage of such reduction in strength as was taking place.

GENERAL SMITH emphasized that the Supreme Commander intended to put into the northern effort every single division which could be maintained logistically. The plan called for an ultimate strength of 36 divisions in the northern thrust. There would also be about ten additional divisions in strategic reserve available to exploit success. A very strong airborne force would be used for the northern crossing. It was, however, impossible to overlook the fact that the northern attack would, of necessity, take place on a narrow four-divisional front and might bog down. The southern advance was not intended to compete with the northern attack but must be of sufficient strength to draw off German forces to protect the important Frankfurt area and to provide an alternate line of attack if the main effort failed. He wished to make clear the Supreme Commander's view of the differentiation between the main and secondary thrusts. Everything that could be put into the main effort would be put there.

TOP SECRET

SIR ALAN BROOKE said that he welcomed this explanation. He had felt that the southern advance might cause the northern attack to bog down.

GENERAL MARSHALL, in referring to a point previously made by Field Marshal Brooke as to the necessity of resting and relieving divisions in the line, agreed that this was vitally important. In his view the considerations involved in the plan were as follows: the most favorable spot logistically, that is, in the North; the fact that it was not safe to rely on one line of advance only; the number of divisions required to maintain security in the non-active parts of the line; the assessment of the number of divisions which could be logistically supported in the northern thrust. He considered it essential that there should be more than one possible line of advance. The strategic reserve should be fed into either advance in the light of how well that advance was succeeding. If extremely heavy casualties were sustained in the northern attack there were the alternatives of either battling through or switching the weight of attack elsewhere. It was his view that it was essential to have some other line of advance to turn to if we bogged down in the North. It was likely that the Germans would put up a heavy resistance in the North and, with the aid of jet-propelled reconnaissance aircraft, would assess the likelihood of our attacking in that area.

SIR ALAN BROOKE pointed out that after crossing the Rhine the strength of the main thrust would be reduced by the necessity for relief and rehabilitation of tired units.

GENERAL SMITH gave the proposed general deployment of divisions. He said that while 36 would be available for the northern thrust they would not all be in the line at the same time. There would also be a strategic reserve of about ten divisions which would permit rotation. About 12 divisions would be used in the secondary attack and the remainder would be holding relatively quiet sectors of the line, where tired divisions could be rotated for rest and refit.

Turning to the employment of French divisions, *GENERAL SMITH* said that every effort was being made to arm the new divisions as quickly as possible. Equipment for the first three of the new divisions was already moving, and they would be ready for action together with their corps troops by the latter part of April. The French had certain odd brigades and other units available at present and these, with the new French divisions, might be used to contain or reduce St. Nazaire and Bordeaux.

TOP SECRET

SIR ALAN BROOKE said that the British Chiefs of Staff had not entirely agreed with the Supreme Commander's plan as set out in SCAF 180. This however had taken on a different complexion in the light of General Smith's explanations. The British Chiefs of Staff were loath therefore to approve SCAF 180, as at present drafted, as had been suggested by the United States Chiefs of Staff in C.C.S. 761/4.

SIR CHARLES PORTAL drew attention to paragraph 20 of SCAF 180 (page 120) which appeared out of keeping with General Smith's explanation

GENERAL SMITH said that as he understood it, it had never been General Eisenhower's intention to sweep the whole area west of the Rhine clear of Germans before effecting crossings.

GENERAL BULL confirmed this view and said that such action had not been intended if heavy fighting and consequent delay was thereby entailed. However, closing up to the Rhine on its whole length was obviously desirable if it could be achieved without delay.

GENERAL SMITH said that if the Germans resisted our attack in the North with their full strength it was likely that they would only have Völksgrenadier divisions available to hold the ground west of the Rhine to the south.

SIR ALAN BROOKE pointed out that the final sentence of paragraph 9 of SCAF 180 (page 118) also implied equally important lines of advance.

ADMIRAL KING drew attention to paragraph 22 (page 121) which he felt clarified the position.

In reply to a question by Sir Alan Brooke, GENERAL SMITH said that the southern thrust was likely to start from some position between the Siegfried Line and the Rhine. He felt that about 12 divisions could successfully achieve this thrust if the Germans concentrated to oppose the main effort and the Siegfried Line would not impose an insuperable obstacle. In general he felt that the Siegfried Line could be "nibbled through" by two or three good divisions in 15 days in almost any position.

SIR ALAN BROOKE said that he felt that rather than approve SCAF 180 at the present time, he would prefer that the Combined Chiefs of Staff should take note of it and should examine the record of General Smith's explanation at their meeting on the following day.

TOP SECRET

THE COMBINED CHIEFS OF STAFF:—

Deferred action on the above subject pending further consideration by the British Chiefs of Staff.

5. *COORDINATION OF OPERATIONS WITH THE RUSSIANS*

SIR ALAN BROOKE said that as he saw it, the only point was to insure that the Combined Chiefs of Staff were still in full agreement with the instructions which they had issued to General Deane and Admiral Archer in FAN 477.

GENERAL MARSHALL confirmed that the United States Chiefs of Staff were still in complete agreement with the contents of this message, no answer to which had yet been received from the Russians. He felt it would be necessary to raise the issue with them during the forthcoming conference.

THE COMBINED CHIEFS OF STAFF:—

Agreed to press the Russians to agree at *ARGONAUT* to the proposals in the Appendix to C.C.S. 741/6 (Fan 477, see page 185).*

6. *THE COMBINED BOMBER OFFENSIVE*
(C.C.S. 166 Series**)

SIR CHARLES PORTAL explained that his object in raising this question was to find out if the United States Chiefs of Staff had any views on the possible move of the Fifteenth Air Force from the Mediterranean to Western Europe. Such a move, involving some 1,000 heavy bombers, would, of course, have considerable effect on the potentialities in other theaters.

GENERAL KUTER explained that C.C.S. 400/2*** did in effect give the commander of the United States strategic air forces the right to move such forces within the two theaters. He understood in fact that General Spaatz had been considering the possibility of moving the Fifteenth Air Force to the United Kingdom but had decided against such a course.

---

* See also C.C.S. 778/1.
**Not published herein.
****SEXTANT* Conference book, page 105.

TOP SECRET

GENERAL MARSHALL said that he had directed an examination of the possibility of using the Fifteenth Air Force, or part of it, from southern France, thus avoiding the bad weather over the Po Valley. This proposal, however, had not commended itself to his staffs.

SIR CHARLES PORTAL pointed out that any large move as between theaters should, he felt, be approved by the Combined Chiefs of Staff since it had a great effect on the strategy in the theaters concerned. The number of bombers available in Italy, for instance, very materially affected the possibility of withdrawing ground forces from that theater.

GENERAL MARSHALL said that as he remembered it, the agreement with regard to the movement of the Fifteenth Air Force was designed to permit the commander of the strategic air forces the freedom of movement and flexibility to employ his forces temporarily in whichever theater provided the best weather at that time. There was in his mind no question of a permanent move of forces.

SIR CHARLES PORTAL said that it had been felt that temporary moves of air units to the United Kingdom was undesirable in view of the difficult weather and the fact that operating out of the United Kingdom was a highly specialized business.

ADMIRAL KING said that he considered the permanent allocations of forces to be the function of the Combined Chiefs of Staff. If necessary, the paper under discussion (C.C.S. 400/2) should be modified to bring it into line with this view.

SIR CHARLES PORTAL said that he was entirely reassured by General Marshall's statement with regard to the future of the Fifteenth Air Force.

THE COMBINED CHIEFS OF STAFF:—

Took note that the United States Chiefs of Staff were not at present contemplating the transfer of any formations of the Fifteenth Air Force from the Mediterranean.

TOP SECRET

7. *PLANNING DATE FOR THE END OF THE WAR WITH GERMANY*
   (C.C.S. 772)

SIR ALAN BROOKE presented a memorandum by the British Chiefs of Staff dealing with the planning date for the end of the war with Germany (C.C.S. 772). He explained that it had been necessary to estimate such a date or dates in order to provide a basis for production and manpower planning.

GENERAL MARSHALL explained that United States production planning was based on a bracket of the first of July and the 31st of December, 1945.

THE COMBINED CHIEFS OF STAFF:—

Deferred action on C.C.S. 772 pending consideration by the United States Chiefs of Staff.

8. *PLANNING DATE FOR THE END OF THE WAR WITH JAPAN*

THE COMBINED CHIEFS OF STAFF:—

Reaffirmed the planning date for the end of the war against Japan as recommended in paragraph 32 of C.C.S. 680/2 (OCTAGON Conference book, page 138).

9. *THE U-BOAT THREAT*

SIR ANDREW CUNNINGHAM explained that at present we were in a somewhat similar position to that of 1918. The ASDIC was proving less effective against present U-boat operations in shallow water where the tide affected the efficiency of the ASDIC. The Germans had discovered this and were working their submarines close inshore around the United Kingdom. At present they were operating principally in the Channel, the Irish Sea, and one had even penetrated the entrance to the Clyde. Our aircraft were also hampered by the extremely small target presented by the schnorkel. This relatively small object was normally used only some three feet above the water and ASV aircraft could therefore only detect it in calm weather.

Further, the Germans were fitting a radar device on their schnorkel which enabled them to detect the ASV emissions before the aircraft contacted the schnorkel.

TOP SECRET

In the last month there had been six sinkings in the Irish Sea, an escort carrier had been torpedoed in the Clyde, and at least four ships sunk in the Channel. He hoped, however, that the position would improve, and, in fact, two submarines had been sunk in the Irish Sea in the last week and a further one south of Land's End. The object was to force the submarines back into deep water where the ASDIC would be effective, and to achieve this deep mine fields were being laid in order to shut the enemy out of the Irish Sea.

THE CHIEF OF THE AIR STAFF explained that from the air point of view new devices were being brought into action, and included an infra-red device. It must be remembered, however, that with a submerged submarine using her schnorkel, the aircraft, even after it had contacted the submarine, found difficulty in sinking it since it could dive in some three seconds and left no swirl at which to aim.

SIR ANDREW CUNNINGHAM explained that the Germans were building new types of submarines which were a vast improvement over those which had been used previously. There were two new types: one of 1600 tons with a speed of up to 18 knots submerged, and carrying twenty torpedoes; the other, a small coastal type, was capable of 13 knots submerged and carried two torpedoes. The larger boat had an extremely long range. It was thought that these new boats would be coming into operation about the middle or end of February.

THE COMBINED CHIEFS OF STAFF:—

Took note with interest of the foregoing statements.

TOP SECRET

ANNEX

PROPOSED PROGRAMME OF WORK

Tuesday,
30th January   1. A. WAR AGAINST GERMANY

                  1. C. CO-ORDINATION OF OPERATIONS
                                    Bomblines, etc.

                  1. E. COMBINED BOMBER OFFENSIVE

                  1. F. PLANNING DATE FOR END OF GERMAN WAR

Wednesday,
31st January   1. B. STRATEGY IN MEDITERRANEAN

                  2.   WAR AGAINST JAPAN

                      A. SOUTH-EAST ASIA

                      B. ALLOCATION OF RESOURCES BETWEEN S.E.A.C. AND CHINA

Thursday,
1st February   2. C. PACIFIC OPERATIONS

                  2. D. PLANNING DATE FOR END OF JAPANESE WAR

                  1. D. U-BOAT THREAT

Friday,
2nd February   3.   REVIEW OF CARGO SHIPPING

          Additional
            Item. OIL STOCKS

                  4.   BASIC UNDERTAKINGS

CASTILLE,
  30.1.45.

TOP SECRET

COMBINED CHIEFS OF STAFF

C.C.S. 183d Meeting

ARGONAUT CONFERENCE

Minutes of Meeting Held in
The Main Conference Room, Montgomery House, Malta,
on Wednesday, 31 January 1945, at 1430.

PRESENT

United States

General of the Army
  G. C. Marshall, USA
Fleet Admiral E. J. King, USN
Maj. Gen. L. S. Kuter, USA
  (Representing General of the
  Army H. H. Arnold)

British

Field Marshal Sir Alan F. Brooke
Marshal of the Royal Air Force
  Sir Charles F. A. Portal
Admiral of the Fleet
  Sir Andrew B. Cunningham

ALSO PRESENT

Lt. Gen. B. B. Somervell, USA
Lt. Gen. W. B. Smith, USA
  (Items 1 to 4 only)
Vice Adm. C. M. Cooke, Jr., USN
Rear Adm. L. D. McCormick, USN
Maj. Gen. H. R. Bull, USA
  (Items 1 to 4 only)
Maj. Gen. J. E. Hull, USA
Maj. Gen. F. L. Anderson, USA
Maj. Gen. W. A. Wood, USA
Brig. Gen. C. P. Cabell, USA
  (Items 1 and 2 only)
Brig. Gen. J. L. Loutzenheiser, USA

Field Marshal Sir H. M. Wilson
Field Marshal Sir H. Alexander
  (Items 1 and 2 only)
General Sir Hastings L. Ismay
Admiral Sir James Somerville
General Sir Thomas Riddell-Webster
Air Marshal Sir James M. Robb
  (Items 1 to 4 only)
Maj. Gen. R. E. Laycock

SECRETARIAT

Maj. Gen. E. I. C. Jacob
Brig. Gen. A. J. McFarland, USA
Brigadier A. T. Cornwall-Jones
Captain E. D. Graves, Jr., USN
Commander R. D. Coleridge, RN
Colonel C. R. Peck, USA

TOP SECRET

1. *APPROVAL OF MINUTES OF C.C.S. 182D MEETING*

SIR ALAN BROOKE referred to the record of General Bull's statement contained in the fourth paragraph of item 4 of the minutes. He had not understood that there was any question about operation *GRENADE* not being launched. He had, on the other hand, understood that operation *VERITABLE* was dependent on operation *GRENADE*. Was it visualized that *VERITABLE* would have to await the launching of *GRENADE?*

GENERAL SMITH explained that General Bradley was endeavoring to advance on the Prüm-Bonn axis. If this advance succeeded in reaching Euskirchen quickly, it would be equally effective in assisting operation *VERITABLE* as would operation *GRENADE*. *VERITABLE* was not, however, dependent on either operation. General Eisenhower was at present at General Bradley's headquarters and was now deciding whether or not to cancel General Bradley's operations and shift forces north in order to undertake *GRENADE* instead.

GENERAL MARSHALL said that in recent discussions General Eisenhower had explained that he would have to take a decision by 1 February as to whether to continue with General Bradley's operations or to stop them and start the movement of troops preliminary to launching *GRENADE.*

GENERAL SMITH said that it was his personal opinion that it would probably be necessary to stop General Bradley's operations and to launch operation *GRENADE.*

GENERAL MARSHALL pointed out that if General Bradley's operations could achieve their objective in time there were certain advantages since the troops were already in position.

THE COMBINED CHIEFS OF STAFF:—

Approved the conclusions of the 182d Meeting and approved the detailed record of the meeting subject to later minor amendments.

2. *OPERATIONS IN THE MEDITERRANEAN*
   (C.C.S. 773)

THE COMBINED CHIEFS OF STAFF had before them a draft directive to the Supreme Allied Commander, Mediterranean, prepared by the British Chiefs of Staff (C.C.S. 773).

TOP SECRET

SIR ALAN BROOKE said that the British Chiefs of Staff had come to the conclusion that the right course of action was to reinforce the decisive Western Front at the expense of the Mediterranean Theater which, of necessity, would then have to revert to the offensive-defensive in Italy. There was now no question of operations aimed at the Ljubljana Gap and in any event the advance of the left wing of the Russian Army made such an operation no longer necessary.

GENERAL MARSHALL stated that the United States Chiefs of Staff were not yet in a position to give their final views on the draft directive, particularly with reference to possible moves of part of the Twelfth Air Force. However, there were certain United States proposals which he would like to put to the British Chiefs of Staff at once. The United States Chiefs of Staff suggested the following amendments: In paragraph 2 the substitution of the word "British" for "our" wherever it occurred; in paragraph 4 the substitution of "five" for "six" divisions; in paragraph 5, first sentence, the deletion of the words "United States" and "in equal proportions."

GENERAL MARSHALL explained that it was felt wiser to leave the Fifth Army intact as a well balanced organic force, and that it would be preferable to reinforce France with British and Canadian divisions in order to increase the strength of Field Marshal Montgomery's army.

The United States Chiefs of Staff agreed to the removal of three divisions, British or Canadian, at once, and the remainder as soon as they could be released from Greece, since this was the only way of finding the additional forces required. The question of the equipment of Greek forces had also been considered, since on this depended the release of the British divisions now in that country, but this was a complicated problem which he would like to consider further. The United States proposal was therefore that five divisions, two of which should be Canadian and the remainder British, should eventually be moved to France. With regard to the transfer of these forces, a preliminary study went to show that use of air transport could expedite the transfer of at least the first two divisions. He felt that if motor transport could be provided for these divisions from the United Kingdom, the date by which they would be available for operations in France would be greatly expedited.

SIR ALAN BROOKE said that the British Chiefs of Staff originally estimated that six divisions could be spared from the theater. With regard to their nationality, there were obviously great advantages in moving the Canadian divisions to enable them to join up with the remainder of the Canadian

TOP SECRET

forces in France. He was prepared to agree that the remaining divisions should be British. He felt it right to accept five divisions as a basis and this figure could be reconsidered later in the light of the situation.

FIELD MARSHAL ALEXANDER said that the Canadian divisions were the easiest to move quickly; one was already out of the line and could be moved at once and the other approximately a fortnight later. He pointed out, however, that it would be difficult to find suitable British divisions since all were now in the line and they had been involved in hard fighting for a long period. He had no reserve divisions. He outlined the composition of the forces available to him in the Mediterranean Theater.

SIR ALAN BROOKE felt it unwise to go into the details of the formations to be moved at this stage. He accepted the United States proposals in principle. Two Canadian and one British divisions could be moved first and the remaining two British divisions as soon as they could be released from Greece.

GENERAL MARSHALL said that the United States Chiefs of Staff had in mind to propose the withdrawal from the Mediterranean of a part of the Twelfth Tactical Air Force to include five fighter groups, one light bomber group, one reconnaissance unit, and two squadrons of night fighters. These air forces would be used to assist the First French Army and the Seventh United States Army.

FIELD MARSHAL ALEXANDER pointed out that if land formations were removed from him it was all the more desirable to keep as much air power as possible in the theater. If it was absolutely necessary to withdraw air forces from him he was most anxious that the United States medium and light bombers should not be taken, since British air forces in Italy were weak in those particular types.

GENERAL SMITH said that he was not asking for light bombers to be withdrawn from the Mediterranean Theater to Northwest Europe.

GENERAL ANDERSON pointed out that the greatest need was for fighter-bombers. The Southern Group of Armies had been robbed of these in order to strengthen the northern forces. He felt that if the Mediterranean Theater was passing to the defensive and the troops were being transferred to Northwest Europe, then the appropriate air components should, if possible, accompany them. The main deficiencies in Northwest Europe were in P-47's which could be used as either fighters or fighter-bombers.

TOP SECRET

GENERAL KUTER explained that the proposal to move the 47th Light Bomber Group from Italy had been made in view of the fact that it was trained for night intruder work which it was felt would be of more value in Northwest Europe than in Italy.

GENERAL SMITH said that he would be delighted to accept this group but only if Field Marshal Alexander could spare it. He was as concerned as Field Marshal Alexander himself as to the security of the Italian Front.

FIELD MARSHAL ALEXANDER said that if General Smith would give him his minimum requirements, he would do his utmost to meet them.

GENERAL SMITH said that the five fighter-bomber groups were his minimum requirement for France and the light bombers, though desirable, were not essential.

FIELD MARSHAL ALEXANDER undertook to examine this proposal at once and to release these forces if this proved at all possible. He fully realized that if his theater was to go on the defensive it was his duty to give up all possible resources, provided only that his front remained reasonably secure.

GENERAL SMITH said that he was entirely prepared to leave the final decision to Field Marshal Alexander.

SIR ALAN BROOKE referred to NAF 841* in which Field Marshal Alexander had requested approval to the equipment of certain additional Greek forces. He (Sir Alan Brooke) was most anxious that a decision on this proposal should be reached before the Combined Chiefs of Staff left Malta since such a decision would greatly accelerate the dates at which the British divisions could be released from Greece.

THE COMBINED CHIEFS OF STAFF:—

Deferred action on this subject.

---

* See page 188.

TOP SECRET

3. **STRATEGY IN NORTHWEST EUROPE**
   (C.C.S. 761/3 and 761/4)

SIR ALAN BROOKE said the British Chiefs of Staff were prepared to accept the Supreme Commander's operations as explained by General Smith and recorded in the minutes of the 182d Meeting. This explanation, however, was not in complete accord with the proposals put forward in SCAF 180. The British Chiefs of Staff therefore were not prepared to approve SCAF 180 as at present drafted.

GENERAL SMITH then presented a redraft of the Supreme Commander's plan as contained in paragraph 21 of SCAF 180 (page 121). This redraft was designed to bring the Supreme Commander's proposals into line with his previous explanation of SCAF 180.

THE COMBINED CHIEFS OF STAFF:—

Deferred action on this subject.

4. **PLANNING DATE FOR THE END OF THE WAR WITH GERMANY**
   (C.C.S. 772)

GENERAL MARSHALL said that he felt it wiser to defer consideration of this item until after discussion with the Russian General Staff.

THE COMBINED CHIEFS OF STAFF:—

Deferred action on this subject until the conclusion of ARGONAUT.

5. a. **OPERATIONS IN SOUTHEAST ASIA COMMAND**
      (C.C.S. 452/35 and 452/36)

   b. **ALLOCATION OF RESOURCES BETWEEN THE INDIA-BURMA AND CHINA THEATERS**

SIR ALAN BROOKE explained that the British Chiefs of Staff in C.C.S. 452/35 had put forward a new draft directive to the Supreme Commander, Southeast Asia.

TOP SECRET

GENERAL MARSHALL said that he felt that the question of a directive to the Supreme Commander should be linked with the problem of the allocation of resources between the India-Burma and China Theaters. He drew attention to a memorandum by the United States Chiefs of Staff (C.C.S. 452/36) which, while concurring in the directive proposed by the British Chiefs of Staff, linked this directive to an understanding as to the allocation of United States resources to the Southeast Asia Command. He felt that the situation was developing to a point where the resources of the China and Burma-India Theaters would be separated. U.S. resources required for China would not be available for operations in Malaysia. It was important that Admiral Mountbatten should be in no doubt as to the circumstances under which United States forces were available to him.

General Wedemeyer had recently estimated that some three squadrons of fighters would be required to protect the air route to China and had further implied that he was prepared to accept the responsibility of protecting with Chinese or United States troops the northern part of the Burma Road. This would, of course, relieve Admiral Mountbatten of these responsibilities. The situation was developing rapidly and the Japanese might well hold out in the Rangoon area in order to deny us that port but, in a matter of weeks, the Japanese sea communications to Burma, Malaysia and the Netherlands East Indies would be cut by air operations out of the Philippines. This would materially reduce Admiral Mountbatten's problems. Further, it would soon be possible to transfer more power to China, not so much additional tonnage but the all-important transport vehicles and light and medium artillery. The striking power then available to us on the far side of the Hump would be very different from that which we now had.

Summing up, *GENERAL MARSHALL* said that the proposed directive to Admiral Mountbatten was acceptable to the United States Chiefs of Staff, provided it was communicated to Admiral Mountbatten together with the policy with regard to the employment of United States forces outlined in C.C.S. 452/36.

SIR ALAN BROOKE explained that the phrase "with the forces at present at your disposal" contained in paragraph 3 of the draft directive was inserted in order to make it clear to Admiral Mountbatten that he should not undertake operations which could not be carried out without an increased allocation of resources.

TOP SECRET

  SIR CHARLES PORTAL asked for clarification of the meaning of the United States Chiefs of Staff memorandum (C.C.S. 452/36). Did this memorandum imply that, although Admiral Mountbatten could use for approved operations in Burma United States forces not required in China, such forces would not be available to him for use in Malaya?

  GENERAL MARSHALL said that the memorandum was meant to make it quite clear that the employment of United States forces outside Burma must be the subject of fresh agreement and that Admiral Mountbatten must not be led to assume that they would be available to him.

  THE COMBINED CHIEFS OF STAFF:—

Deferred action on C.C.S. 452/36 pending further study by the British Chiefs of Staff.

6. *ESTIMATE OF THE ENEMY SITUATION—EUROPE*
(C.C.S. 660/3)

  THE COMBINED CHIEFS OF STAFF:—

Took note of C.C.S. 660/3.

7. *BOMBING OF U-BOAT ASSEMBLY YARDS AND OPERATING BASES*
(C.C.S. 774)

  SIR ANDREW CUNNINGHAM said that he would prefer to consider this memorandum at the same time as the paper he was putting forward with regard to the U-boat threat.

  THE COMBINED CHIEFS OF STAFF:—

Deferred action on C.C.S. 774 pending study by the British Chiefs of Staff.

TOP SECRET

COMBINED CHIEFS OF STAFF

C.C.S. 184th Meeting

ARGONAUT CONFERENCE

MINUTES OF MEETING HELD IN
THE MAIN CONFERENCE ROOM, MONTGOMERY HOUSE, MALTA,
ON THURSDAY, 1 FEBRUARY 1945, AT 1430.

PRESENT

United States

General of the Army
  G. C. Marshall, USA
Fleet Admiral E. J. King, USN
Maj. Gen. L. S. Kuter, USA
  (Representing General of the
  Army H. H. Arnold)

British

Field Marshal Sir Alan F. Brooke
Marshal of the Royal Air Force
  Sir Charles F. A. Portal
Admiral of the Fleet
  Sir Andrew B. Cunningham

ALSO PRESENT

Lt. Gen. B. B. Somervell, USA
Lt. Gen. W. B. Smith, USA
Vice Adm. C. M. Cooke, Jr., USN
Rear Adm. L. D. McCormick, USN
Maj. Gen. H. R. Bull, USA
Maj. Gen. F. L. Anderson, USA
Maj. Gen. J. E. Hull, USA
Maj. Gen. W. A. Wood, USA
Brig. Gen. J. L. Loutzenheiser, USA
Brig. Gen. C. P. Cabell, USA
  (For items 1 and 2 only)

Field Marshal Sir H. M. Wilson
Field Marshal Sir H. Alexander
  (For items 1 and 2 only)
General Sir Hastings L. Ismay
Admiral Sir James Somerville
General Sir Thomas Riddell-Webster
Maj. Gen. R. E. Laycock

SECRETARIAT

Maj. Gen. E. I. C. Jacob
Brig. Gen. A. J. McFarland, USA
Brigadier A. T. Cornwall-Jones
Captain E. D. Graves, Jr., USN
Commander R. D. Coleridge, RN

TOP SECRET

1. *APPROVAL OF MINUTES OF C.C.S. 183D MEETING*

GENERAL MARSHALL said that he would like the first statement attributed to him in item 1 of the minutes amended to read as follows:—

"*GENERAL MARSHALL* said that in recent discussions General Eisenhower had explained that he would have to take a decision by 1 February as to whether to continue with General Bradley's operations or to stop them and start the movement of troops preliminary to launching GRENADE."

THE COMBINED CHIEFS OF STAFF:—

Approved the conclusions of the minutes of the C.C.S. 183d Meeting, and approved the detailed record of the meeting, subject to the amendment proposed by General Marshall and to later minor amendments.

2. *STRATEGY IN THE MEDITERRANEAN*
(C.C.S. 773/1 and 773/2)

FIELD MARSHAL BROOKE referred to the amended draft directive contained in C.C.S. 773/1. He suggested that paragraph 4 *b.* of this directive should read as follows:—

"Further complete formations as the forces now in Greece are released from that country."

It was explained that this amendment was consequent upon the reduction of the number of divisions to move to Northwest Europe from six to five. Three divisions would go from Italy and therefore it would only be necessary for two of the three divisions in Greece to follow them.

SIR CHARLES PORTAL referred to paragraph 5 of the draft directive. He felt that Field Marshal Alexander might well prefer to retain the Twelfth Air Force, since he was losing three divisions at once, in order to enable him to carry out that part of his directive contained in paragraph 7 *c.*, which instructed him to be prepared to take immediate advantage of any weakening or withdrawal of the German forces. He might also require it to maintain the security of his front, though it might well be possible to release it after the Germans had withdrawn to the Adige. A further point was that since it was proposed to move the first three divisions quickly, it might not be possible to transfer air forces at the same time.

In reply to a question, *SIR CHARLES PORTAL* confirmed that it was his view that the Twelfth Air Force should remain in the Mediterranean in the event that the German forces did not retire.

GENERAL MARSHALL said that in his view it was important to transfer such air forces as was possible to the decisive theater.

SIR CHARLES PORTAL suggested that the remainder of the directive should be approved and, in lieu of paragraph 5, the Supreme Commander should be informed that the question of the transference of parts of the Twelfth Air Force was still under consideration.

GENERAL MARSHALL said he was not in favor of this proposal.

GENERAL KUTER suggested that General Eisenhower might require parts of the Twelfth Air Force before the ground troops which were being transferred to him.

GENERAL SMITH said that General Eisenhower's first requirement, before any of the land forces, was for two groups of fighter-bombers. These were urgently required in view of the lack of such types on the southern part of the front. The move of these two groups could, he believed, be very quickly accomplished.

THE COMBINED CHIEFS OF STAFF:—

Deferred action on this subject until their next meeting.

3. *EQUIPMENT FOR ALLIED AND LIBERATED FORCES*
   (C.C.S. 768/1)

   THE COMBINED CHIEFS OF STAFF:—

   Deferred action on C.C.S. 768/1 until their next meeting.

TOP SECRET

4. a. *OPERATIONS IN SOUTHEAST ASIA COMMAND*
   (C.C.S. 452/35, C.C.S. 452/36)

   b. *ALLOCATION OF RESOURCES BETWEEN THE INDIA-BURMA AND CHINA THEATERS*
   (C.C.S. 747/7 (ARGONAUT)

The Combined Chiefs of Staff discussed the wording of the final sentence of paragraph 2 of C.C.S. 452/36.

GENERAL MARSHALL said that he understood that the British Chiefs of Staff wished to delete the words "British forces engaged in." This he felt fundamentally altered the sense of the sentence. It implied that operations rather than forces should not be placed in jeopardy. It might result in lengthy discussions each time the question of the possibility of moving forces to China arose.

SIR CHARLES PORTAL explained that the British Chiefs of Staff were asking only that discussion should take place before such a move was ordered. He felt that the crowning success of an approved operation might well be jeopardized by the withdrawal of United States forces without the British Chiefs of Staff or the Supreme Commander having an opportunity of laying before the Combined Chiefs of Staff the full consequences of such a withdrawal.

After further discussion, *THE COMBINED CHIEFS OF STAFF* agreed on the following wording of the final sentence of paragraph 2 of C.C.S. 452/36:

"Any transfer of forces engaged in approved operations in progress in Burma which is contemplated by the United States Chiefs of Staff and which, in the opinion of the British Chiefs of Staff, would jeopardize those operations, will be subject to discussion by the Combined Chiefs of Staff."

SIR ALAN BROOKE said that in the light of this redrafting, the British Chiefs of Staff would withdraw C.C.S. 747/7 (ARGONAUT).

GENERAL MARSHALL said that the United States Chiefs of Staff accepted the draft directive put forward by the British Chiefs of Staff in C.C.S. 452/35, subject to the communication to the Supreme Commander of the policy recorded in C.C.S. 452/36 and amended in the course of discussion.

TOP SECRET

THE COMBINED CHIEFS OF STAFF:—

a. Approved the policy set out in the first and second paragraphs of C.C.S. 452/36, subject to the amendment of the last sentence of the second paragraph as agreed above. (The policy, as amended and approved, subsequently circulated as C.C.S. 452/37.)

b. Approved the directive to the Supreme Allied Commander, Southeast Asia contained in C.C.S. 452/35, subject to the addition of a paragraph drawing his attention to the policy set out in C.C.S. 452/37.

c. Took note that the British Chiefs of Staff withdraw C.C.S. 747/7 (ARGONAUT).

5. *PACIFIC OPERATIONS*
(C.C.S. 417/11)

At the request of Sir Alan Brooke, **GENERAL MARSHALL** and **ADMIRAL KING** explained the future course of operations in the Pacific and various plans and projects which were under examination by the United States Chiefs of Staff. Plans had been prepared aiming at an attack on Kyushu in September of 1945 and the invasion of the Tokyo Plain in December of 1945. However, these operations involved the use of forces which would have to be redeployed from Europe after the defeat of Germany. The actual dates of these operations were therefore dependent on the date of the defeat of Germany. The length of time required for redeployment varied between four and six months, depending on whether the troops involved had actually been committed in Europe. At the present time all ground forces allocated to the Pacific were already in that theater and there would be no additional formations which could be moved there until the end of the German war. It was important, however, that during the necessary interval before the attack on the Empire itself could be carried out that the Japanese should be given no respite. It was intended to use this interval to obtain positions designed to assist in the final defeat of Japan. There were various possible courses of action after the capture of the Ryukyus and Bonins to achieve this object. The possible operations now under consideration were:—

(1) *An attack on the Island of Hainan.* This had the advantage not only of securing an air base to assist in cutting Japanese sea and land communications but also afforded a new airway into the heart of China, thereby assisting the Chinese to take a more active part in operations.

(2) *An attack on North Borneo.* The advantages of such an operation were that it secured to the United Nations the valuable oil supplies in that area. In this connection it was interesting to note that certain of these oil wells afforded fuel which required but little refinement before it was ready for use.

(3) *An operation against the Chusan-Ningpo area.* This operation was extremely valuable in broadening the base for air attack against the Island Empire. In addition, it had the great merit of throttling Japanese communications up the Yangtze River. The area concerned contained a series of islands and a peninsula and was therefore one in which operations against the Japanese could be undertaken without permitting the enemy to deploy large land forces against us.

When Okinawa had been seized a decision could be taken as to which of the courses of action outlined above was likely to afford the most valuable results. At the same time it might be found desirable to capture additional islands in the Ryukyus either to the north or south of Okinawa.

In general, future operations in the Pacific were designed to avoid full-scale land battles against Japanese forces, involving heavy casualties and slowing up the conduct of the campaign.

With regard to operations in the Philippines it was not visualized that major United States forces would be used in mopping-up operations nor that the island of Mindanao and others to the south would be assaulted by United States forces. Rather, it was hoped that with U.S. troops holding certain key positions, the rearmed Philippine Army and guerillas would be able to carry out the necessary mopping-up operations.

In view of the above considerations it was hoped to avoid an assault on Formosa and to isolate and bomb Japanese forces in the island from positions in the Ryukyus and Luzon.

The dates on which any of the possible alternative operations could be undertaken and the choice of such operations was dependent on the results of present operations in Luzon and on the date of the termination of the war in Europe. It was unlikely that both Hainan and North Borneo could be undertaken.

The importance of adequate bases and staging points was stressed. A fleet base was being developed on the southeast tip of Samar and it was estimated that three months' work could be achieved on this base before any work

TOP SECRET

could be done to render Manila available to the fleet. It might, in fact, be decided not to recondition the Manila base at all. A base had also been developed in Ulithi which was some 1100 miles to the westward of Eniwetok which had previously been used as a base and staging point.

The difficulties of developing the northern sea route to Russia were emphasized. The two divisions which had been earmarked for an assault on the Kuriles had now been diverted to Europe and it was unlikely that further forces would be available for this operation. Further, the sea lane to Russian ports was rendered difficult and in certain instances impossible during the winter months due to ice conditions.

The Russians had asked for some 85 additional ships to enable them to stock up their eastern armies. The provision of such ships would of course affect the course of operations elsewhere. In order to make a sea route safe and effective it would be necessary to seize an island in the Kuriles from which air cover could provide safe passage either to the north or south of it. Unless such an operational base was seized by the first of July its value would be lost due to ice conditions preventing the passage of ships. At present ships flying the Russian flag were convoying "civilian-type" supplies to the Maritime Provinces.

To sum up, it was unlikely that the operation against Kyushu could be undertaken until four months after the defeat of Germany. In the period intervening before such an operation could be undertaken, further operations would be carried out with the forces available. These operations would be designed to secure positions best calculated to assist the final attack on the Empire.

In further discussion the shortage of service troops was stressed. These forces would be the first to be redeployed from Europe. They were in short supply throughout the world and additional commitments were caused by the inability of the French to provide service forces to maintain their own troops.

With regard to the employment of Australian troops, it was explained that these forces were relieving United States divisions wherever possible. They were carrying out mopping-up operations in New Guinea and were garrisoning such points as Bouganville and the Admiralty Islands. Two Australian divisions had also been included in a plan to assault Mindanao, which might not now be used.

THE COMBINED CHIEFS OF STAFF:—

Took note of the plans and operations proposed by the United States Chiefs of Staff in C.C.S. 417/11.

6. *a. U-BOAT THREAT*
   (C.C.S. 774/1 and 774/2)

   b. BOMBING OF ASSEMBLY YARDS AND OPERATING BASES
   (C.C.S. 774)

GENERAL MARSHALL said the United States Chiefs of Staff suggested that C.C.S. 774/1 should be noted and the situation with regard to estimated shipping losses should be reviewed on the first of April.

SIR ANDREW CUNNINGHAM agreed with General Marshall.

SIR CHARLES PORTAL, referring to C.C.S. 774, said that he felt the proposals contained in the memorandum by the United States Chiefs of Staff would not be implemented by the suggested directive to the air forces. He felt that if persistent bombing of U-boat assembly yards was now undertaken the effect of this action on the attacks on the vital oil targets would be unacceptable. Both the oil targets and the submarine targets necessitated visual bombing and there were very few days in the month available for such operations in Northwest Europe at the present time of year. His proposal was that the "marginal effort" should be used against submarine targets and explained that such a decision would mean that, when an attack against an oil target had been ordered and it was found that the weather over the oil target prevented visual bombing, the aircraft concerned would divert their efforts to a submarine target if one existed with clear weather over it.

He felt it right to point out that the issuance of the draft directive proposed by the United States Chiefs of Staff would not materially increase the weight of bombs dropped on submarine targets.

GENERAL KUTER said that some directive on the subject of the submarine menace would be valuable in focusing attention upon it.

ADMIRAL KING said that the Combined Chiefs of Staff should record their views with regard to the submarine menace and issue a directive on the action to be taken to counter it.

TOP SECRET

SIR ANDREW CUNNINGHAM said that the Naval Staff would have liked to see some additional emphasis being placed on the bombing of submarine targets. He had, however, been convinced that the attacks on oil targets would in fact pay a more valuable dividend.

THE COMBINED CHIEFS OF STAFF then considered the summary of countermeasures set out in C.C.S. 774 and 774/2. It was agreed that the action proposed in paragraph 10 of this paper should be communicated to the appropriate authorities in the form of a directive.

THE COMBINED CHIEFS OF STAFF:—

a. Took note of C.C.S. 774/1 and agreed to review this paper on 1 April 1945.

b. Directed the Secretaries to draft and circulate for approval a directive based on C.C.S. 774 and C.C.S. 774/2.

7. *STRATEGY IN NORTHWEST EUROPE*
(C.C.S. 761/5 and 761/6)

In closed session,

THE COMBINED CHIEFS OF STAFF:—

Took note of SCAF 180,* as amended by SCAF 194** of 31 January, and as amplified by Message No. S-77211** of 31 January to General Smith.

---

* Enclosure "B" to C.C.S. 761/3 (Page 116).
**Appendices "A" and "B" to C.C.S. 761/6 (Pages 123, 124).

TOP SECRET

COMBINED CHIEFS OF STAFF

C.C.S. 185th Meeting

ARGONAUT CONFERENCE

Minutes of Meeting Held in
The Main Conference Room, Montgomery House, Malta,
on Friday, 2 February 1945, at 1200.

PRESENT

United States

General of the Army
  G. C. Marshall, USA
Fleet Admiral E. J. King, USN
Maj. Gen. L. S. Kuter, USA
  (Representing General of the
  Army H. H. Arnold)

British

Field Marshal Sir Alan F. Brooke
Marshal of the Royal Air Force
  Sir Charles F. A. Portal
Admiral of the Fleet
  Sir Andrew B. Cunningham

ALSO PRESENT

Lt. Gen. B. B. Somervell, USA
Lt. Gen. W. B. Smith, USA
Vice Adm. C. M. Cooke, Jr., USN
Rear Adm. L. D. McCormick, USN
Maj. Gen. H. R. Bull, USA
Maj. Gen. F. L. Anderson, USA
Maj. Gen. J. E. Hull, USA
Brig. Gen. J. L. Loutzenheiser, USA
Brig. Gen. C. P. Cabell, USA
  (For items 1 to 5 only)

Field Marshal Sir H. M. Wilson
Field Marshal Sir H. Alexander
  (For items 1 to 5 only)
General Sir Hastings L. Ismay
Admiral Sir James Somerville
General Sir Thomas Riddell-Webster
  (For items 1 to 4 only)
Air Marshal Sir James M. Robb
Maj. Gen. R. E. Laycock

SECRETARIAT

Maj. Gen. E. I. C. Jacob
Brig. Gen. A. J. McFarland, USA
Brigadier A. T. Cornwall-Jones
Captain E. D. Graves, Jr., USN
Commander R. D. Coleridge, RN

TOP SECRET

1. *APPROVAL OF MINUTES OF C.C.S. 184TH MEETING*

   THE COMBINED CHIEFS OF STAFF:—

   Approved the conclusions of the minutes of the C.C.S. 184th Meeting and approved the detailed record of the meeting, subject to later minor amendments.

2. *EQUIPMENT FOR ALLIED AND LIBERATED FORCES*
   (C.C.S. 768/1)

   SIR ALAN BROOKE said that he understood that the question of equipment for Allied and liberated forces had been under discussion by General Somervell and General Riddell-Webster. It was understood that the requirement for internal security for mobile military labor and miscellaneous units could be cut from a total commitment of 460,000 to 400,000 and equipped on the scale of British forces rather than a United States scale — a commitment which he believed that the British could undertake. It would however be necessary to confirm this with the War Office, which would be done as quickly as possible.

   THE COMBINED CHIEFS OF STAFF:—

   a. Took note that SCAEF's requirements in liberated manpower could be reduced from 460,000 to 400,000.

   b. Agreed to the implementation of the proposals in NAF 841* upon assurance by the British Chiefs of Staff that, subject to confirmation from London, this implementation would not:—

      (1) Interfere with the provision already affirmed in principle of equipment, on the scale for British forces, for Allied and liberated forces in Northwest Europe, nor

      (2) Result in subsequent direct or indirect charges against U.S. resources.

---

* See page 188.

TOP SECRET

3. *REVIEW OF CARGO SHIPPING*
   (C.C.S. 746/8 and C.C.S. 746/10)

SIR ALAN BROOKE suggested the substitution of the word "some" for the word "present" in the first sentence of paragraph 4 of the enclosure to C.C.S. 746/10. With regard to paragraph 6 *d.*, he felt that it should be made clear that the shipping and resources annex to the final report by the Combined Chiefs of Staff at *ARGONAUT* should be completed before the conference ended. To enable this to be achieved it would be necessary for the shipping team to go to *MAGNETO* unless it could be definitely decided that the conference would be continued at *CRICKET* after the *MAGNETO* discussions had been concluded. It was generally agreed that the shipping staffs should remain at *CRICKET*.

GENERAL MARSHALL suggested the deletion of the word "other" before the word "programs" in paragraph 5 *b.*

Turning to C.C.S. 746/8, *SIR ALAN BROOKE* said that the British Chiefs of Staff accepted the proposals put forward by the United States Chiefs of Staff, provided that a sentence could be added to paragraph 4 to make it clear that coordination should also be effected with the Combined Shipping Adjustment Board.

THE COMBINED CHIEFS OF STAFF:—

   a. Approved C.C.S. 746/10 subject to the substitution of "some" for "present" in the first line of paragraph 4 and the deletion of "other" in the fourth line of paragraph 5 *b.*

   b. Approved the recommendation of the United States Chiefs of Staff in paragraph 4 of C.C.S. 746/8 subject to the addition to that paragraph of the following:

   "Coordination should also be effected with the Combined Shipping Adjustment Board."

   c. Agreed that during the absence of the Combined Chiefs of Staff in *ARGONAUT*, the shipping staffs would continue their studies at *CRICKET* with a view to the submission of a report to the Combined Chiefs of Staff prior to the conclusion of *ARGONAUT*.

TOP SECRET

4. LEVELS OF SUPPLY OF PETROLEUM PRODUCTS IN U.K. AND NORTHWEST EUROPE
(C.C.S. 625/10 (ARGONAUT))

GENERAL MARSHALL asked for an explanation as to why the British Chiefs of Staff felt it essential for stocks in Northwest Europe to be expressed in fixed quantities rather than in days of forward consumption.

GENERAL RIDDELL-WEBSTER said that the British Chiefs of Staff were prepared to depart from the principle of expressing requirements in fixed quantities except in certain particular items. One of these special items was Admiralty fuel oil. Stocks had to be maintained at a large number of points in order to maintain the flexibility of naval operations. A cut below the figure asked for would result in the necessity for using tankers to transfer stocks from one base to another. With regard to aviation fuel, negotiations had been in progress and although the Air Ministry were loath to allow stocks to fall below 1,150,000 tons, it had finally been agreed to accept a figure of 1,000,000 tons. In this case the same considerations with regard to a fixed figure applied as in the case of Admiralty fuel oil.

GENERAL RIDDELL-WEBSTER, continuing, outlined the position concerning certain other oil products.

GENERAL SOMERVELL said that the figure 59 days forward consumption proposed for motor spirits seemed reasonable. He felt, however, that the requirement for similar fuels in which the War Department was interested should be reduced to the same figure. The whole problem had been referred to the Combined Administrative Committee in Washington and he felt that discussions should not take place on this matter in two places.

GENERAL MARSHALL said that he appreciated the complicated situation in the United Kingdom where the whole economy of the country was affected, but felt that he must point out that difficulties with regard to stock levels were also being experienced in other theaters.

After further discussion it was suggested that the Combined Administrative Committee should be instructed to expedite consideration of the problem and to signal an early report to the Combined Chiefs of Staff.

TOP SECRET

THE COMBINED CHIEFS OF STAFF:—

Directed the Secretaries to call for the report of the Combined Administrative Committee on C.C.S. 625/3,* 625/6,* and 625/9* to reach them at *ARGONAUT* by 1800 hours on 5 February, *ARGONAUT* time.

5. *TRANSFER OF TACTICAL AIR FORCES FROM SACMED TO SCAEF* (C.C.S. 773/1 and 773/2)

GENERAL MARSHALL said that as he saw it the British proposal left the matter of the transfer of aircraft open for consideration later. He felt that the two commanders concerned should be allowed to negotiate direct. He considered that the Twelfth Air Force should move to Northwest Europe, which was the decisive theater in which additional air power would produce the most valuable results. A move of the tactical air force to the southern part of the line in France was complementary to the British Chiefs of Staff's desire to strengthen the northern thrust.

SIR ALAN BROOKE said that he felt that the offensive on the Western Front would be assisted by action on the Italian Front.

GENERAL MARSHALL pointed out that there was considerable air strength in Italy. He agreed that the final decision on moves should be taken by the Combined Chiefs of Staff but felt that the commanders should consult and put up agreed proposals.

SIR CHARLES PORTAL said that he felt a valuable opportunity might be afforded us in Italy if the enemy started to withdraw. In such an event the United States' P-47's would be of the utmost help in cutting communications beyond the limits of the shorter ranged British fighters. He pointed out that the tactical air forces comprised 4,300 aircraft on the Western Front as opposed to 1,950 in the Mediterranean; including strategic air forces there were 9,000 aircraft on the Western Front as opposed to 3,580 in the Mediterranean.

There was another point involved: the move of the tactical air force to France might interfere with the agreed troop movement. The commander concerned must of course say which he required first, but there were also political factors involved. The public were more impressed with the number of

---

* Not published herein.

divisions taking part in a battle than with the number of aircraft. It seemed to him that to withhold a movement of the tactical air force for the present fitted in well with this political consideration since the divisions could move to France first, thus leaving the tactical air force in Italy to exploit any opportunity which arose. However, to meet the views put forward by the United States Chiefs of Staff he was prepared to accept a liberal interpretation of the words "substantial reduction" in paragraph 2 of C.C.S. 773/2. This he felt should not be allowed to rule out the immediate move of the two fighter-bomber groups particularly required by General Eisenhower. He understood that such a move was agreeable to Field Marshal Alexander and would leave three fighter-bomber groups in Italy. He understood, however, that it was important that the headquarters of the Twelfth Air Force should remain in Italy since they administered and controlled the medium bombers and troop carriers of the Twelfth Air Force.

GENERAL MARSHALL said he understood that the 6th Army Group was inadequately supplied with air staffs and that the headquarters of the Twelfth Air Force was important to them.

GENERAL KUTER said that he personally felt that the whole of the Twelfth Air Force should be transferred to France to assist in the main effort. All this force should be made available to General Eisenhower to move when he required it.

GENERAL MARSHALL said that the French forces in the South were inadequately provided with air support and the air forces in question were urgently required for the reduction of the Colmar pocket.

SIR ALAN BROOKE felt that when this pocket had been eliminated the Allied line in this sector would be very strong.

FIELD MARSHAL ALEXANDER said he was anxious to retain the Twelfth Air Force headquarters but he had many able officers in the theater from among whom he would be glad to provide General Eisenhower a new air headquarters in southern France.

THE COMBINED CHIEFS OF STAFF:—

Approved the directive to the Supreme Allied Commander, Mediterranean, contained in C.C.S. 773/1 subject to the substitution of the following for the existing paragraph 5:

TOP SECRET

"5. Two fighter groups of the Twelfth Air Force will be moved to France at once. The Combined Chiefs of Staff intend to move to France in the near future as much of the Twelfth Air Force as can be released without hazard to your mission. You should consult with SCAEF and submit agreed proposals for confirmation by the Combined Chiefs of Staff."

6. *PROVISION OF LVT'S FOR THE MEDITERRANEAN*
   (C.C.S. 755/3)

SIR ALAN BROOKE said that he thought it essential that Field Marshal Alexander should be provided with offensive power in order to take advantage of any enemy weakness.

FIELD MARSHAL ALEXANDER undertook to re-examine his requirements in LVT's in the light of the new directive which was about to be issued to him and to report to the Combined Chiefs of Staff at an early date.

THE COMBINED CHIEFS OF STAFF:—

Invited the British Chiefs of Staff to request the Supreme Allied Commander, Mediterranean, to review his requirements in LVT's along the lines indicated in C.C.S. 755/3.

7. *U-BOAT THREAT*

THE COMBINED CHIEFS OF STAFF had before them a draft directive prepared by the Secretariat in accordance with Conclusion 6 *b.* of the C.C.S. 184th Meeting.

THE COMBINED CHIEFS OF STAFF:—

Approved the draft directive submitted by the Secretaries and invited the United States and British Chiefs of Staff to dispatch it to all appropriate commanders. (Subsequently circulated as C.C.S. 774/3.)

8. *BASIC UNDERTAKINGS*
   (C.C.S. 775)

In reply to a question from Sir Alan Brooke, *GENERAL MARSHALL* outlined the strategic reasons which rendered the maintenance of Russian goodwill of such vital importance. He appreciated, however, the importance of insuring also that a state of affairs did not arise in France which would hinder our operations based on that country.

THE COMBINED CHIEFS OF STAFF then discussed the effect of various proposals to amend the basic undertakings contained in paragraph 6 *h.* of the interim report to the President and Prime Minister (C.C.S. 776).

GENERAL MARSHALL explained that the British proposal would introduce a new category of basic undertakings which would affect the availability of shipping for military operations. He recalled the difficult decision which had been necessitated when, in considering the timing of operations against the Bonins and Ryukyus, a deficiency of some forty sailings had arisen. Simultaneously, a demand for an additional forty ships to increase the bread ration in Italy had been put forward.

GENERAL SOMERVELL pointed out that requirements to prevent disease and unrest and requirements to implement the U.S. military manufacturing programs in liberated areas were already included under the military shipping requirements.

After further discussion,

THE COMBINED CHIEFS OF STAFF:—

Deferred action on this subject.

9. *INTERIM REPORT TO THE PRESIDENT AND PRIME MINISTER* (C.C.S. 776)

THE COMBINED CHIEFS OF STAFF agreed that paragraph 6 *h.* of C.C.S. 776 should be left blank with a notation to the effect that it was still under discussion.

SIR ALAN BROOKE pointed out that the paragraph dealing with cargo shipping could not yet be inserted since British acceptance of C.C.S. 746/10 was conditional upon the rewording of paragraph 6 *h.* of the interim report along the lines indicated in C.C.S. 775.

THE COMBINED CHIEFS OF STAFF:—

Approved the draft interim report as amended during the discussion.

TOP SECRET

COMBINED CHIEFS OF STAFF

C.C.S. 186th Meeting

ARGONAUT CONFERENCE

MINUTES OF MEETING HELD IN THE
CHATEAU VORONTSOV, ALUPKA, RUSSIA,
ON TUESDAY, 6 FEBRUARY 1945, AT 1000.

PRESENT

United States

General of the Army
  G. C. Marshall, USA
Fleet Admiral E. J. King, USN
Maj. Gen. L. S. Kuter, USA
  (Representing General of the
  Army H. H. Arnold)

British

Field Marshal Sir Alan F. Brooke
Marshal of the Royal Air Force
  Sir Charles F. A. Portal
Admiral of the Fleet
  Sir Andrew B. Cunningham

ALSO PRESENT

Lt. Gen. B. B. Somervell, USA
Vice Adm. C. M. Cooke, Jr., USN
Rear Adm. L. D. McCormick, USN
Maj. Gen. H. R. Bull, USA
Maj. Gen. F. L. Anderson, USA
Maj. Gen. J. E. Hull, USA
Brig. Gen. J. L. Loutzenheiser, USA

Field Marshal Sir H. M. Wilson
Field Marshal Sir H. Alexander
General Sir Hastings L. Ismay
Admiral Sir James Somerville
Maj. Gen. R. E. Laycock

SECRETARIAT

Maj. Gen. E. I. C. Jacob
Brig. Gen. A. J. McFarland, USA
Brigadier A. T. Cornwall-Jones
Captain E. D. Graves, Jr., USN
Commander R. D. Coleridge, RN

TOP SECRET

1. *APPROVAL OF MINUTES OF THE 185TH MEETING*

    THE COMBINED CHIEFS OF STAFF:—

    Approved the conclusions of the minutes of the C.C.S. 185th Meeting and approved the detailed record of the meeting, subject to later minor amendments.

2. *LEVELS OF SUPPLY OF PETROLEUM PRODUCTS IN U.K. AND NORTHWEST EUROPE*
    (C.C.S. 625/10 (ARGONAUT) and 625/11)

    THE COMBINED CHIEFS OF STAFF had before them a telegram reporting the fact that the Combined Administrative Committee had been unable to reach agreement on C.C.S. 625/3,* 625/6* and 625/9.* The basis of disagreement lay in the fact that the British considered the absolute minimum below which stocks should not fall should be expressed in terms of fixed quantities, whereas the U.S. view was that the desirable minimum was the emergency reserve level and that this could and should be expressed in days of forward consumption.

    Some discussion took place as to whether or not the requirements could be stated in terms of days forward consumption, and *GENERAL SOMERVELL* put forward certain suggestions as to the number of days' stocks required in certain categories of oil.

    THE BRITISH CHIEFS OF STAFF said that they would like to see General Somervell's proposals in writing, but meanwhile pointed out that they could not accept any reduction in the requirements they had already put forward in respect of Admiralty fuel and aviation gas.

    THE COMBINED CHIEFS OF STAFF:—

    a. Took note that the United States Chiefs of Staff would circulate a further paper on this matter.

    b. Agreed to appoint a combined *ad hoc* committee to consider this subject and put forward recommendations in time for consideration at 1000 on Thursday, 8 February 1945.

---

* Not published herein.

TOP SECRET

3. *PLANNING DATE FOR THE END OF THE WAR AGAINST GERMANY*
(C.C.S. 772)

THE COMBINED CHIEFS OF STAFF:—

Agreed to accept for planning purposes the following dates for the end of the war with Germany:—

a. Earliest date, 1 July 1945.

b. Date beyond which war is unlikely to continue, 31 December 1945.

4. *PROVISION OF LVT'S FOR THE MEDITERRANEAN*
(C.C.S. 755/4)

THE COMBINED CHIEFS OF STAFF had before them a memorandum by the British Chiefs of Staff.

Without discussion,

THE COMBINED CHIEFS OF STAFF:—

a. Approved as an immediate measure the reduction of the assignment to the Mediterranean Theater of LVT's from 600 to 400.

b. Approved the diversion to 21st Army Group of the 200 LVT's surrendered by Field Marshal Alexander.

c. Agreed that consideration of the final requirements of the Mediterranean Theater should await the result of the detailed study of the position by Allied Force Headquarters in the light of the new directive.

5. *ALLOCATION OF ZONES OF OCCUPATION IN GERMANY*
(C.C.S. 320/35)

THE COMBINED CHIEFS OF STAFF had before them a memorandum by the United States Chiefs of Staff proposing the acceptance of an agreement regarding the Bremen and Bremerhaven enclave and the use of the railway from Bremen to the southwest zone, on the understanding that this agreement did not involve the question of command of the Bremen-Bremerhaven area.

TOP SECRET

GENERAL MARSHALL referred to the fact that the letter at Enclosure "B" (page 5) visualized the necessity for making a more detailed form of agreement, covering a variety of circumstances. He felt strongly that no such detailed agreement was necessary. The broad policy had been decided and the good will was there. Details could be left very largely to local commanders and any problems of overlapping authority which did arise could be referred to the Combined Chiefs of Staff when the time came.

THE COMBINED CHIEFS OF STAFF then agreed to the following amendments to the Appendix to Enclosure "B" of C.C.S. 320/35:—

   a. In paragraph 1 delete the words "but will be generally administered as a sub-district of a larger British controlled area."

   b. In the second sentence of paragraph 1, delete the words "larger district" and substitute "British zone."

   c. In the second sentence of paragraph 2, delete the word "responsible" and substitute the word "responsive."

THE COMBINED CHIEFS OF STAFF:—

   a. Endorsed the views expressed by General Marshall above and approved the Appendix to Enclosure "B" of C.C.S. 320/35 as amended in discussion. (Subsequently circulated as C.C.S. 320/37.)

   b. Agreed to take no further action on the detailed recommendations included in the letter at Enclosure "B" to C.C.S. 320/35.

6. *BASIC UNDERTAKINGS*
(C.C.S. 775)

THE COMBINED CHIEFS OF STAFF had before them a memorandum by the British Chiefs of Staff recommending a substitution for the existing paragraph 6 *h.* in C.C.S. 680/2.*

SIR ALAN BROOKE said that the British Chiefs of Staff were now in a position to agree to this subparagraph *h.*, as it had been amended informally in discussion at a previous C.C.S. meeting when this had been discussed.

---
* *OCTAGON* Conference book, page 132.

TOP SECRET

THE COMBINED CHIEFS OF STAFF:—

Agreed to the following revised subparagraph *h.*:

"*h.* Provide assistance to such of the forces of the liberated areas in Europe as can fulfill an active and effective role in the war against Germany and/or Japan. Within the limits of our available resources to assist other co-belligerents to the extent they are able to employ this assistance against the Enemy Powers in the present war. Having regard to the successful accomplishment of the other basic undertakings, to provide such supplies to the liberated areas as will effectively contribute to the war-making capacity of the United Nations against Germany and/or Japan."

7. *LIAISON WITH THE SOVIET HIGH COMMAND OVER ANGLO-AMERICAN STRATEGIC BOMBING IN EASTERN GERMANY*
   (C.C.S. 778)

THE COMBINED CHIEFS OF STAFF had before them a memorandum by the British Chiefs of Staff suggesting a line that might be taken with the Soviet General Staff at a meeting which was to be held later the same day to discuss the matter of the bombline.

THE COMBINED CHIEFS OF STAFF discussed the desirability of putting forward this fresh memorandum in the place of the one recently submitted in FAN 477.*

THE COMBINED CHIEFS OF STAFF:—

Agreed that the United States Chiefs of Staff should put forward to the Russians the views expressed in C.C.S. 778, as amended in discussion.

8. *NEXT MEETING, COMBINED CHIEFS OF STAFF*

THE COMBINED CHIEFS OF STAFF:—

Agreed to meet again, provisionally at 1000 on Thursday, 8 February 1945, to finish off any outstanding items on the *ARGONAUT* Agenda.

---

* See page 185.

TOP SECRET

COMBINED CHIEFS OF STAFF

C.C.S. 187th Meeting

ARGONAUT CONFERENCE

MINUTES OF MEETING HELD IN
CONFERENCE ROOM "A," BUILDING "A," LIVADIA PALACE, RUSSIA,
ON THURSDAY, 8 FEBRUARY 1945, AT 1200.

PRESENT

United States	*British*
Fleet Admiral W. D. Leahy, USN	Field Marshal Sir Alan F. Brooke
General of the Army G. C. Marshall, USA	Marshal of the Royal Air Force Sir Charles F. A. Portal
Fleet Admiral E. J. King, USN	Admiral of the Fleet Sir Andrew B. Cunningham
Maj. Gen. L. S. Kuter, USA (Representing General of the Army H. H. Arnold)	

ALSO PRESENT

Lt. Gen. B. B. Somervell, USA	Field Marshal Sir H. M. Wilson
Vice Adm. C. M. Cooke, Jr., USN	General Sir Hastings L. Ismay
Rear Adm. L. D. McCormick, USN	Admiral Sir James Somerville
Maj. Gen. H. R. Bull, USA	Maj. Gen. R. E. Laycock
Maj. Gen. F. L. Anderson, USA	Maj. Gen. N. G. Holmes
Maj. Gen. J. E. Hull, USA	Lord Leathers
Brig. Gen. J. L. Loutzenheiser, USA	(For items 1 and 2 only)

SECRETARIAT

Maj. Gen. E. I. C. Jacob
Brig. Gen. A. J. McFarland, USA
Brigadier A. T. Cornwall-Jones
Captain E. D. Graves, Jr., USN
Commander R. D. Coleridge, RN

TOP SECRET

1. *APPROVAL OF THE MINUTES OF THE 186TH MEETING OF THE COMBINED CHIEFS OF STAFF*

THE COMBINED CHIEFS OF STAFF:—

Approved the conclusions of the minutes of the C.C.S. 186th Meeting and approved the detailed record of the meeting subject to later minor amendments.

2. *LEVELS OF SUPPLY OF ALL PETROLEUM PRODUCTS IN ALL THEATERS*
(C.C.S. 625/13)

ADMIRAL LEAHY said that the United States Chiefs of Staff suggested that the footnote under paragraph 6 of the enclosure to C.C.S. 625/13 should read: "Emergency level for this theater takes special cognizance of the complexity of the distribution systems."

SIR ALAN BROOKE accepted this proposal and said that the British Chiefs of Staff had two minor amendments to suggest. They would like the words "or other appropriate authorities" added to the end of paragraph 2 of the enclosure, and the words "of the armed services" deleted from paragraph 5 c. There was one further point. The British Chiefs of Staff wished note to be taken of the omissions of the following oils which could not be expressed in terms of days of forward consumption and which did not appear in the paper: tar oil, 100,000 tons; and crude and process oils, aviation components, and bitumen, 400,000 tons. It was understood that these stocks would be provided under other agreements.

ADMIRAL LEAHY said that Sir Alan Brooke's proposals were acceptable.

THE COMBINED CHIEFS OF STAFF:—

a. Approved C.C.S. 625/13 subject to the following amendments to the enclosure:

(1) Add to paragraph 2 "or other appropriate authorities."

(2) Delete from the seventh line of paragraph 5 the words "of the armed services."

(3) Amend the footnote to read:

"Emergency level for this theater takes special cognizance of the complexity of the distribution systems."

b. Took note of the omission from the above paper of the following oil stocks, for which provision would be made under other agreements:—

	Tons
Tar oil	100,000
Crude and process oils, aviation components, and bitumen	400,000

(Agreement as amended and approved subsequently circulated as C.C.S. 625/14.)

3. OVER-ALL REVIEW OF CARGO SHIPPING
(C.C.S. 746/11)

ADMIRAL LEAHY said that the United States Chiefs of Staff had examined this paper and it was acceptable to them with one amendment. They would like to change the date referred to in the first sentence of paragraph 4 b. (1) (d) on page 4 of the enclosure from 30 April to 1 April.

LORD LEATHERS said that this amendment would suit him personally very well if the staffs concerned could prepare the study in time.

ADMIRAL LEAHY said that the United States staffs believed this would be possible.

SIR ALAN BROOKE said that the British Chiefs of Staff were quite prepared to accept the first of April as a target date for the report concerned.

Continuing, Sir Alan Brooke suggested that paragraph 4 b. (1) of the enclosure required clarification as to the order of priority in which the tasks referred to were to be undertaken. For instance, the fixing of priorities for the continuance of the war against Japan referred to in paragraph 4 b. (1) (b) might well have to take place before the preparation of the combined redeployment plan or at least concurrently with it.

TOP SECRET

GENERAL SOMERVELL explained that the tasks referred to in paragraph 4 *b*. (1) were not set out in the sequence in which they would necessarily be undertaken.

SIR ALAN BROOKE suggested that the Combined Chiefs of Staff should decide on the agencies to undertake the preparation of a combined redeployment plan, and the fixing of priority for continuance of the war against Japan. He felt that the Combined Staff Planners and the Combined Administrative Committee, in consultation, would be the best bodies to undertake this work. They would, of course, as set out in paragraph 4 *b*. (1) (c) confer with the Combined Military Transportation Committee and the appropriate shipping authorities.

THE COMBINED CHIEFS OF STAFF:—

a. Approved C.C.S. 746/11, subject to the change of the date in the third line on page 4 from 30 April to 1 April 1945.

b. Directed the Combined Staff Planners, in collaboration with the Combined Administrative Committee, to take the action outlined in paragraph 4 *b*. (1).

c. Invited the combined shipping authorities to take the action outlined in paragraph 4 *b*. (2).

4. *RECIPROCAL AGREEMENT ON PRISONERS OF WAR*
   (C.C.S. 777/1)

SIR ALAN BROOKE said there were two points the British Chiefs of Staff would like to make. With regard to Article 6, certain of the Dominion Governments had raised objections to the conclusion of an agreement whereby their prisoners of war should work for the Russians on any but a voluntary basis. He suggested therefore the insertion of the words "on a voluntary basis" after the words "They may also be employed" in the second sentence of Article 6.

As he saw it, the proposed agreement was susceptible to alteration by the State Department or Foreign Office, and all that was required was the assurance of the Combined Chiefs of Staff that they saw no objection to it in principle.

TOP SECRET

ADMIRAL LEAHY said that he had understood the Combined Chiefs of Staff should agree on the wording of the document and recommend its acceptance to the State Department and Foreign Office as a basis for discussion with the Russians.

Replying to a question by General Marshall, *SIR CHARLES PORTAL* explained that the Dominion Governments concerned had pointed out that their forces were enrolled on a voluntary basis and were not conscripts. For political reasons, therefore, they felt it important that such troops who might be prisoners of war, should not be made to work by the Russians except on a voluntary basis.

ADMIRAL LEAHY said the proposed amendment was acceptable.

Continuing, *SIR ALAN BROOKE* said that the second point which the British Chiefs of Staff wished to put forward was with regard to Article 8. They felt that this article introduced a new subject which had not previously been considered and might not be acceptable to the Russian authorities who might well object to agreeing that their prisoners of war falling into the hands of United States or British troops should, without their consent, be transferred by one of these powers to the other.

ADMIRAL LEAHY pointed out that such transfers might be operationally necessary.

SIR CHARLES PORTAL said that as he read it, there was nothing in the remainder of the agreement which prohibited such transfers but he regarded it as a matter more for mutual arrangement between the United States and British authorities concerned than for discussion with the Russians.

GENERAL MARSHALL said that he was prepared to agree that paragraph 8 should be deleted.

THE COMBINED CHIEFS OF STAFF:—

Approved C.C.S. 777/1 subject to the following amendments:

Article 6: In the fifth line, after "employed," insert "on a voluntary basis."

Article 8: Delete this article and renumber the succeeding article as Article 8.

(Amended paper subsequently circulated as C.C.S. 777/2.)

5. EQUIPMENT FOR GREEK FORCES
(C.C.S. 185th Mtg., Item 2; C.C.S. 768/1; NAF 841*)

SIR ALAN BROOKE reminded the Combined Chiefs of Staff that at their 185th Meeting, 2 February 1945, it had been agreed that the British would undertake the equipment of an additional 60,000 Greek forces upon receipt from London of certain assurances. The British Chiefs of Staff were now in a position to assure the United States Chiefs of Staff that the implementation of the proposals contained in NAF 841:

a. Would not interfere with the equipment for Allied and liberated forces in Northwest Europe; and

b. Would not result in subsequent direct or indirect charges against United States resources.

The British would therefore go ahead with the equipping of the forces concerned. The British Chiefs of Staff would also formalize this matter by putting out a memorandum on the lines he had just mentioned.

GENERAL MARSHALL said that these assurances were satisfactory.

THE COMBINED CHIEFS OF STAFF:—

a. Took note of the assurance of the British Chiefs of Staff that the implementation of NAF 841 would not:
   (1) Interfere with the equipment for Allied and liberated forces in Northwest Europe;
   (2) Result in subsequent direct or indirect charges against U.S. resources.
b. Pursuant to the above, agreed to the implementation of the proposals in NAF 841.*

6. FINAL REPORT TO THE PRESIDENT AND PRIME MINISTER
(C.C.S. 776/1)

ADMIRAL LEAHY raised the question of the preparation of the final report to the President and Prime Minister. He understood that such a report

---
* See page 188.

TOP SECRET

would be ready for consideration on the following morning. He understood also that the Prime Minister had suggested a plenary meeting at noon, on Friday, 9 February. He would seek the wishes of the President in this matter.

SIR ALAN BROOKE suggested that it might be well for the Combined Chiefs of Staff to meet an hour before the plenary meeting in order to clear any final points with regard to the report itself or any other matters which might arise.

THE COMBINED CHIEFS OF STAFF:—

a. Agreed to request a plenary meeting for 1200 hours on Friday, 9 February 1945.

b. Agreed to meet one hour prior to the plenary meeting, whatever the hour selected, to consider the final report.

7. *OPERATIONS ON THE WESTERN FRONT*

GENERAL MARSHALL read out the latest information available on the course of ground and air operations on the Western Front. He felt it of particular interest to note that at the present time there were 49 Allied divisions in the line with 33 in reserve.

THE COMBINED CHIEFS OF STAFF:—

Took note with interest of the above statement.

TOP SECRET

COMBINED CHIEFS OF STAFF

C.C.S. 188th Meeting

ARGONAUT CONFERENCE

MINUTES OF MEETING HELD IN
CONFERENCE ROOM "A," BUILDING "A," LIVADIA PALACE, RUSSIA,
ON FRIDAY, 9 FEBRUARY 1945, AT 1100.

PRESENT

United States

Fleet Admiral W. D. Leahy, USN
General of the Army
  G. C. Marshall, USA
Fleet Admiral E. J. King, USN
Maj. Gen. L. S. Kuter, USA
  (Representing General of the
  Army H. H. Arnold)

British

Field Marshal Sir Alan F. Brooke
Marshal of the Royal Air Force
  Sir Charles F. A. Portal
Admiral of the Fleet
  Sir Andrew B. Cunningham

ALSO PRESENT

Lt. Gen. B. B. Somervell, USA
Vice Adm. C. M. Cooke, Jr., USN
Rear Adm. L. D. McCormick, USN
Maj. Gen. J. E. Hull, USA
Maj. Gen. J. R. Deane, USA
Captain A. S. McDill, USN
Commander R. N. S. Clark, USN

Field Marshal Sir H. M. Wilson
General Sir Hastings L. Ismay
Admiral Sir James Somerville

SECRETARIAT

Maj. Gen. E. I. C. Jacob
Brig. Gen. A. J. McFarland, USA
Brigadier A. T. Cornwall-Jones
Captain E. D. Graves, Jr., USN
Commander R. D. Coleridge, RN
Colonel D. Capel-Dunn

TOP SECRET

1. *APPROVAL OF THE MINUTES OF THE 187TH MEETING OF C.C.S.*

THE COMBINED CHIEFS OF STAFF:—

Approved the conclusions of the minutes of the C.C.S. 187th Meeting and approved the detailed record of the meeting subject to later minor amendments.

2. *DRAFT FINAL REPORT TO THE PRESIDENT AND PRIME MINISTER* (C.C.S. 776/2)

THE COMBINED CHIEFS OF STAFF considered those paragraphs of the draft final report which had been added since they had approved C.C.S. 776/1.

SIR ALAN BROOKE drew attention to the directive to the Supreme Allied Commander, Mediterranean, contained in Appendix "A" of C.C.S. 776/2. He pointed out that in paragraph 4 c. of the directive it was stated that, "The nomination of ground formations to be withdrawn and the arrangements for their transfer will form the subject of a separate instruction." In order to avoid any possible delay in the movement of these forces he suggested that the Combined Chiefs of Staff should send an instruction to the Supreme Allied Commander, Mediterranean repeated to the Supreme Commander, Allied Expeditionary Force in the following sense:

"Reference paragraph 4 c. of the directive issued to you in FAN 501. The move of two Canadian and three British divisions should proceed under plans to be agreed between yourself and SCAEF, without awaiting any further instructions from the Combined Chiefs of Staff."

GENERAL MARSHALL said that this proposal was acceptable.

THE COMBINED CHIEFS OF STAFF:—

a. Approved the text of the report to the President and Prime Minister on the *ARGONAUT* Conference (C.C.S. 776/2).

b. Approved the dispatch of the telegram proposed by Field Marshal Sir Alan Brooke. (Subsequently dispatched as FAN 504 and FACS 155.)

TOP SECRET

3. *LIAISON WITH THE SOVIET HIGH COMMAND WITH REGARD TO STRATEGIC BOMBING IN EASTERN GERMANY*
(C.C.S. 778, C.C.S. 186th Mtg., Item 7, Two Tripartite Military Meetings)

SIR CHARLES PORTAL referred to the discussions which had been taking place between himself and General Kuter and Marshal of Aviation Khudyakov. At the meeting a draft agreement had been drawn up and agreed and submitted to the three High Commands. It was acceptable to the British and, he understood, to the United States Chiefs of Staff. However, on the previous evening identical letters had been received by General Kuter and himself from Marshal Khudyakov setting out a considerably revised draft agreement. This was unacceptable to himself and to General Kuter.

GENERAL KUTER said he had redrafted the Russian proposals in such a way as to make them acceptable to the U.S. and British; he proposed putting this new draft to the Russians. If this were not acceptable to the Russians, it would probably be wisest to inform them that we planned to continue with the previous arrangements.

SIR CHARLES PORTAL explained the main difference between the Russian proposals and the draft which had been agreed at the meeting of the Heads of Air Staffs. In the original draft the Allied air forces could bomb a target to the east of the line, provided 24 hours' notice was given to the Soviet High Command and no objection was raised. In the Russian proposal, however, it was necessary to obtain agreement for any Allied bombing east of the line 24 hours before the attack was to take place. It had been his understanding in conversations with Marshal Khudyakov, that the Russian Staff was more interested in preventing incidents between Allied and Soviet aircraft than they were in protecting their ground forces.

GENERAL KUTER pointed out that there was one further important change in the Russian proposals. The Soviet Staff had now proposed that a rigid line should exist which would be moved from time to time by the Soviet Staff whereas in the original agreement the bombline was to move forward automatically at a given distance from the Russian front line. An example of the difficulties which would arise under Marshal Khudyakov's proposals had recently occurred. Marshal Tito had asked that the town of Brod be bombed on a certain day and a request for permission to do so had been made by General Deane in Moscow. General Deane had written letters to the Staff on this subject four consecutive days without receiving any reply and in fact no answer had yet been received. In his view the present Russian proposal was an entirely unworkable procedure.

TOP SECRET

THE COMBINED CHIEFS OF STAFF then discussed the best method of handling further action with regard to the Russian proposals.

THE COMBINED CHIEFS OF STAFF:—

Agreed that Marshal of the Royal Air Force Sir Charles Portal and General Kuter should each reply separately to Marshal of the Soviet Air Force Khudyakov, making it clear that the revised agreement proposed by the Soviet High Command differed substantially from that which it was thought had been agreed between the Heads of the three Air Forces on 6 February; that these differences made acceptance of the revised agreement impracticable; and that the British/United States High Command therefore intended to continue with the arrangements in force prior to the Crimean Conference.

4. CONCLUDING REMARKS

ADMIRAL LEAHY said he would like to express on behalf of the United States Chiefs of Staff their appreciation for the cooperation and assistance received from the British Chiefs of Staff during the present conference. He felt that progress had been made on the general plans of the war as a whole, and that much had been accomplished.

SIR ALAN BROOKE said that he would like to reciprocate on behalf of the British Chiefs of Staff the feelings expressed by Admiral Leahy. He was convinced that great progress had been made during the present conference.

MINUTES OF

**TRIPARTITE
MILITARY MEETINGS**

TOP SECRET

ARGONAUT CONFERENCE

Minutes of the First Tripartite Military Meeting
Held in the Soviet Headquarters, Yalta,
on Monday, 5 February 1945, at 1200.

PRESENT

United States

Fleet Admiral W. D. Leahy
General of the Army
  G. C. Marshall
Fleet Admiral E. J. King
Major General L. S. Kuter
  (Representing General of the
  Army H. H. Arnold)
Vice Admiral C. M. Cooke, Jr., USN
Major General J. R. Deane, USA
Major General H. R. Bull, USA
Major General F. L. Anderson, USA
Major General J. E. Hull, USA

British

Field Marshal Sir Alan F. Brooke
Marshal of the Royal Air Force
  Sir Charles F. A. Portal
Admiral of the Fleet
  Sir Andrew B. Cunningham
Field Marshal Sir H. Alexander
General Sir Hastings L. Ismay
Rear Admiral E. R. Archer

U.S.S.R.

Army General Antonov
  Deputy Chief of Staff, Red Army
Marshal of Aviation Khudyakov
  Chief of Soviet Air Staff
Admiral of the Fleet Kuznetsov
  Peoples Commissariat for the Navy
Lieutenant General Grizlov
  Assistant to Deputy Chief of Staff
Vice Admiral Kucherov
  Deputy Chief of Staff of the Navy
Commander Kostrinski
  Deputy Chief of Foreign Relations

TOP SECRET

SECRETARIAT

Brigadier General A. J. McFarland, USA
Brigadier A. T. Cornwall-Jones
Captain E. D. Graves, Jr., USN
Commander R. D. Coleridge, RN

INTERPRETERS

Captain Hill Lunghi
Captain Henry Ware, USA
Lieutenant Joseph Chase, USNR
Mr. Potrubach

TOP SECRET

At the suggestion of General Antonov, Field Marshal Brooke agreed to take the chair.

1. COORDINATION OF OFFENSIVE OPERATIONS

SIR ALAN BROOKE suggested that the meeting should begin by considering the coordination of the Russian and U.S.-British offensives. At the Plenary Meeting on the previous day, General Antonov had put forward certain Russian requirements. He had asked, first, that during the month of February the Allied armies in the West should carry out offensives. As General Marshall had explained, the Allied offensive in the West would start in the North on the eighth of February and some eight days later the Ninth U.S. Army would also start an offensive. These operations would be carried out during most of February. In addition to these operations in the North, operations were now being carried out by United States and French armies to push the Germans back to the Rhine in the Colmar area. It was therefore clear that the immediate coordination of Allied and Russian offensives was already being carried out. It was necessary, however, to look into the matter of coordination of offensives in the spring and summer months. As far as operations in the West were concerned these would be more or less continuous throughout the spring. There were, of course, bound to be intervals between operations, though such intervals would not be of long duration. For instance, after clearing the western bank of the Rhine on the northern part of the front, preparations would have to be made for the final crossing of the Rhine. From a study of conditions of the river it was hoped to effect a crossing during the month of March. After establishing the crossing it would have to be widened and improved before the final advance into the heart of Germany could be undertaken.

Should operations in the North aimed at the Ruhr be held up, it was the intention to carry out further operations in the South. It was safe to say, therefore, that during the months of February, March and April, active operations would be in progress during almost the entire time.

The actual crossing of the Rhine presented the greatest difficulties and it was during the period of this crossing that the Allies were anxious to prevent a concentration of German forces against the armies in the West. It was therefore hoped that during March operations on the Eastern Front would be able to continue. *SIR ALAN BROOKE* said he appreciated the difficulties in March and early April due to the thaw and mud which would interfere with communications. He also realized that after their present great advances the Russian armies would want to improve their communications. He would much like to hear General Antonov's views on what operations could be undertaken by the Soviet armies during March and April.

GENERAL MARSHALL said that during the Tripartite Plenary Meeting on the previous day the number of divisions, the amount of artillery, and the number of tanks on the Eastern Front had been enumerated. In considering the Western Front it was important to bear in mind that operations must be conducted to meet the special conditions existing. In the West there was no superiority in ground forces. There were delicate lines of sea communications, particularly in the Scheldt Estuary. The Allies, however, did enjoy a preponderance of air power, but in this connection the weather was an important consideration. If the Allies were unable to take full advantage of their air superiority they did not have sufficient superiority on the ground to overcome enemy opposition. Operations must therefore be conducted on this basis. Another restriction arose from the fact that there were only a small number of favorable locations for crossing the Rhine. It was therefore most important to insure that the enemy could not concentrate strongly at the point of attack.

The enemy were now operating behind the Rhine and the Siegfried line and therefore had great freedom of maneuver. We must therefore arrange to occupy the Germans as much as possible to prevent them from concentrating against us on the very narrow bridgehead area available to us.

With regard to air forces, on the Western Front some 3,000 to 4,000 fighter-bomber sorties could be undertaken each day. There was about one-third of this strength on the Italian Front. This did not include the power of the great four-engine bombers with their escorting fighters.

GENERAL ANTONOV said that, as Marshal Stalin had pointed out, the Russians would continue the offensive in the East as long as the weather permitted. There might be interruptions during the offensive and, as Sir Alan Brooke had said, there was the need to reestablish Russian communications. The Soviet Army would, however, take measures to make such interruptions as short as possible and would continue the offensive to the limit of their capacity.

In connection with the western offensive in February, it was not believed that the Germans could transfer forces from the Eastern Front to the West in large numbers. The Soviet Staff, however, was also interested in the Italian Front, from where the Germans had the opportunity of transferring troops to the Eastern Front. In view of this, the Soviet General Staff would like to know the potentialities of the Allied armies now fighting the Germans in Italy.

TOP SECRET

SIR ALAN BROOKE said that the situation on the Italian Front was being carefully examined as it developed. Kesselring's forces had now been driven into northern Italy where the country was very well suited for defense or for systematic retirement. There was a series of rivers which could be used for rear-guard actions while withdrawing his forces gradually. The enemy would have to retreat through the Ljubljana Gap or the passes of the Alps. The coast in the Bay of Venice was not suitable for amphibious operations, and therefore outflanking operations in the Adriatic did not appear fruitful. So far there had been continuous offensive operations which had driven the enemy out of the Apennine line and into the Valley of the Po. Winter weather and floods had, however, brought these offensive operations almost to a standstill.

At present our troops were preparing for further offensive action when the weather improved. It had, however, been decided that it would be better to transfer some of the forces now in Italy to the Western Front, where at present we did not have sufficient superiority in ground forces. Five divisions were therefore now to be transferred from Italy to France and certain air forces would accompany them. The forces remaining in Italy had been instructed to carry out offensive operations and to seize every opportunity to inflict heavy blows on the enemy. Their object was to retain as many of Kesselring's forces as possible by offensive action. However, owing to the topography of the country, it was believed that Kesselring could carry out a partial withdrawal without the Allies being able to stop it. The rate of withdrawal was estimated at some one and one-half divisions per week. Thus, any withdrawal which he did undertake could only be gradual.

To sum up, it was proposed to take what action was possible to stop the German withdrawal in Italy, though it was not thought that this could be entirely prevented. For this reason, it had been decided to withdraw certain forces from Italy to the vital front in Northwest Europe.

GENERAL MARSHALL said that he agreed with Sir Alan Brooke's summary of the position but felt that a reference should be made to the value of our air power in Italy.

GENERAL ANTONOV asked the number of German troops believed to be in Italy.

FIELD MARSHAL ALEXANDER said that at present the German forces in Italy consisted of 27 German divisions and 5 Italian divisions.

TOP SECRET

SIR ALAN BROOKE said that all these forces could not be held down in Italy by offensive action. If the Germans decided to retire to the line of the Adige, it was estimated that they would be able to withdraw some ten divisions from Italy.

SIR CHARLES PORTAL said that on the Western and Italian Fronts together the United States and British air forces consisted of some fourteen thousand aircraft. This figure did not include the reserve behind the front line. Should the land campaign have to halt, the war in the air would continue, so far as weather permitted, even more strongly than before. Everything possible would be done, as General Marshall had stated, to bring the greatest possible air assistance to the vital points of attack in the land offensive. Such air assistance included the operations of a number of airborne divisions, for which the necessary transport was available.

So far as the requirements of the land battle permitted, it was the intention to concentrate the strategic bomber forces on the enemy's oil supply. Evidence was available almost daily that the destruction of his oil production capacity was imposing limitations on the enemy's operations. It was believed that the destruction of enemy oil was the best contribution which the air forces could make, both to the offensive on land and in the air. Much had been done and would continue to be done to disorganize the enemy's rail communications, but it was our experience that an attempt to cut all railways in the middle of Germany to stop troop movements would produce disappointing results in view of the relative ease with which the enemy could repair such destruction.

It was known that the Germans intended to assemble a strong force of jet-propelled fighters during the course of the present year. It had therefore been decided that, in order to maintain our air superiority into the summer, a proportion of our air effort must be devoted to attacks on the German jet-propelled fighter manufacturing plants. Nevertheless, it was an agreed principle that when the land offensive began, everything in the air that could contribute to its success should be so used.

Before the advance of the Soviet armies, Allied air power had been brought to bear as far afield as Koenigsberg, Danzig, Posen and Warsaw. The great range of our strategic air forces made it most necessary that Allied air operations should be coordinated with the advance of the Soviet armies both to prevent accidents and to obtain the best value from our bomber effort.

TOP SECRET

GENERAL MARSHALL invited Field Marshal Alexander to comment on the capability of air forces in Italy to prevent a German withdrawal.

FIELD MARSHAL ALEXANDER said that it had been his experience in Italy that our greatly superior air forces were a most powerful weapon while the enemy was withdrawing, if it was possible to force the pace of his withdrawal. If, however, he was in a position to withdraw at his own pace the air forces were less effective since the withdrawal could be undertaken mostly under cover of darkness.

In the Valley of the Po there was a series of extremely strong holding positions and it would therefore be difficult to force the enemy to withdraw faster than he planned. Nevertheless, when the weather improved from May onwards, considerable damage could be done to the withdrawing German forces and to their lines of communication. However, in February, March and April the weather was bad, with low clouds, which hindered the air effort to a great extent. Further, the Germans had destroyed nearly all the bridges over the River Po and had replaced them with some 30 to 40 pontoon bridges which were not kept in position during the day but were hidden along the banks. The destruction of these bridges was therefore extremely difficult.

To sum up, the better the weather the more damage could be done to the enemy by air action but however successful the air action, he did not believe that it would be possible entirely to prevent a German withdrawal by this means.

GENERAL MARSHALL said that at the Tripartite Plenary Meeting on the previous day the desire had been expressed that every effort should be made to stop the movement of German forces from west to east by air action and, in particular, to paralyze the vital rail junctions of Berlin and Leipzig. In this connection a report he had received that day summarizing Allied air operations in the last few days was of interest. On Friday, the second of February, the Royal Air Force had flown 2,400 sorties, concentrating on rail and road targets in Euskirchen and Coblenz. The latter, in particular, was of vital importance in the transfer of German forces to the East. Similar destruction of rail targets had taken place east of Alsace. On the same night a thousand of our bombers had attacked Wiesbaden, Karlsruhe and synthetic oil plants elsewhere. On the following day, Saturday, the third of February, four-engined United States bombers had attacked Marienberg railway yards and 550 RAF bombers had attacked targets in the same area.

TOP SECRET

In relation to the destruction of communications and the interference with enemy movements the following data had been received relating to the effect of air attacks carried out on the 22d and 23d of January: On these two days alone 2,500 motor cars and trucks had been destroyed and 1,500 damaged; a thousand railway cars had been destroyed and 700 damaged; 93 tanks and self-propelled guns had been destroyed and a further 93 damaged; 25 locomotives had been destroyed and 4 damaged; 50 horse-drawn vehicles had been destroyed and 88 damaged. In addition, 62 known gun positions had been wiped out and 21 marshalling yards damaged. These very large results had been obtained on the two days he had referred to, but similar attacks were carried out on almost every fine day by the Allied air forces. He had referred on the previous day to the thousand-bomber attack on Berlin carried out on the third of February. There was also ready a plan to carry out a similar attack on Leipzig.

MARSHAL KHUDYAKOV said that, as Marshal Stalin had pointed out, more than 8,000 Soviet planes were being used in the main thrust. In spite of weather conditions, between the 12th of January and the first of February 80,000 sorties had been flown in support of the Russian advance. More than a thousand enemy planes had been captured on airfields which had been overrun by the Russian troops. These aircraft had been prevented from flying away by bad weather. In addition, 560 planes had been shot down in air combat. If better weather prevailed air operations could be carried out on objectives further in the enemy rear but fog at this time of year rendered such deep operations to the west of Berlin almost impossible. He agreed with Sir Charles Portal that there were too many railroads in Germany to destroy all of them. He hoped that Field Marshal Alexander's operations could be aimed at hampering the movement of German divisions from Italy to the Eastern Front.

FIELD MARSHAL ALEXANDER said that this object was contained in his directive.

MARSHAL KHUDYAKOV said that he was glad to hear of this. In Italy there were fewer railways to assist the enemy withdrawal.

FIELD MARSHAL ALEXANDER explained that the Germans in Italy largely used roads for their withdrawals.

GENERAL ANTONOV said that in addition to the Soviet offensives in the North, offensives would also continue in the direction of Vienna and west

TOP SECRET

of Lake Balaton. It was for this reason that Allied action in Italy was of importance to the Soviets. It seemed to him expedient that Allied land offensives should be directed toward the Ljubljana Gap and Graz. He now understood that this was not possible.

SIR ALAN BROOKE said that it must be remembered that the Allies had no great superiority in land forces. They had come to the conclusion that in conjunction with the vital death blows being dealt by the Soviet armies in the East, the correct place for the western death blow was in Northwestern Europe. For this reason it had been decided to transfer divisions from Italy to the Western Front and to limit operations in Italy to holding as many German forces in that theater as possible. In the event of a German withdrawal from northern Italy, we had forces strong enough to take advantage of such a withdrawal, and possibly at a later date to be able to operate through the Ljubljana Gap. Such action, however, must remain dependent on the withdrawal of a proportion of the German forces at present in the north of Italy.

2. MOVEMENT OF GERMAN FORCES FROM NORWAY

GENERAL ANTONOV said that the Germans were transferring forces from Norway to Denmark. He asked if there was any way in which such a movement could be stopped.

SIR ANDREW CUNNINGHAM said as far as was known, these movements were being carried out by rail and road to Oslo and not by sea. The troops were then being moved across the short sea passage to Denmark. It was not possible in view of heavy mining to operate surface forces in the Skagerrak and thus prevent the enemy making this short sea passage.

SIR CHARLES PORTAL said that the action of the air forces in this connection could be divided into two parts: firstly, by such attacks as could be made on shipping in the Kattegat, and with four-engined bombers operated on almost every fine night in an endeavor to bomb enemy ships. Several ships had recently been set on fire in this area. The second form of air action was by mine-laying aircraft. Approximately 1,000 mines were being laid by this method each month. Each aircraft carried some six mines. Sir Andrew Cunningham had just told him that recently these mines had sunk or damaged four enemy transports. German minesweepers did endeavor of course to sweep up our mines but it was now planned to increase the number of air attacks made on these minesweepers. However, there were so many varying tasks for the air forces to carry out that all could not be undertaken equally well.

TOP SECRET

SIR ALAN BROOKE said an examination had also been made of the possibility of stopping the movement of German forces from Norway by land action in Norway itself. There were, however, insufficient forces to undertake this without weakening our main effort on the Western Front.

3. *USE OF ARTILLERY AND AIR IN FUTURE OPERATIONS*

GENERAL ANTONOV said he felt it would be interesting to exchange information with regard to the method of carrying out operations in the autumn, winter and spring when, by reason of weather, it was not always possible to make use of air power. On these occasions the role of artillery became one of particular importance. As Marshal Stalin had said on the previous day, the Russians were establishing special artillery divisions of some 300 to 400 guns each, which were used for breaking through the enemy line. This method enabled a mass of artillery of some 230 guns of 76 millimeters and upwards to be concentrated on a front of one kilometer. He would be very glad to know what degree of artillery density would be used on the Western Front when the February offensive commenced.

GENERAL BULL said that the northern army group, which would take part in the next offensive, possessed some 1,500 guns of 105 millimeters and upwards, and the United States army group which would also take part in the offensive, had some 3,000 guns of similar calibers. The army commanders concerned, by concentrating their artillery power on a narrow front, would be able to use some 200 guns to the mile in the area of the break-through. To this offensive power should be added the power of the air forces. In the three days preceding the attack on the eighth of February, it could be expected that some 1,600 heavy bombers would be used, capable of delivering 4,500 tons of bombs on the first day. For the remaining two days before the offensive, a slightly less weight of bombs could be dropped, but closer to the point of attack. Not only would communications behind the front be bombed, but also positions known to be strongly held.

On the day of the attack itself, "carpet bombing" would be used, and some 4,000 tons could be dropped on an area two miles square. He felt the effect of the air attack and the artillery concentration should produce a break-through, thus allowing our armor to operate in the enemy's rear. A similar pattern of attack had been used on previous occasions with great success.

MARSHAL KHUDYAKOV asked what action would be taken if it was found that weather prohibited the air from operating on the day of attack.

TOP SECRET

GENERAL BULL explained that the attack was normally timed for a day on which it was predicted that the weather would enable "carpet bombing" to be carried out. During the actual attack the bombing was carried out some 2,000 yards ahead of our own front line, but earlier bombing on targets further behind the line could be undertaken through overcast.

MARSHAL KHUDYAKOV explained that all Russian operations in winter were planned on the supposition that bad weather would exist, and no air operations would be possible. He felt that the Allies should bear this point in mind in planning their own operations.

GENERAL MARSHALL said that he had endeavored to explain that the Allies did not possess the same superiority in ground forces as did the Russians. The Allies did not have 300 divisions, nor was it possible to produce them. It was therefore essential to make full use of our air superiority. He would like to point out the advance across France had, in fact, been accomplished with the same number of divisions as the enemy himself had. This was made possible by a combination of ground and air power.

GENERAL ANTONOV said that he now had a very clear picture of Allied offensive intentions. Were there any questions which the British or United States Chiefs of Staff would like to ask?

4. *LIAISON ARRANGEMENTS*

ADMIRAL LEAHY said that in view of the very frank discussion of plans which was taking place, he would like to bring up the question of liaison between the Eastern and Western Fronts. The distance between the two armies was now so short that direct liaison was a matter of great importance. He had been directed by the President to bring up this question of liaison before the British, Russian and United States Chiefs of Staff. It was the opinion of the United States Chiefs of Staff, who had not yet discussed it with their British colleagues, that arrangements should be made for the Allied armies in the West to deal rapidly with the Soviet commanders on the Eastern Front through the Military Missions now in Moscow. He would be glad to take back to the President the views of the Soviet and British Chiefs of Staffs on this matter.

SIR ALAN BROOKE said that the British Chiefs of Staff were equally anxious to have the necessary liaison in order that plans could be concerted. They felt that such liaison required organizing on a sound basis. Military Missions were already established in Moscow, and these should, he felt, act as a link

TOP SECRET

on a high level between the United States, British and Soviet Chiefs of Staffs. In addition to this, closer liaison was required between the commanders of Allied theaters with the commanders of the nearest Russian armies. For example, on the Italian Front, Field Marshal Alexander required direct liaison with the Russian commander concerned.

In the case of the Supreme Commander on the Western Front, he would require direct liaison with the commanders of the Russian armies in the East. Thus there would be coordination between the high commands dealing with future action and in addition, direct coordination between the Allied and Soviet armies, who were closely in contact, on such matters as the employment of air forces and the coordination of day-to-day action.

GENERAL ANTONOV said that the question of liaison between the general staffs was very important and, as had already been mentioned, could be undertaken through the Missions in Moscow. In the present state of the offensives, this should be perfectly satisfactory until the forces came closer into contact with each other. Later, as operations advanced, the question of liaison between Army commanders could be reviewed and adjusted. These proposals would be reported to Marshal Stalin.

GENERAL MARSHALL said that he had not entirely understood the necessity for limiting liaison.

GENERAL ANTONOV explained that his proposal was to limit liaison to that through the General Staff in Moscow and the U.S. and British Missions. Such arrangements, however, could be revised and adjusted later to meet changing conditions.

GENERAL MARSHALL pointed out that difficulties and serious results had already occurred in air operations from Italy over the Balkans. Such operations were directed from day to day and even from hour to hour, depending on weather and other conditions. If contact had to be maintained between the armies concerned through Moscow, difficulties would be certain to arise.

If this round-about method of communications through many busy people had to be adopted, there was a risk that our powerful air weapon could not be properly used.

GENERAL ANTONOV said that the accident to which General Marshall referred had occurred not because of lack of liaison but due to the pilots concerned losing their way. They had, in fact, made a navigational mistake with regard to the correct point for bombing.

TOP SECRET

GENERAL MARSHALL said that he recognized this. However, the bombline at that time excluded roads crowded with retreating Germans who could not be bombed by the Allied forces without an approach being made through Moscow. A powerful air force was available and good weather existed but the Allied air force was unable to act and the Germans profited thereby.

SIR ALAN BROOKE said he entirely agreed with General Marshall that, through lack of liaison, we are losing the full force of the air power at our disposal.

GENERAL ANTONOV said that at the present time no tactical coordination was required between Allied and Russian ground forces. We should, he believed, aim at planning the strategic requirements of our air forces. The use of all Soviet air forces was dictated by the Soviet General Staff in Moscow. It was for this reason that the coordination of the air effort should, in his view, be carried out through the Soviet General Staff in Moscow, who alone could solve the problems. It was possible to agree on the objectives for strategic bombing irrespective of a bombline.

SIR CHARLES PORTAL said that in the British view there were two distinct problems with regard to liaison. The first was the necessity for the form of liaison referred to by General Antonov, i.e., the coordination of the Allied long-range bomber effort over eastern Germany and its relation to the advance of the Red Army. The Allied long-range strategic bomber force was not controlled by the Supreme Commander in the West except when it was undertaking work in close cooperation with the ground forces but was controlled by the United States and British Chiefs of Staff. It was right, therefore, that the United States and British Chiefs of Staff or their representatives should deal direct with Moscow on this matter.

The second problem was in respect to the constant air operations out from Italy in relation to Russian operations in the Balkans and Hungary. In that theater liaison was required, not so much on policy as on an interchange of information. The British Chiefs of Staff entirely agreed with the United States view that it was inefficient for liaison between Field Marshal Alexander and the Russian commanders to be effected through Moscow. It was, therefore, essential that some machinery should be set up to deal with day-to-day liaison between General Alexander and the Russian headquarters which controlled the southern front. Without such direct liaison it was impossible to take advantage of the many opportunities presented to hit the Germans from the air.

TOP SECRET

MARSHAL KHUDYAKOV said that concerning air action into Germany itself, this could be done through the General Staff in Moscow as suggested by Sir Charles Portal, using the U.S. and British Military Missions. This liaison on policy was one which took time to arrange and was not a matter for great speed. With regard to direct liaison between Field Marshal Alexander and the Russian left wing he felt this was a matter which should be reported to Marshal Stalin.

GENERAL ANTONOV asked if it could not be agreed that a bombline should be established running from Berlin to Dresden, Vienna and Zagreb, all these places being allotted to the Allied air forces. Such a line could, of course, be changed as the front changed.

ADMIRAL LEAHY and SIR ALAN BROOKE asked that this matter be deferred one day for consideration.

5. NAVAL OPERATIONS IN SUPPORT OF THE LAND OFFENSIVE

ADMIRAL KUZNETSOV asked if plans had been made for any naval operations in direct assistance to the land attack which was shortly to be carried out. He referred not so much to the normal naval operations in the defense of communications and day-to-day operations of the fleet to control the seas but rather to direct operations in support of a land offensive.

SIR ANDREW CUNNINGHAM explained that projected operations were too far inland to be directly affected by any operations which could be carried out by the fleet except the routine operations of keeping open communications. He asked if Admiral Kuznetsov had any particular operations in mind.

ADMIRAL KUZNETSOV said he had no particular operation in mind but rather the possibility of some operation in the neighborhood of Denmark that would not have any direct tactical connection with the army operations but would have a strategic connection.

SIR ANDREW CUNNINGHAM said that possible operations to outflank the Rhine had been studied. However, landing on the coast of Holland would prove extremely difficult and the necessary land forces were not available to enable an operation against Denmark to be undertaken.

TOP SECRET

SIR ALAN BROOKE said that owing to the difficulty of forcing a crossing of the Rhine when that river was in flood, a very detailed examination had been carried out of the coastline from the Scheldt to the Danish coast, but operations in this area had not been found practicable since: firstly, large areas of Holland could be flooded and, secondly, operations further to the north would be too far detached from the main thrust to be of value.

ADMIRAL KING asked if Admiral Kuznetsov would outline the successes which the Soviet Fleet had been able to obtain in amphibious operations or operations to interfere with the transport of troops from the Baltic states to Germany.

ADMIRAL KUZNETSOV said that operations of the Soviet Fleet to cut German communications in the Baltic had been undertaken by submarines and naval aircraft. When the area of Memel was reached, it became possible to transfer torpedo boats to augment Russian naval activity in that area. However, all operations were at present hampered by ice conditions and, further, the Gulf of Finland and the Gulf of Riga were heavily mined by the enemy, and mine clearance was hampered by weather conditions and ice.

ADMIRAL KING said that he appreciated that ice conditions were now limiting operations but had asked this question in view of earlier Soviet communiques mentioning the damage or destruction of German shipping.

ADMIRAL KUZNETSOV said that the earlier destruction of German shipping had been carried out by naval air forces and submarines.

6. *DATE OF THE END OF THE WAR WITH GERMANY*

ADMIRAL LEAHY said that the United States Chiefs of Staff were engaged in making logistic plans for that phase of the war following the collapse of Germany. It had been suggested that such plans should now be based on a probable date of the first of July for the earliest possible collapse of Germany. Before deciding on such a date he was anxious to have the views of the Soviet Staff on this matter.

GENERAL ANTONOV said that until the eastern and western offensives developed it was difficult if not impossible to predict the date of the collapse of Germany.

ADMIRAL LEAHY said he entirely appreciated the uncertainty but for planning purposes he would be glad to know if the Soviet Staff regarded the first of July as the earliest date as a reasonable assumption.

TOP SECRET

GENERAL ANTONOV said he regarded such assumptions as being difficult to make. He could assure Admiral Leahy that the Soviet General Staff would concentrate every effort on the earliest possible defeat of Germany.

GENERAL MARSHALL explained that a year ago it had been necessary to assume a date for the defeat of Germany on which to base calculations on such matters as production and the construction of shipping. It was necessary to revise this date from time to time, particularly in connection with the handling of shipping throughout the world. It had been proposed to take two target dates, one the earliest and one the latest likely date for the defeat of Germany. Such dates were now under consideration between the United States and British Chiefs of Staff who were in agreement that the first of July was the earliest likely date but differed by two months with regard to the latest likely date. The United States assumption in this connection was the 31st of December. Did General Antonov regard the first of July as improbable as the earliest likely date?

GENERAL ANTONOV said that he regarded the summer as the earliest date and the winter as the latest. The first of July should be a reasonably certain date for the defeat of Germany if all our efforts were applied to this end.

7. FUTURE BUSINESS

A brief discussion took place on future business.

SIR ALAN BROOKE suggested that a meeting should be held on the following day at 12 noon in the Soviet Headquarters, and that the following subjects should be discussed: (1) Coordination of Air Operations; (2) Shuttle Bombing; and (3) A Short Discussion on the War in the Far East.

ADMIRAL KING said he would be prepared to make a statement on operations taking place in the Pacific and his conception of the future development of the war in that theater. He would welcome any questions which the Soviet Staff might wish to ask on this subject.

GENERAL ANTONOV said he would be glad to listen to a description of the situation in the Far East and operations in that area, but as far as discussion of the matter was concerned the Soviet General Staff would prefer that this should take place after the war in the Far East had been considered by the Heads of Government.

TOP SECRET

ARGONAUT CONFERENCE

Minutes of the Second Tripartite Military Meeting
Held in the Soviet Headquarters, Yalta,
on Tuesday, 6 February 1945, at 1200.

PRESENT

United States

Fleet Admiral W. D. Leahy
General of the Army
  G. C. Marshall
Fleet Admiral E. J. King
Major General L. S. Kuter
  (Representing General of the
  Army H. H. Arnold)
Vice Admiral C. M. Cooke, Jr., USN
Major General J. R. Deane, USA
Major General H. R. Bull, USA
Major General F. L. Anderson, USA
Major General J. E. Hull, USA

British

Field Marshal Sir Alan F. Brooke
Marshal of the Royal Air Force
  Sir Charles F. A. Portal
Admiral of the Fleet
  Sir Andrew B. Cunningham
Field Marshal Sir H. M. Wilson
General Sir Hastings L. Ismay
Admiral Sir James Somerville
Rear Admiral E. R. Archer

U.S.S.R.

Army General Antonov
  Deputy Chief of Staff, Red Army
Marshal of Aviation Khudyakov
  Chief of Soviet Air Staff
Admiral of the Fleet Kuznetsov
  Peoples Commissariat for the Navy
Lieutenant General Grizlov
  Assistant to Deputy Chief of Staff
Vice Admiral Kucherov
  Deputy Chief of Staff of the Navy
Commander Kostrinski
  Deputy Chief of Foreign Relations

SECRETARIAT

Brigadier General A. J. McFarland, USA
Brigadier A. T. Cornwall-Jones
Captain E. D. Graves, Jr., USN
Commander R. D. Coleridge, RN

INTERPRETERS

Captain Hill Lunghi
Lieutenant Joseph Chase, USNR
Mr. Potrubach

TOP SECRET

CHAIRMANSHIP

GENERAL ANTONOV requested Admiral Leahy to serve as Chairman of the 2d Tripartite Meeting.

ADMIRAL LEAHY thanked General Antonov but suggested that in the interest of continuity, Field Marshal Brooke continue to preside.

1. *BOMBLINE AND LIAISON ARRANGEMENTS*

SIR ALAN BROOKE suggested that the first item to be discussed should be General Antonov's proposal for a bombline running from Stettin through Berlin, Vienna and Zagreb. He asked the United States Chiefs of Staff to express their views on this proposal since they were most intimately concerned with it.

GENERAL KUTER said he would like to read a statement on behalf of the United States Chiefs of Staff, setting out their views on this matter. This statement read as follows:

"1. Our wishes are:—

   (a) To continue to do the greatest possible damage to the German military and economic system.

   (b) To avoid interference with or danger to the Soviet forces advancing from the East.

   (c) To do what is possible to assist the advance of the Soviet Army.

"2. To achieve the first wish, that is, maximum damage to the Germans, it is essential to avoid as far as possible any restriction of strategic bomber action. It is not our wish to draw a line on the map which would exclude our bombers from attacking any targets which are important to the warmaking power of the enemy, whether against the Soviet or the British and American forces.

"3. To achieve the second wish, that is, avoidance of interference with Soviet land operations, we must rely upon the Soviet High Command to inform the British and United States Missions in Moscow of the positions of the Red Army from day to day. We also invite the Soviet High Command to inform the British and United States Missions if there are any particular objectives, for example, railway centers or centers of road communication close in front of their armies which they wish us *not* to attack. We should require at least 24, and preferably 48 hours' notice for action upon such requests.

"4. A regular daily meeting between the British and United States Missions in Moscow and a responsible officer of the Soviet General Staff seems to us to be essential.

"5. To achieve the third wish, that is, assistance to the Russian advance, we should be glad to receive through the British and American Missions in Moscow any suggestions from the Soviet High Command. This suggestion would have to be considered in the light of other commitments and such factors as the distance and the weather.

"6. To summarize, we suggest:—

 (a) That there should be no rigid division of eastern Germany into spheres of action of the Soviet and British and American strategic bombers respectively;

 (b) That day-to-day liaison should be established between a responsible officer of the Russian High Command and representatives of the British and American Missions in Moscow, in order to exchange information upon which we can regulate the action of the Anglo-U.S. strategic bombers in accordance with the development of Soviet operations on land.

"7. When the Soviet Air Force is ready to undertake strategic bombing deep into Germany from the East, the coordination of policy should be discussed by Soviet, American and British Staff representatives in London or in Moscow. Some further machinery for the closer coordination of operations would appear to be necessary at that time."

GENERAL KUTER said that he would like to add that in addition to his objection to the principle of a fixed line on the map, there was the further objection that there were valuable strategic targets to the east of the proposed line. From among some 20 such strategic targets which would be denied to Allied air power he would mention a few. These included the oil targets at Politz, the main production center of high octane gasoline and main source of fuel supply for the German Air Force; Ruhrland, second only in importance to Politz, and one of the four major synthetic oil plants in Germany. In addition there were several other oil targets. Further the proposed line would appear to prohibit attacks on some industrial and communication targets in the neighborhood of Berlin and Dresden. The line would also prohibit attack on three tank and self-propelled gun factories; and, lastly, and of great importance, it would prevent attacks on three jet-propelled fighter engine factories where components of the Juno jet engines were made and the engines themselves were assembled. He would point out that the oil targets referred to required repeated attacks in view of the German's ability to repair them rapidly.

There was one further point he would like to make. Apart from the strategic implication of the line, it was unacceptable in view of topographical considerations. A bombline must be clearly visible to a pilot in the air, both from high and low altitudes.

GENERAL MARSHALL said he would like to add an additional illustration of the point made by General Kuter. He had that morning received a message from the Commanding General of the United States heavy bombers operating from the United Kingdom, reporting an attack on Berlin carried out three or four days previously by a thousand heavy bombers supported by some 600 fighters. These fighters were practically over the Russian lines and, in fact, destroyed a number of German aircraft taking off from an airfield east of Berlin. The Commanding General pointed out that, with good liaison parties and proper radio communication, not only could valuable information be given to the Russians before such an attack but also that the most recent information with regard to enemy and Russian movements could be communicated to him.

With the speed of modern fighters the aircraft taking part in this raid were involved in operations only five minutes flying time from the Russian ground forces. Yet it must be remembered that these aircraft were bombing a definite point which the Russian staff had requested should be attacked. Unless better methods of handling liaison were evolved, it would mean that the most powerful weapon of the war would be denied its proper use in assisting the Russians. He asked that an immediate and really practical solution should be found to this problem.

SIR CHARLES PORTAL then explained the point of view of the British Chiefs of Staff. Owing to the fact that United States bombers operated by day while the Royal Air Force bombers operated mainly by night, this problem

TOP SECRET

affected the United States forces more than it did the British. Nevertheless, the problem for both air forces was almost identical. Already complete integration of control of the United States and British bomber effort from the West and from the South had been achieved.

Speaking for the British Air Staff, he fully supported the proposals which had been put forth by General Kuter which would entirely cover British requirements.

GENERAL ANTONOV explained that in putting forward at the previous meeting his proposal with regard to the bombline, he had in mind the wishes expressed by the United States and British Chiefs of Staff which had been put forward by General Deane and Admiral Archer. These wishes expressed a desire that the bombline should be as near as possible to the Soviet front. The line that he now suggested was only some 60 to 75 kilometers in front of the Soviet lines. There was no possibility of moving the bombline further to the eastward as this would hinder the action, not only of the Soviet ground forces but also the Soviet air forces. He appreciated that there were a number of important targets to the east of the proposed line which should be bombed. In connection with the bombing of such individual targets, each one could be considered separately. He would ask also that consideration should be given to the fact that the Soviets had a large number of aircraft themselves. He had mentioned on the previous day the 8,000 aircraft now being employed on the central front. If all the targets to the east of the line were made available to the Allied air forces, then there would be nothing left for the Soviet forces to attack. The line now proposed was only a very general line drawn in the light of considerations put forward by General Deane and Admiral Archer and would have to be worked out in detail and, in particular, altered to enable Allied flyers easily to identify it. With regard to changes in the line necessitated by changes in the position of Soviet forces, full information with regard to this would be provided daily through the missions in Moscow. Through the same channel, the efforts of the Soviet air forces could also be coordinated.

SIR CHARLES PORTAL said that as he understood it, General Antonov's view was that if the line which he had proposed was to be moved further to the east, there would be nothing left for the Soviet Air Force to attack. He felt there had been some misunderstanding on this point since the United States and British air staffs were entirely agreeable that any strategic target should be attacked by all three air forces. This was one of the reasons why he was opposed to the drawing of any line which would divide Germany into two parts from the point of view of strategic bombing.

TOP SECRET

GENERAL KUTER said he would like to comment on two points. He was glad to learn that the Soviet wishes were similar to his own, as indicated by General Antonov's reference to constant liaison to enable coordination to be achieved. Secondly, he would like to refer to the results achieved during the advance across the western desert. In this operation, as the result of excellent air-ground liaison, it was possible to place the bombline not at some specific distance ahead of the front line but at a point which it was expected that our own ground forces might be able to reach in eight hours.

GENERAL MARSHALL asked confirmation that General Antonov's view was that the bombline he proposed should be altered so that it could be better defined topographically and that at the same time arrangements could be made for Allied forces to bomb critical points on the Soviet side of this line.

GENERAL ANTONOV said the line which he had indicated was a rough guide only. He felt that the Heads of the Air Staffs could work out the details of this line so as to insure its recognition from the air. This redefinition of the line could, he believed, be undertaken at the present conference. He also supported the statement made by Sir Charles Portal that there could be no line established which would entirely divide the targets of the three strategic air forces. It was for this reason that he considered that the action of the Soviet strategic air force should be coordinated with the Allied air effort through the missions in Moscow. If it was desirable for the Allied air forces to bomb targets to the east of the line, such action could be discussed in Moscow and the necessary decision taken.

SIR ALAN BROOKE said he regarded the bombline as a line of demarcation between the action of air forces and land forces and not as a line of demarcation between the action of strategic air forces. In Allied operations on the Western Front there was no line of demarcation between the action of the United States and British strategical air forces but there were bomblines on the various fronts closely connected with the action of the land forces and designed to insure close cooperation between land and air forces. He asked if it were to be assumed from General Antonov's statement that the proposed bombline now being discussed was to be considered as the bombline which would ensure coordination of action between land and air forces but not designed to restrict the action of the strategic air forces, which action would be regulated through the missions in Moscow on a day-to-day basis.

SIR CHARLES PORTAL said he would like to put the question in a different way. Was it the intention of the Soviet Staff that the improved liaison which it had been suggested should take place through the missions in

TOP SECRET

Moscow, would be in lieu of the line proposed and should be such as to safeguard the Soviet ground forces from the action of strategic bombers?

GENERAL ANTONOV said that the line he had proposed was designed to secure Soviet land forces from the possibility of accidental bombardment by the Allied air forces. Such a line could not be permanent and would be changed frequently to conform to changes in the land front. The actions of the strategic air forces, both Soviet and Allied, would not be bound by this line, however. It was drawn so close to the Soviet front that he presumed that the Allied strategic air forces would not find many targets to the east of this line though such targets might exist and in this case action against any of them could be decided upon individually. As to the Soviet strategic air force it would appear that in most cases their attacks would take place to the west of the line.

ADMIRAL LEAHY suggested that, since there appeared to be a large measure of agreement, time would be saved if the three air staffs met together and worked out the details of the proposed bombline.

SIR CHARLES PORTAL said he would like to suggest an amendment to Admiral Leahy's proposal. He felt that instead of the air staffs trying to work out the details of the line they should work out the requirements for safeguarding the interests and security of the Soviet forces, having regard to the need for the destruction of as many important German installations as was possible. There seemed to be little difference between the various views expressed and what differences there were could, he felt sure, be settled quite easily.

ADMIRAL LEAHY said that he accepted Sir Charles Portal's amendment to his suggestion.

GENERAL ANTONOV said that he agreed with Admiral Leahy's view that the matter should be referred to the air staffs to work out a detailed line in accordance with the principles which had been discussed.

It was agreed that Marshal Khudyakov, General Kuter and Sir Charles Portal should meet together immediately to consider this matter.

SIR ALAN BROOKE said that there was one further related question which remained unsettled. This was the question of liaison on a lower level. General Antonov had undertaken, at the previous meeting, to seek the views of Marshal Stalin on this point.

TOP SECRET

GENERAL ANTONOV said he had reported on this matter to Marshal Stalin. Marshal Stalin had pointed out that there had so far been no close contact between Soviet and Allied land forces and therefore wished that liaison should take place through the Staff of the Red Army and the Military Missions in Moscow.

2. COORDINATION OF OFFENSIVE OPERATIONS

SIR ALAN BROOKE said that the forthcoming offensives had been fully discussed at the previous meeting and coordination had been broadly settled. There remained, however, the question of the offensives during March and April. General Antonov had mentioned also a summer offensive. Could he give any further information as to the probable date of the commencement of this summer offensive and whether it would be in great strength? Further did he foresee any long periods between the end of the present offensive and the commencement of the summer offensive?

GENERAL ANTONOV said that Soviet offensive action had started and would continue. The Soviet forces would press forward until hampered by weather. With regard to the summer offensive, it would be difficult to give exact data with regard to the interval between the end of the winter and beginning of the summer attack. The most difficult season from the point of view of weather was the second part of March and the month of April. This was the period when roads became impassable.

GENERAL MARSHALL asked, with regard to General Antonov's comment on the bad weather period between the winter and summer offensives, whether it was anticipated that it would be possible to carry out any important action until the summer offensive could be started.

GENERAL ANTONOV said that, if during this period operations in the West were carried out actively, the Soviets would take every possible action on the Eastern Front wherever this could be done.

GENERAL MARSHALL emphasized that the interval between the winter and summer offensives would probably be the period at which the Allies would be trying to cross the Rhine. He was therefore most anxious that the enemy should not be able to concentrate forces against the Allies on the Western Front at that particular time.

TOP SECRET

GENERAL ANTONOV said that he could assure General Marshall that the Soviets would do everything possible to prevent the transference of German forces from east to west during this period.

3. EXCHANGE OF INFORMATION WITH REGARD TO RIVER-CROSSING TECHNIQUE AND EQUIPMENT

ADMIRAL LEAHY said that at the first meeting between the Heads of State, the British Prime Minister had raised the question of exchanging information with regard to technique and equipment employed by the Soviet forces in river crossings. At the present time in view of the Allied proximity to the River Rhine this was a most immediate problem for the Allied forces. There were now two officers present from General Eisenhower's headquarters and it appeared highly desirable that they should meet with the appropriate Soviet experts on the subject of the technique and equipment employed by the Red Army in major river crossings which they had undertaken. Thus the Allies on the Western Front could obtain the benefit of the experience of the Red Army in this matter. He would therefore very much appreciate if General Antonov would indicate whether this could be done and if so would make such arrangements as were practicable for the officers from General Eisenhower's headquarters to meet with the appropriate Soviet officers.

GENERAL ANTONOV said that the Soviet Army was always ready to share its battle experience with its allies. However, at the moment there were no specialists in this technique available and he would like therefore time to look into this matter. He would furnish the required information later.

ADMIRAL LEAHY thanked General Antonov for this very satisfactory reply.

4. BASES FOR U.S. STRATEGIC BOMBER FORCES IN THE VIENNA-BUDAPEST AREA

GENERAL MARSHALL said that as the Soviet advance proceeded it would be found logistically possible to move U.S. strategic bomber forces now in Italy, with their protecting fighters, to bases in the Vienna-Budapest area. It was very desirable for such aircraft to operate from that vicinity. It was therefore the hope of the United States Chiefs of Staff that this could be arranged by having a staging area or zone of passage in that area so that it could be arranged for some 670 individual heavy bomber sorties to be undertaken each month. This would require the support of about 1,800 fighter missions in the same period. To effect this it would be necessary to carry out certain construction work for which some 2,000 United States personnel could be provided from Italy and 200 from elsewhere. The greatest difficulty would be the transfer of the necessary supplies and equipment. 22,000 tons would be required initially and a further 8,300 tons a month thereafter. The President of the United States was likely to present this project to Marshal Stalin with a request for his approval. It would involve the use of two airfields in the Budapest area and also agreements that the Soviet authorities should undertake the movement of the necessary stores to the Budapest area by road, rail or barge.

GENERAL ANTONOV said that the matter would probably be decided between Marshal Stalin and the President. He personally felt that it could conveniently be undertaken and suggested that the Heads of the Air Forces should consider the problem.

GENERAL MARSHALL said he would be very happy for this to be arranged.

5. PROVISION OF SOVIET AIRFIELDS FOR DAMAGED BRITISH NIGHT BOMBERS

SIR CHARLES PORTAL said he had one request to make. It would be extremely helpful if the Soviet General Staff could allocate air bases with night landing equipment at various points distributed along their front at which British night bombers, damaged in night combat over Germany, could land instead of having to fight their way back over the heavy defenses of Germany. If these aircraft were so badly damaged that they could not get back, and no such airfields were available, the crews had no alternative but to bail out and lose their aircraft. If the Soviet authorities could agree to this request he suggested that details could be arranged through the missions in Moscow.

MARSHAL KHUDYAKOV said that he regarded this as a technical question. Up to the present the Soviet forces had never denied assistance to Allied fliers, who had always been met and taken care of. He suggested the details of Sir Charles Portal's proposal should be worked out after the conference.

6. ENEMY INTELLIGENCE

GENERAL ANTONOV said that at the previous Conference he had referred to the fact that the Germans would endeavor to stop the Russian offensive on the line of the Oder. Quite possibly they would not only adopt a passive defense on this line but would try to gather together counterattack forces for a break-through. He would be glad to know if the Allied commander in the West had any intelligence with regard to the collection of such forces, their movements or the likely point for such an attack. He was particularly interested in the transference of the Sixth S.S. Panzer Army.

GENERAL BULL said that when he left General Eisenhower's headquarters a short time ago evidence existed that the Sixth Panzer Army was leaving the Western Front and possibly an additional two divisions from north of the Vosges. General Eisenhower had taken immediate action to put the maximum possible air effort on these German movements. He was not up to date with regard to the direction of these moves but he was certain that such information as was available at the Supreme Commander's headquarters could be sent to the Soviet General Staff. He would be glad to take this matter up with General Eisenhower immediately on his return.

GENERAL MARSHALL said that he had received a message on the previous day which gave definite information of the moves of certain divisions of the Sixth Panzer Army from the Western Front. This message had also given the new total of enemy divisions on the Western Front as 69. This morning's operational report raised this total to 70 since a newly formed parachute division had appeared on the Western Front on the right of Field Marshal Montgomery's forces, in a position somewhere east of Venlo. He would get an exact statement on this matter and give it to General Antonov.

SIR ALAN BROOKE said that his information was very similar to that given by General Marshall. It was known that the Fifth Panzer Army had also been pulled out of the line but there were no indications yet of its moving to the eastward. The British experts believed that this move was unlikely to take place. If General Antonov wished, a telegram could be sent asking for the latest information.

GENERAL ANTONOV said he was very grateful for the information given him and was particularly interested in the transfer of the Sixth Panzer Army to the eastward.

SIR ALAN BROOKE said, with regard to the Italian Front, that as far as was known only one division was being withdrawn although there were indications of considerable movement.

GENERAL MARSHALL said it might be helpful, if the Soviet Staff was not already aware of them, to give details of the attack in the Ardennes. This

TOP SECRET

attack had been made by the Fifth and Sixth Panzer Armies. Prior to the attack the Sixth Panzer Army had been out of the line for several months and had been located northeast of the Ruhr with five divisions. The Fifth Panzer Army had been in the front line or close to it. The Sixth Panzer Army had crossed to the west of the Rhine a month or six weeks before the offensive had taken place but had not been located until the attack was launched. The Sixth Panzer Army had been the first to be withdrawn from the attack and the Fifth Panzer Army was finally also withdrawn though it was not known if it had left the front.

MARSHAL KHUDYAKOV asked if the losses in the Fifth Panzer Army were known.

GENERAL MARSHALL said it was difficult to differentiate between losses incurred by the Fifth and Sixth Panzer Armies. At the meeting on the previous day he had given information with regard to the destruction inflicted on one or the other of these armies in the course of two days' operations. It was believed that very heavy casualties had been inflicted on the motor vehicles and tanks of almost all the divisions of both the Fifth and Sixth Panzer Armies.

GENERAL BULL said the Fifth Panzer Army had attacked in the center and, of the two, made the most progress. The Sixth Panzer Army had attacked in the north in the direction Malmedy-Liege. Both the Fifth and the Sixth Armies had suffered considerable losses in armor and two divisions of the Fifth Army in particular were known to have suffered heavily.

7. PACIFIC OPERATIONS

ADMIRAL KING said that the general principles for the conduct of the war against Germany and Japan were: firstly, the defeat of both Germany and Japan at the earliest possible date; secondly, that Germany was the principal enemy; thirdly, that continuous and unremitting pressure would be maintained against the Japanese forces. Efforts would be made to attain positions from which the final attack on Japan could be staged when the necessary forces became available from Europe. There had been no fixed schedule but endeavor had been made to go as fast and as far as the available means permitted. At the present time our operations were hampered chiefly by lack of shipping and the shortage of service and auxiliary troops. It was worthy of note that all operations in the Pacific had, of necessity, been amphibious operations and some were carried out over great distances.

TOP SECRET

In general, the forward line now held included Attu, the Marianas, and Luzon. In addition, we had control of the sea and air not only up to this line, but beyond it to China, Formosa, the Ryukyus, and even to the coast of Japan itself. The present fighting was taking place on the island of Luzon, about 1,500 sea miles from Japan itself. The Japanese appeared to prefer to keep the fighting at that distance from their homeland. What was important was that it was still possible to inflict casualties on the Japanese navy, air forces, and shipping. The British Pacific Fleet was now available, and had been reported to him as being available for operations about the 15th of March.

Regarding future operations, it was proposed to continue the liberation of the Philippines and to establish air bases in Luzon from which to interdict enemy air and shipping in the north part of the China Sea, including the China coast and the area of Formosa. On the 19th of February the United States forces would seize the Bonin Islands, which would be used chiefly as a base for fighters accompanying the heavy bombers on raids on Japan. About the first of April it was proposed to go into Okinawa in the Ryukyus for the purpose of establishing air bases and an advance naval base, and to intensify the sea and air blockade of Japan.

Though no decision had been taken, planning was proceeding on an operation to go into the Chusan Archipelago to broaden the base for intensifying the air and sea blockade of Japan. This would also assist interdiction of communications in the Shanghai-Hankow area, including the great water highway of the Yangtze.

In the North Pacific, air operations were being conducted from the Aleutians and occasional ship bombardments of the Kuriles, chiefly against the islands of Paramushiru and Shushima in the extreme north of the chain. The weather for air operations in this area was particularly bad, and consequently there had been a number of forced landings by United States aircraft in Kamchatka. He would like to express his deep appreciation for the care and assistance which had been rendered to these airmen by the Soviet authorities.

For a period of about a year examination and study had been continuing of the possibility of securing a safe sea passage through the Kuriles by seizing an island, preferably in the central part of the chain, whose topography was such as to permit the establishment of airfields. Lack of means made it unlikely that such operations would take place during 1945 unless they became so vitally important that ways and means would have to be

TOP SECRET

found to do them, even though the over-all means available for the war against Japan were limited.

ADMIRAL KUZNETSOV asked if the capture of an island in the Kuriles was planned for 1945.

ADMIRAL KING said that means were not available to undertake it as well as the other operations which had been planned; however, as always, it was a question of the relative importance of the various operations under consideration.

GENERAL MARSHALL said he would like to add that from the point of view of the Army, plans were kept up to date in great detail, particularly with regard to shipping, in order to effect the most rapid possible movement of forces from Europe to the Pacific. These plans were so arranged that the movement would start one week after the termination of the war in Europe. The total transfer would, however, take a long time. Air would move first, accompanied by the service units needed to support the air forces and to prepare bases for the other troops. The necessity for these plans was one of the reasons why an estimated date for the end of the war against Germany had been required.

GENERAL ANTONOV said that, as he had mentioned on the previous day, it would be more convenient to discuss questions concerning the Far East after this matter had been considered by the Heads of State.

8. VLR BOMBER OPERATIONS AGAINST JAPAN

GENERAL KUTER said that the B-29's, the heavy long-range United States bombers, were organized into the Twentieth Air Force commanded by General Arnold. The operations of the Twentieth Air Force had been following a plan somewhat similar to that used by the strategic air forces in Europe. The Japanese aircraft industry had been selected as the first priority target. At the present time this air force had approximately 350 operational B-29's. About a third of that number had been operating from China bases since May 1944 and the remainder had begun operating from the Marianas in July 1944. It was expected to build up a force of approximately 1,800 operational B-29's. The latest operation carried out was on the previous Sunday, when 120 B-29's had attacked Kobe. Broadly speaking, the relatively small force of B-29's which had so far been employed had exceeded the anticipated results for the number of attacks that had been carried out.

TOP SECRET

9. OPERATIONS IN BURMA AND CHINA

SIR ALAN BROOKE said that during 1944 the Japanese had delivered a serious attack in north Burma. This attack was stopped and the Japanese were driven back by the British forces in north Burma, assisted by Chinese forces under United States direction which had been trained by United States officers in India. Land communications to China had now been opened through north Burma. The road was not good but motor vehicles and guns could now be delivered by that road to China. Operations in Burma were continuing southward with the object of ultimately clearing the Japanese out of Burma, which would then provide a suitable base for further operations against the Japanese in those parts. In addition, as Admiral King had mentioned, British naval forces had been dispatched to take part in operations in the Pacific. Carrier attacks had also been carried out against the oil targets in Palembang on the island of Sumatra.

SIR CHARLES PORTAL said that it was of interest to add that the British advanced forces operating in the Mandalay area and to the west of it, were almost entirely dependent on air supply provided by United States and British transport aircraft.

GENERAL MARSHALL said that the United States maintained a considerable air force in China, consisting, at the present time, of some 600 planes with more to come. The sole source of supply for these forces was over the 17,000-foot mountains between northeast Burma and Kunming. These operations presented an extremely difficult proposition from every point of view. As Sir Alan Brooke had said, the Japanese had in the previous spring attacked towards the line of communication to China. This was the line of communication not only for the British forces in Burma but also for the Chinese forces in Burma, and the United States air transport force flying supplies into China. In spite of all the difficulties, 44,000 tons of supplies had been flown over the Himalayas last month. A transport plane left airfields in Burma every two minutes of the day and night. It was necessary to provide not only gasoline for the air forces operating out of China but to provide also for the ground forces in China who had little food or equipment. United States transport aircraft had moved Chinese forces to India from where, after training, they had again been transferred by air to the seat of operations where they had joined up with their equipment. More recently the Chinese forces had been flown back over the mountains, thus providing the only really dependable well-equipped fighting force in China. They were, however, without armored fighting vehicles or medium artillery. Now that the road was open, armored fighting vehicles, trucks and artillery could be sent to them. There had been

TOP SECRET

almost a complete lack of motor transport in China and what there had been was now worn out. It was under these circumstances that the United States Chiefs of Staff had asked assistance from the Soviets in order to get 500 trucks to the Chinese. He very much appreciated the efforts the Soviets had made and fully understood their difficulties. Fortunately, these vehicles could now be sent to China direct by road.

A United States general (General Wedemeyer) was now acting as chief of staff to the Generalissimo in an effort to coordinate the various activities of the Chinese forces. This was of particular importance in relation to United States action in the Pacific. Operations in China were of increasing importance now that naval forces were so close to the coast of China. General Wedemeyer was endeavoring to restore a very serious situation and, with armored cars and trucks now available, his task should prove easier. As he (General Marshall) had previously mentioned, in the face of unparalleled difficulties 44,000 tons had been flown over the Himalayas last month. He mentioned this because to him it meant the accomplishment of the greatest feat in all history. In the face of such achievements cooperation by the staffs now seated around the table should be relatively easy.

GENERAL ANTONOV asked if the operations in Burma were regarded as decisive operations or secondary operations.

SIR ALAN BROOKE said that they were decisive operations aimed at the clearing of Burma of all Japanese forces.

GENERAL ANTONOV asked if it was considered that there were enough troops for decisive action on the two fronts — the Far East and Europe. Would not concentration on the main front hasten the end of the war in Europe and thus hasten the end of the war against Japan by making additional forces available?

SIR ALAN BROOKE explained that mainly local forces were being used in Burma, the majority of them being from the Indian Army. Indian divisions had been taken from India and had been engaging Germans since the beginning of the war. However, it had been essential to protect India's eastern frontier and at the same time to open up a land route to China. Far greater forces were required in this theater to carry out all the desired operations. As General Marshall had mentioned, plans were ready to transfer forces as fast as possible upon the completion of the war with Germany in order

TOP SECRET

to finish the war against Japan. Up to the present time Germany was regarded as the main enemy and Japan as the secondary enemy, to be taken on with full forces immediately Germany was defeated.

GENERAL MARSHALL explained that the policy of the United States Government played a great part in the decisions with regard to operations in Burma. The United States Government placed great importance on the maintenance of the present regime in China. From the military point of view it would be a very serious matter if all China passed into Japanese control. Only relatively small American forces had been used except for transport aircraft.

It was imperative, however, that operations should not stand still in the Pacific. This would enable the Japanese to build up a solid line in the occupied areas. In the first year of the war only small land and air forces had been available to assist the strong naval force in the Pacific. These forces had, however, pushed forward by by-passing Japanese positions. At present some 200,000 to 300,000 Japanese troops had been cut off in these by-passed positions and a comparable number could now be considered as cut off in Malaya, the Netherlands East Indies, and even Burma.

ADMIRAL KUZNETSOV asked for information with regard to the area of the United States submarine operations in the Pacific.

ADMIRAL KING said that the United States submarine force had always operated where the most Japanese shipping was to be found. The main submarine force used Hawaii as its main base and worked generally north of the latitude of 20° N. A further submarine force was based on Australia and was now supplemented by a considerable number of British submarines. This force worked in the area of the East Indies. Allied submarines in the Pacific had taken a heavy toll of Japanese shipping, which was now reduced from a maximum of some seven million tons to two million tons. These Japanese losses had been inflicted by submarines, by air forces and by naval surface vessels. United States submarine losses had remained relatively constant at about two per month. The number of United States submarines operating was still increasing. It was clear that the closer operations come to Japan the tougher would be the opposition not only for submarines but also for air and naval forces and for ground troops.

ADMIRAL KUZNETSOV asked if it was intended that United States submarines should operate in the Sea of Japan.

TOP SECRET

ADMIRAL KING said that so far they had not operated in the Sea of Japan though they operated in the Yellow Sea.

ADMIRAL KUZNETSOV suggested that the Japanese were likely to shift their sea lines of communication to the Sea of Japan.

ADMIRAL KING explained that such a line of communications already existed as did a Japanese sea line of communications to Manchuria and to the North China coast.

10. *FUTURE BUSINESS*

After a brief discussion it was agreed that all the necessary subjects had already been covered and that no further meetings were called for until such time as the Heads of State might submit additional problems to the military staffs.

In reply to a question from Sir Alan Brooke, *GENERAL ANTONOV* said that he felt that for the present no written report to the Heads of State was necessary, but rather that each staff should report individually to its own Head of State. Should a written report be required, this could easily be prepared later.

In conclusion, *SIR ALAN BROOKE* said he would like to thank General Antonov for his hospitality in receiving the United States and British Chiefs of Staff in Yalta and for his cooperative attitude during the meetings.

MINUTES OF
PLENARY MEETINGS

TOP SECRET

ARGONAUT CONFERENCE

MINUTES OF 1ST PLENARY MEETING BETWEEN THE U.S.A. AND GREAT BRITAIN, HELD IN THE PRESIDENT'S CABIN ON BOARD THE "USS QUINCY," MALTA, ON FRIDAY, 2 FEBRUARY 1945, AT 1800.

PRESENT

United States	*British*
The President	The Prime Minister
Fleet Admiral W. D. Leahy	Field Marshal Sir Alan F. Brooke
General of the Army G. C. Marshall	Marshal of the Royal Air Force Sir Charles F. A. Portal
Fleet Admiral E. J. King	Admiral of the Fleet Sir Andrew B. Cunningham
Major General L. S. Kuter (Representing General of the Army H. H. Arnold)	Field Marshal Sir H. M. Wilson General Sir Hastings L. Ismay

SECRETARIAT

Major General E. I. C. Jacob
Brigadier General A. J. McFarland

TOP SECRET

THE MEETING had under consideration an interim report to the President and the Prime Minister by the Combined Chiefs of Staff (C.C.S. 776/1).

THE PRESIDENT expressed his appreciation of the amount of progress which had been made in so short a time in the military discussions.

The report was then considered paragraph by paragraph.

a. *Paragraph 6 h.*

THE PRESIDENT and *THE PRIME MINISTER* were informed that discussion was proceeding upon the wording of the basic undertaking to be included in this paragraph.

GENERAL MARSHALL said that the wording proposed by the British Chiefs of Staff raised a new question which involved placing supplies for liberated areas, over and above those required for the prevention of disease and unrest, in the same category as operational requirements. This would entail a change in the general priority at the expense of essential military requirements, which the United States Chiefs of Staff were disinclined to accept.

THE PRIME MINISTER inquired whether the British import program would be affected. He pointed out that Great Britain had had less than half her pre-war imports for over five years, and he was afraid lest the requirements of liberated areas, and even certain of the military requirements, would necessitate a reduction in the tonnage which it was hoped to import into Great Britain in 1945.

SIR ALAN BROOKE explained that the wording of the proposed basic undertaking was still under discussion, and the matter was not submitted for consideration at the present meeting.

THE PRIME MINISTER, referring to paragraph 6 *f.*, thought that great efforts should now be made to pass supplies to Russia via the Dardanelles.

ADMIRAL KING said that this was all in hand and the first convoy was expected to go through on 15 February. The delay had been caused by the fact that the port of Odessa had not previously been ready to receive the supplies.

b. *The U-Boat War (paragraphs 7 and 8)*

THE PRIME MINISTER expressed his agreement with this paragraph. He thought the time had not yet come to take drastic measures at the expense of other operations, though it might be necessary to do so if the U-boat campaign developed in the way expected.

c. *Operations in Northwest Europe (paragraphs 9 and 10)*

THE PRESIDENT and *THE PRIME MINISTER* were informed that complete agreement had been reached on this question.

THE PRIME MINISTER referred to the importance of having plenty of divisions available for the support of the main operation in the North, so that tired divisions could be replaced.

SIR ALAN BROOKE said that this had been allowed for. Ten divisions would be in reserve and available to replace tired divisions in the battle. Other divisions could also be taken from the less active parts of the front.

THE PRIME MINISTER inquired what action had been taken on SCAF 180.

SIR ALAN BROOKE explained that the Combined Chiefs of Staff had taken note of this telegram. General Bedell Smith had given further explanations of General Eisenhower's proposed operations, and two further telegrams had been received from the latter. SCAF 180 should be read in the light of these additional explanations and telegrams.

THE PRIME MINISTER questioned the meaning of the words "to close the Rhine" which occurred in paragraph 10 of the report.

It was explained that these words were a quotation from General Eisenhower's signal, and were understood to mean making contact with, or closing up to, the Rhine.

TOP SECRET

d. Strategy in the Mediterranean (paragraphs 11, 12, and 13)

THE PRESIDENT inquired whether the Combined Chiefs of Staff were satisfied that if the forces proposed were withdrawn from the Italian Front, enough troops would be left behind for the task in hand.

SIR ALAN BROOKE said that Field Marshal Alexander had been consulted and had agreed to the withdrawal of three divisions forthwith, and two further divisions as soon as they could be released from Greece.

THE PRIME MINISTER said that there should be no obligation to take forces away from Greece until the situation there admitted of their withdrawal. It was necessary to build up a Greek National Army under a broad-based government.

SIR ALAN BROOKE drew attention to paragraph 4 of the proposed directive to the Supreme Allied Commander, Mediterranean (Appendix "A" to the report), in which it was stated that further complete formations after the first three divisions would be sent as they could be released from Greece.

THE PRIME MINISTER said that he expected that by the time the first three divisions had moved it would be possible to start withdrawing troops from Greece. He was in full agreement with the course proposed, and was particularly glad that General Marshall had taken the view that Canadian and British troops should be withdrawn. There were special reasons for desiring the transfer to France of the Canadian Corps. He was also anxious that the British contribution to the heavy fighting which would be taking place in Northwest Europe should be as great as possible.

In reply to an inquiry by the President, SIR HENRY MAITLAND WILSON said that he was in complete agreement with the course proposed.

With regard to the proposed withdrawal of air forces, SIR CHARLES PORTAL explained, in reply to an inquiry by the President, that the move of five groups was in question. Two were to go now, and proposals for further moves were to be made by the Supreme Commanders in consultation.

THE PRIME MINISTER agreed that it would be unwise to make any significant withdrawal of amphibious assault forces from Italy, as to do so would be to relieve the Germans of an ever-present anxiety.

Referring to paragraph 7 of the proposed directive to the Supreme Allied Commander, Mediterranean, THE PRIME MINISTER said that he attached great importance to a rapid follow-up of any withdrawal or of any surrender of the German forces in Italy. He felt it was essential that we should occupy as much of Austria as possible as it was undesirable that more of Western Europe than necessary should be occupied by the Russians.

Referring to paragraph 8 of the proposed directive, dealing with support to the Yugoslav Army of National Liberation, THE PRIME MINISTER said that he presumed that the phrase "the territory of Yugoslavia" should be interpreted to mean the existing or lawful territory of Yugoslavia. There were certain territories which were claimed by both Yugoslavia and Italy and he was unwilling to give any suggestion of support to the claims of either side. For example, Trieste ought to be a valuable outlet to Southern Europe and the question of sovereignty in that area should be entirely reserved.

THE PRESIDENT agreed and said that he was unwilling to see either the Yugoslavs or the Italians in complete control.

SIR ALAN BROOKE pointed out that the phrase as used in the report applied to the present territory of Yugoslavia.

THE WAR AGAINST JAPAN

e. Operations in Southeast Asia Command (paragraphs 18 and 19)

THE PRIME MINISTER said that the main object of the operations to clear the enemy from Burma was to liberate the important army engaged there for further operations against Japan. He inquired whether the Staffs had come to any conclusion on what these further operations should be.

SIR ALAN BROOKE referred to Appendix "C" of the report, which contained the proposed directive to the Supreme Allied Commander, Southeast Asia Command. The directive gave as the next task the liberation of Malaya and the opening of the Straits of Malacca.

THE PRIME MINISTER hoped there would be time to review this matter in accordance with developments. For example, if the Japanese forces in Java or Sumatra were greatly weakened, small detachments might be able to go in and liberate these countries. His object, however, was to go where a good opportunity would be presented of heavy fighting with the

TOP SECRET

Japanese, particularly in the air, as this was the only way which the British had been able to discover of helping the main American operations in the Pacific.

SIR ALAN BROOKE pointed out that the Supreme Allied Commander was directed to submit his plans, and it would then be possible to review the matter.

THE PRIME MINISTER inquired whether paragraph 18 meant that there would be no help from United States air forces in operations in the Kra Peninsula, Malaya, et cetera.

SIR CHARLES PORTAL pointed out that any such help would be the subject of a separate agreement when the plan had been received.

THE PRIME MINISTER inquired whether the President had not been somewhat disappointed at the results achieved by the Chinese, having regard to the tremendous American efforts which had been made to give them support.

THE PRESIDENT said that three generations of education and training would be required before China could become a serious factor.

GENERAL MARSHALL pointed out that the picture in China was now considerably changed. In the first place certain well-trained Chinese troops were now in China, having been transferred there from Burma. Secondly, the opening of the Burma Road had meant that the first artillery for the Chinese Army had been able to go through. Thirdly, if operations in Burma continued to go well, additional trained Chinese troops could move back to China, and it was hoped that an effective reinforced Chinese corps would soon be in existence.

THE PRIME MINISTER said that it now appeared that the American and British operations in this part of the world were diverging. The American effort was going on into China and the British effort was turning to the south. He inquired whether any consideration had been given to the move of British or Indian divisions from Burma into China to take part in the operations there.

SIR ALAN BROOKE said that the facilities for sending equipment and supplies into China allowed of the support of Chinese forces, who required a considerably lower scale than British troops. These facilities certainly could not support British troops as well.

GENERAL MARSHALL agreed that the maintenance of British forces in China was not a practical proposition. There was only one reinforced United States brigade in China, which would act as a spearhead for critical operations. There was the reinforced Chinese corps, which had a stiffening of United States personnel in their tanks, armored cars, tank destroyers, et cetera, and there was an effective air force. These forces should now be able to insure that the Japanese could no longer go wherever they pleased in China. The aid which could be given by these forces to the American arrival on the Chinese Pacific Coast would be important. A pincer movement against the Japanese could in this way be initiated — one arm of the pincer being represented by the forces assaulting the selected spot on the Chinese Pacific Coast. This arm would be strong. The other arm of the pincer would be the Chinese and American forces in China. This arm would be weak, but nevertheless of value. The progress of the American main operations in the Pacific and the campaign in the Philippines had changed the picture in Southeast Asia, and would make further operations by Admiral Mountbatten's forces much easier. He felt that it was important that Admiral Mountbatten should know what forces would be available to him in these operations, and that he should not plan on a false assumption. The American military authorities in Southeast Asia would know what United States forces could at any time not be supported logistically in China. These could be made available to Admiral Mountbatten in Burma. It might even be possible to bring air forces back from China for specific operations. Admiral Mountbatten should, however, be under no illusion as to what forces he could count on for his operations.

THE PRIME MINISTER repeated that if the Americans made any request for British troops to go into China he would certainly be prepared to consider it.

ADMIRAL LEAHY said that all the transportation available was fully required for the forces now in China, or earmarked for China.

GENERAL MARSHALL agreed, and said that he did not think it would be practicable to increase the forces in China until a port had been secured. Up to the present it had been possible to do only a very little in the way of equipping the Chinese ground army. Nearly all the transportation had had to be used for the needs of the American air forces. It would now be possible to handle the requirements of the Chinese ground forces.

Referring to paragraph 17, and Appendix "B," which contained an outline of the plans and operations proposed by the United States Chiefs

TOP SECRET

of Staff for the Pacific, *THE PRIME MINISTER* inquired whether it had been decided to delay the assault on Japan until after the close of the German war.

GENERAL MARSHALL said that this delay had been necessitated by the fact that until the German war ended, shipping, air forces, and service troops, could not be made available in sufficient quantities to enable the main operations against Japan to be carried out. If the German war had ended in December of 1944, it would have been possible to operate against Kyushu in the autumn of 1945. There were also certain seasonal limitations on operations in this area.

Summing up, *THE PRIME MINISTER* said that he was glad to see that such a great measure of agreement had been reached. He understood that the present report was merely designed to keep the President and himself abreast of the progress of the discussions, and that a final report would be rendered later.

THE PRESIDENT agreed, and again expressed his appreciation of the work which had been accomplished.

Discussion then turned upon the conduct of future discussions, and *SIR ALAN BROOKE* explained that arrangements were being made to keep all the accommodations available at Malta so that the conference could be resumed there if necessary after the discussions with the Russians.

THE PRESIDENT and *THE PRIME MINISTER* expressed their agreement with this action, and said that although final plans need not be made until later, it appeared highly probable that a short meeting at Malta on the return journey would be desirable.

THE MEETING then adjourned.

TOP SECRET

ARGONAUT CONFERENCE

Minutes of 2d Plenary Meeting Between the U.S.A. and Great Britain, Held at Livadia Palace, Yalta, on Friday, 9 February 1945, at 1200.

PRESENT

United States

The President

Fleet Admiral W. D. Leahy
General of the Army
   G. C. Marshall
Fleet Admiral E. J. King
Major General L. S. Kuter
   (Representing General of the
   Army H. H. Arnold)

British

The Prime Minister

Field Marshal Sir Alan F. Brooke
Marshal of the Royal Air Force
   Sir Charles F. A. Portal
Admiral of the Fleet
   Sir Andrew B. Cunningham
Field Marshal Sir H. M. Wilson
General Sir Hastings L. Ismay
Admiral Sir James Somerville

SECRETARIAT

Major General E. I. C. Jacob
Brigadier General A. J. McFarland

TOP SECRET

REPORT TO THE PRESIDENT AND THE PRIME MINISTER
(C.C.S. 776/2)

THE MEETING had before them the draft of the final report to the President and the Prime Minister, containing the results of the Combined Chiefs of Staff *ARGONAUT* discussions (C.C.S. 776/2).

The report was accepted and approved by the President and the Prime Minister without amendment.

In the course of the ensuing discussion, the following matters were touched on briefly:

a. There was a discussion of possible developments after the defeat of Germany and the possible action of Russia at that time.

THE PRIME MINISTER expressed the opinion that it would be of great value if Russia could be persuaded to join with the United States, the British Empire, and China in the issue of a four-power ultimatum calling upon Japan to surrender unconditionally, or else be subjected to the overwhelming weight of all the forces of the four powers. Japan might ask in these circumstances what mitigation of the full rigour of unconditional surrender would be extended to her if she accepted the ultimatum. In this event it would be for the United States to judge the matter; but there was no doubt that some mitigation would be worth while if it led to the saving of a year or a year and a half of a war in which so much blood and treasure would be poured out. Great Britain would not press for any mitigation but would be content to abide by the judgment of the United States. Whatever the decision, Great Britain would see the matter through to the end.

THE PRESIDENT thought that this was a matter which might well be mentioned to Marshal Stalin. He doubted whether the ultimatum would have much effect on the Japanese, who did not seem to realize what was going on in the world outside, and still seemed to think that they might get a satisfactory compromise. They would be unlikely to wake up to the true state of affairs until all of their islands had felt the full weight of air attack.

b. THE PRIME MINISTER expressed his thanks to the Combined Chiefs of Staff for the work which they had accomplished. He said that the Combined Chiefs of Staff was a wonderful institution which smoothed out so many difficulties, issued clear directions to the commanders in the field

TOP SECRET

and would without doubt be held up in years to come as a model of cooperation between Allies. He hoped very much that the Combined Chiefs of Staff could be kept in being for three of four years more. There would be many problems affecting the security of the two nations in this period, the solution of which would be greatly facilitated if the Combined Chiefs of Staff could continue to operate.

THE PRESIDENT agreed that there would be many matters affecting the two countries, such as the use of bases, which would have to be effectively handled.

In response to an inquiry by the Prime Minister, *GENERAL MARSHALL* expressed his personal opinion that the continuance of the Combined Chiefs of Staff would be advantageous. Its existence had certainly simplified the solution of the problems which had confronted the two nations during the war.

c. There was a short discussion upon the provision of intelligence to the Russian armies, and the President and the Prime Minister were informed of certain steps which had been agreed in discussion between General Marshall and Field Marshal Brooke.

THE MEETING then adjourned.

TOP SECRET

ARGONAUT CONFERENCE

Minutes of the Plenary Meeting Between the U.S.A., Great Britain and the U.S.S.R., Held in Livadia Palace, Yalta, on Sunday, 4 February 1945, at 1700.

PRESENT

United States

The President

Fleet Admiral W. D. Leahy
General of the Army
  G. C. Marshall
Fleet Admiral E. J. King
Major General L. S. Kuter
  (Representing General of the
  Army H. H. Arnold)
Major General J. R. Deane
Brigadier General A. J. McFarland
Mr. E. R. Stettinius
Mr. W. Averill Harriman
Mr. C. E. Bohlen

British

The Prime Minister

Mr. Anthony Eden
Field Marshal Sir Alan F. Brooke
Marshal of the Royal Air Force
  Sir Charles F. A. Portal
Admiral of the Fleet
  Sir Andrew B. Cunningham
Field Marshal Sir H. Alexander
General Sir Hastings L. Ismay

U.S.S.R.

Marshal Stalin

Mr. Molotov
Army General Antonov
Marshal of Aviation Khudyakov
Admiral of the Fleet Kuznetsov
Ambassador to the United States Gromyko
Ambassador to Great Britain Gusev
Mr. Pavlov

TOP SECRET

MARSHAL STALIN asked the President to open the meeting.

THE PRESIDENT said that he was very happy to open such a historic meeting in such a lovely spot. In view of the conveniences and comforts that had been provided the visiting delegations, he wished to thank Marshal Stalin for all that he had found time to do in this regard in the midst of the prosecution of the war. He said that the United States, British and Russian delegations would understand each other better and better as we go along. We could therefore proceed informally to discuss frankly and freely among ourselves the matters necessary to the successful prosecution of the common cause in which we all are engaged. There was much that required discussion, the whole map in Europe in fact. Today, however, the conversations by common agreement would be concerned with Germany. In this connection he felt sure that the British and American people were viewing with a satisfaction as deep as must be that of the Soviet people themselves the successful advances of the Soviet armies against the common enemy.

MARSHAL STALIN said that Colonel General Antonov, Deputy Chief of the Russian General Staff, would outline the situation existing on the Eastern Front.

GENERAL ANTONOV made the following statement:

Soviet forces from the 12th to the 15th of January went into attack on the front from the Niemen River to the Carpathians, a distance of 700 kilometers. Forces of General Cherniakhovsky advanced towards Koenigsberg; forces of Marshal Rokossovsky, along the north bank of the Vistula cutting off East Prussia from central Germany; forces of Marshal Zhukov, south of the Vistula against Poznan; forces of Marshal Konev, against Chenstokhov-Breslau; forces of General Petrov, in the area of the Carpathians against Novo Targ. The greatest blow was delivered by the army groups of Rokossovsky, Zhukov, and Konev on the Ostrolenka-Crakow front, 300 kilometers.

TOP SECRET

Because of the unfavorable weather conditions, this operation was to commence at the end of January when weather conditions were expected to improve. Since the operation was planned and prepared as an operation in full strength, it was hoped to carry it out under the most favorable conditions possible. Nevertheless, in view of the difficult circumstances on the Western Front in connection with the German attack in the Ardennes, the High Command of the Soviet Army gave an order to commence the attack not later than the middle of January, not waiting for improvement in weather.

The enemy grouping, after the Soviet forces reached the Narev and Vistula Rivers, was the most concentrated on the central sector of the front, since striking from this sector led our troops out along the shortest route to the vital centers of Germany. In order to create for ourselves more advantageous conditions for attack, the Supreme Soviet Command decided to extend it to the central group of the enemy. For this purpose this operation was conducted as a subsidiary against East Prussia, and the advance in Hungary toward Budapest was continued. Both of these attacks were for the Germans very painful, and they quickly reacted to our attack by a swift transfer of power onto the flank at the expense of the central sector of our front; thus, out of 24 tank divisions on our front, representing the principal German striking power, 11 tank divisions were drawn in to the Budapest sector, 6 tank divisions on the East Prussian (3 tank divisions were located in Courland), and thus on the central part of the front there remained only 4 tank divisions. The aim of the High Command was accomplished.

On the front from Ostrolenka to Crakow, that is, in the area of our greatest attack, the enemy had up to 80 divisions. We set up a grouping calculated on having a superiority over the enemy: in infantry, more than double; in artillery, tanks and aviation, a decided superiority.

The massing of artillery on the sectors of the break-through amounted to 220-230 guns (from 75mm. and above) on one kilometer of the front.

The advance was begun under extremely unfavorable weather conditions—low visibility and fog, which completely ruled out the possibility of air operations and limited artillery observation to several hundred meters.

Due to good preliminary reconnaissance of the enemy positions and a powerful artillery advance, the fire power of the enemy was overwhelmed and his fortifications destroyed. This situation permitted our troops during the first day of the advance to move forward 10 to 15 kilometers, that is, to completely break through the entire tactical depth of the enemy defense.

TOP SECRET

The following results were achieved:

a. During the 18 days of the advance, the Soviet troops moved forward up to 500 kilometers in the direction of the main offensive.

Thus the average speed of forward movement was 25-30 kilometers per day.

b. The Soviet troops came out onto the Oder River on the sector from Kyustrin (north of Frankfurt) and south and seized the Silesian industrial area.

c. They cut across the main roads and cut off enemy groups in East Prussia from central Germany; thus, in addition to the Courland group (26 divisions) isolated 27 divisions of the enemy group; a series of divisional groupings were surrounded and annihilated in the region of Lodz, Torne, Poznan, Shneidmul and others, an approximate total of up to 15 divisions.

d. Break-throughs in force of long duration of German defensive positions in East Prussia in the Koenigsberg and Latvian directions.

e. Destroyed 45 German divisions against which we sustained the following losses:

Prisoners — about 100,000 men
Casualties — about 300,000 men
    Total — approximately 400,000 men.

Probable enemy action:

a. The Germans will defend Berlin for which they will try to hold up the movement of the Soviet troops in the area of the Oder River, setting up the defense here at the expense of withdrawn troops and at the expense of reserves being moved over from Germany, Western Europe and Italy.

For the defense of Pomerania they will try to use their Courland grouping, moving it over by sea beyond the Vistula.

b. The Germans will probably cover the direction leading to Vienna more strongly, strengthening this sector at the expense of troops now in action in Italy.

TOP SECRET

The shifting of enemy troops:

a. On our front there have already appeared:

From the central regions of Germany	— 9 divisions
From the Western European Front	— 6 divisions
From Italy	— 1 division
Total	16 divisions

b. In the process of being shifted:

> 4 tank divisions
> 1 motorized division
>
> 5 divisions

c. It is probable that there will yet be shifted up to 30-35 divisions (at the expense of the Western European Front, Norway, Italy, and reserves located in Germany).

In this manner there can appear on our front an additional 35 to 40 divisions.

Our wishes are:

a. To speed up the advance of the Allied troops on the Western Front, for which the present situation is very favorable:

(1) To defeat the Germans on the Eastern Front.

(2) To defeat the German groupings which have advanced into the Ardennes.

(3) The weakening of the German forces in the West in connection with the shifting of their reserves to the East.

It is desirable to begin the advance during the first half of February.

b. By air action on communications hinder the enemy from carrying out the shifting of his troops to the East from the Western Front, from Norway, and from Italy.

In particular, to paralyze the junctions of Berlin and Leipzig.

c. Not permit the enemy to remove his forces from Italy.

TOP SECRET

THE PRESIDENT asked whether the Russians proposed to change the gauge of the railroad rolling stock captured from the Germans or to widen the gauge of the lines.

GENERAL ANTONOV replied that much of the equipment was unfit for use. At present the Russians are widening the gauge of those lines that are most vital to supply. These lines were being widened only as a matter of necessity as, manifestly, the available resources are not sufficient to widen all the railroads in Germany. The greater part of the German lines will remain intact.

THE PRIME MINISTER stated that the British Delegation would have a number of questions to address to the Russians. As these were of a technical and military nature, he thought it would be more advantageous if they could be brought up between the military staffs.

THE PRIME MINISTER then suggested that General Marshall explain to Marshal Stalin the impending operations on the Western Front.

THE PRESIDENT pointed out the increasing necessity for coordinating the operations of the three Allies now that the British and American armies are getting so close to the Russians. By reason of the short distance separating the Western and Eastern Fronts the Germans are now able to transfer their reserves quickly from one front to the other.

GENERAL MARSHALL then gave a resumé of the operations planned for the Western Front. He said that the German bulge in the Ardennes had now been eliminated and the Allied forces have advanced in some areas beyond the line originally held. During the past week General Eisenhower has been regrouping his forces and conducting operations designed to eliminate enemy pockets in the southern part of the line north of Switzerland. At the same time he has been maintaining pressure in the Ardennes area in order to determine whether the Germans were present in sufficient forces to resist a movement northeast towards Bonn. Because of the resistance encountered, it was decided four days ago to cease operations and to transfer divisions further north. In the southern end of the line, operations were being directed towards the elimination of the German positions in the vicinity of Mulhausen and Colmar. Colmar has now been occupied but the advance of the First French Army north of Mulhausen has been very slow.

TOP SECRET

North of Strasbourg the small German bridgeheads across the Rhine are being eliminated. As soon as the Rhine is reached it will be possible to reduce the number of divisions in the front line and release them for other employments. Some released divisions are even now moving north in preparation for the larger operations.

Field Marshal Montgomery, in command of the 21st Army Group and Ninth U.S. Army, is preparing an operation designed to strike towards the southeast in order to reach the line of the Rhine from Dusseldorf north. A complementary operation has been planned in a northeast direction towards the same objective, which it is hoped can be launched about a week later than the first operation. By means of these two operations it is hoped to drive the Germans east of the Rhine north of Dusseldorf and then to cross the river north of the Ruhr. This crossing will constitute the main effort of the British and American armies and into it will be put all of the divisions which it is logistically possible to support. In addition, airborne troops in large numbers will land east of the Rhine.

From the standpoint of weather, the passage of the Rhine is considered possible after 1 March. A crossing will be attempted as soon as the river is reached, but it is recognized that ice will make hazardous any crossing prior to 1 March. Three good crossing sites are available for the operation and a fourth may be attempted. However, the front of the assault will accommodate initially only five divisions.

Plans have been made for a secondary effort in the vicinity of Frankfurt which can be exploited if the main effort in the North should fail to go through. The troops composing the left of the American First Army are now conducting an operation designed to capture the two dams controlling the water in the Roer River. As long as these dams are in the hands of the Germans, there is a danger that the bridges established for the river crossing may be swept away by the release of the impounded water.

The opening of the port of Antwerp has relieved the limitation on operations on the Western Front imposed by a lack of supplies. It is now possible to bring in from 75,000 to 80,000 tons of dry cargo a day. The Germans have realized the importance of Antwerp in the Allied supply scheme and have made a continuous effort to interfere with the operations of that port through the use of robot bombs and rockets. This constitutes a danger as there is, of course, always a chance of a lucky hit being made against the Antwerp lock gates. Only scattered attacks have been made by air.

TOP SECRET

United States and British fighters and light bombers supporting the ground troops have destroyed a great deal of German transport. Considerable effort has been directed against trains operating in the vicinity of Cologne and on the east bank of the Rhine. Although definite final reports have not yet been received, there is every indication of severe damage having been done to panzer divisions withdrawing from the Ardennes.

The heavy bombers have been employed primarily against German oil supplies in order to reduce the German supply of fuel for airplanes and motor transport. Present data indicate that these operations have resulted in a reduction of German oil production to 20 percent of the former capacity. The heavy bombers have also been used against German rail communications and assembly yards and a continuous effort has been maintained to destroy German fighter forces. These planes have also struck heavily at tank factories. The air forces in these operations include United States heavy bombers operating from the Italian Front. When weather prevents profitable operations in the Po Valley, they are directed against communications leading into Germany.

There are now about 32 enemy divisions on the Italian Front, 27 German and 5 Italian. The number of Allied divisions is approximately equal. The Allied forces have great superiority in fighter airplanes and these, in good weather, are able to ravage the Po Valley. The destruction of rail lines and rolling stock has been heavy.

Indications point to a serious resumption of the German submarine war as the result of technical developments which are making the detection of the submarines increasingly difficult. The submarines have developed considerable skill in operating in shallow waters where the tide makes it difficult for ASDIC to locate them. In order to counter this submarine resurgence, heavy bombers are being employed to strike at submarine assembly points whenever these operations do not interfere with the bombing of the German oil supplies.

In concluding, *GENERAL MARSHALL* said he would be glad to have Field Marshal Sir Alan Brooke amplify his remarks in any way he thought desirable.

THE PRIME MINISTER stated he would be very glad for Field Marshal Brooke to do this and stated that he would like for Admiral Cunningham also to say a word about the submarine operations.

TOP SECRET

THE PRIME MINISTER pointed out that Danzig is the place where much of the assembling of the submarines is done and expressed satisfaction in the thought that the city is now not far from the Russian front lines, which are daily drawing closer.

In answer to a question from Marshal Stalin, the *PRIME MINISTER* said that other submarine assembling points were Kiel and Hamburg.

FIELD MARSHAL BROOKE said that General Marshall had fully covered the situation now existing on the Western Front and the operations which are contemplated for the future. He said that the British Chiefs of Staff were in full accord with the plan for the future operations which General Marshall had outlined.

THE PRIME MINISTER stated that both the British and Americans have amphibious branches in their services. The officer commanding the British amphibious branch is at present in *ARGONAUT* and he, the Prime Minister, would like very much to have him meet with the Russian amphibious experts and obtain from them any information which the Russians would be kind enough to provide.

In reply to a question from Marshal Stalin, *GENERAL MARSHALL* explained that the front of the main effort in the impending operations covered three crossings over a distance of 25 or 30 miles and afforded room for not more than five divisions. The front eventually would extend all along the Rhine down as far as Dusseldorf, a total of some 50 or 60 miles. He pointed out that, as was the case in Normandy, it will be necessary to assault initially on a narrow front but this front would be expanded as rapidly as possible. He said that the Ruhr was very heavily fortified and for that reason would be by-passed. However, troops attacking on this front would soon get into good tank country.

In answer to a question from Marshal Stalin, *GENERAL MARSHALL* said the reserves available for the proposed attack were believed to be ample.

MARSHAL STALIN said that he asked the question because in the Russian central campaign 9,000 tanks were used up. He would like to know how many tanks the Allies expected to employ.

GENERAL MARSHALL said that roughly one in every three divisions employed would be a tank division. He said that on March 1st General Eisenhower will have 89 divisions at his disposal to cover the front from the Mediterranean to Holland, not including Italy; nine of these were French and all the remainder were either British or American.

TOP SECRET

Through answers to his questions it was made clear to Marshal Stalin that there are nearly 10,000 Allied tanks in the European Theater. The British divisions number 18,000 men, the American divisions 14,000, and armored divisions contain 10,000. There will be available 4,000 heavy bombers, each carrying up to 3,000 pounds of bombs.

MARSHAL STALIN explained that in their attack on the central German position, the Russians employed 100 divisions, which was 20 more than the Germans had. He was interested in the preponderance that the British and Americans would have over the Germans.

THE PRIME MINISTER pointed out that the British and American forces had overwhelming preponderance in airplanes and armored troops but not great preponderance in infantry. He stressed the necessity of exploiting to the full such superiority in strength as existed.

MARSHAL STALIN said that the British and Americans had asked the Russians to express their wishes. He would like to know now what the wishes of the British and Americans were.

THE PRIME MINISTER said that his greatest wish was to express profound gratitude and admiration as he witnessed the marvelous advance of the Russian troops. He said the British and Americans recognized the hard and difficult task lying before them in their impending operations but had full confidence in their power to execute it. All they could ask from the Russians was that the Russians continue to do as they are doing now.

MARSHAL STALIN said there had been no demand from the British and Americans for the Russian winter offensive and no pressure was exerted by them to bring it about.

THE PRESIDENT had asked that information of the offensive be given to General Eisenhower in order to assist him in his planning and Air Marshal Tedder, who came to Moscow as General Eisenhower's representative, had requested that the Russian offensive continue to the end of March but this was understood to be a request from the military leaders.

MARSHAL STALIN said they had staged their winter offensive because they felt it to be their duty as Allies to do it. They greatly appreciated the attitude manifested by both the President and the Prime Minister in this matter.

TOP SECRET

THE PRIME MINISTER said the reason that neither the British nor Americans had made any attempt to bargain with Marshal Stalin was because of their faith in him and in the Russian people and the realization that they could be depended on to do the right thing. It was his opinion that regardless of the discussions which had been held with Air Marshal Tedder, matters should be fully discussed now by the three Staffs in order to determine what is the best course to pursue with respect to the coordinating of the action on the Western and Eastern Fronts. It was imperative that the two offensives should be integrated so as to get the best results.

MARSHAL STALIN agreed that the offensives had not been fully synchronized at first and that action should be taken to do this now. He thought it would be well also to consider a summer offensive as he was not at all certain that the war would be over by that time.

ADMIRAL CUNNINGHAM said that he would like to add something to General Marshall's statement on the submarine warfare. He said while the submarine threat was potentially great it was not very serious at the moment. The point is, however, that the Germans are building large numbers of new types of U-boats. As these will have high underwater speed and embody all the latest technical devices, it will be very difficult for the Allied air and surface craft to deal with them. In Bremen, Hamburg and Danzig the new submarines were being built by prefabrication methods. His greatest wish as a naval man was for the Russians to take Danzig as quickly as possible for in that city about 30 percent of the U-boats were being constructed.

In answer to a question by the President, *MARSHAL STALIN* stated that Danzig was not yet within artillery range of the Russian guns but it was hoped that it soon would be.

Discussion then turned upon the time and place of the next meeting. After discussion, it was agreed that the Staffs of the three nations would meet at 1200 on Monday, 5 February, at the headquarters of the Russian Delegation.

TOP SECRET

INDEX

A

AACHEN SECTOR

SCAEF's account of the development of operations in Northwest Europe, 110

ADMIRALTY ISLANDS

Employment of Australian troops, 221

ADRIATIC

(*See also* Mediterranean Theater)

Directive to SACMED, 143, 167

AGENDA FOR "ARGONAUT"

Agenda for *ARGONAUT* Tripartite Conference, 125, 128

Agenda for U.S.-U.K. conference at Malta, 129, *192, 204*

AIRCRAFT (*See also* Forces)

Allied use of aircraft in "carpet bombing," 260

Effect of Allied bombing on German aircraft production, 35

Employment of B-29's against Japan, *281*

Employment of war-weary bombers against industrial targets in Germany, *193*

General Anderson's remark regarding need of P-47's in Northwest Europe, 209

German employment of available aircraft, 37

Number of U.S. and British air forces on the Western and Italian Fronts, 256

Prime Minister's statement regarding American-British preponderance over Germans in aircraft, *308*

ALEXANDER, FIELD MARSHAL SIR H.

Statements in reference to:
Allied action to prevent German withdrawal from Italy, 257
Employment of the 47th Light Bomber Group in Northwest Europe, 210
Number of German and Italian enemy divisions in Italy, 255
Provision of LVT's for the Mediterranean, 231
Transfer of forces from the Mediterranean Theater to ETO, 209
Withdrawal from the Mediterranean of part of the Twelfth Tactical Air Force, 209

ALLOCATIONS

British memorandum regarding allocation of resources between India-Burma and China Theaters, 101

Employment of U.S. resources in Southeast Asia, 16, *211, 218*

Provision of LVT's for the Mediterranean, 105, *231 235*

Sir Charles Portal and Admiral King's statements regarding allocation of forces, a function of the Combined Chiefs of Staff, *201*

AMPHIBIOUS TECHNIQUE

(*See* Technique)

ANDERSON, MAJOR GENERAL F. L.

Statement regarding need for P-47's in Northwest Europe, 209

ANTONOV, COLONEL GENERAL

Statements in reference to:
Allied operations directed toward Ljubljana Gap, *258*
Bases for U.S. strategic bomber forces in the Vienna-Budapest area, *277*
Bombline arrangements and employment of Russian air forces against important German targets, *272*
Coordination in air operations, *263*
Coordination of offensive operations in Europe during the spring and summer of 1945, *254, 275*
Date for the end of the war with Germany, *265*
Enemy intelligence and movement of enemy forces among various fronts, *277*
Exchange of information on river-crossing technique and equipment, *276*

Note: Italic numerals refer to pages in minutes of meeting.
Plain type numerals refer to pages in C.C.S. Papers.

INDEX

ANTONOV, COLONEL GENERAL

(Cont'd)

    Liaison arrangements between the British-U.S. and Russian armies, *262*
    Measures to prevent movement of German forces from Norway, *259*
    Operations in Burma and China, *283*
    Operations in the Far East, *266*
    Outline of the situation existing on the Eastern Front, *300*
    Russian intentions in Europe, *303*
    Technique of employing artillery in offensive operations, *260*
    Widening the gauge of captured German railroad rolling stock, *304*

ANTWERP

    Possibility of German suicide attacks on vital targets, *194*
    Resumé of operations planned for the Western Front, *305*
    SCAEF's account of the development of operations in Northwest Europe, 109

ARDENNES REGION

    General Bull's remarks regarding projected operations in Northwest Europe, *194*
    Resumé of operations planned for the Western Front, *304*
    SCAEF's account of the development of operations in Northwest Europe, 109

"ARGONAUT" CONFERENCE

    Agenda for *ARGONAUT* Tripartite Conference, 126, 128
    Agenda for U.S.-U.K. conference at Malta, 129, *192, 204*
    Chairman for the conferences, *192*
    Admiral Leahy and Field Marshal Brooke's statements regarding accomplishments during *ARGONAUT* Conference, *250*

ARTILLERY TECHNIQUE (*See* Technique)

AUSTRALIA

    Employment of Australian troops, *221*

AUSTRIA

    Prime Minister's statement regarding U.S.-British occupation of Austria, *290*

B

B-29 AIRCRAFT

    (*See* Twentieth Air Force)

BALKANS

    (*See also* Mediterranean Theater)

    Directive to SACMED, 142, 166
    Discussion with regard to liaison for coordination of air operations, *263*

BASES

    General Marshall and General Antonov's statements regarding bases for U.S. strategic bomber forces in the Vienna-Budapest area, *276*
    Sir Charles Portal and Marshal Khudyakov's statements regarding provision of Soviet airfields for damaged night bombers, *277*

BASIC UNDERTAKINGS

    CCS approve wording for sub-paragraph *h*, Basic Undertakings in Support of Over-All Strategic Concept, *237*
    General Marshall's statement regarding effect of suggested new category of basic undertakings on availability of shipping for military operations, *232, 288*
    General Somervell's remarks regarding extent of relief requirements included under military shipping, *232*

BASTOGNE

    SCAEF's account of the development of operations in Northwest Europe, 112

BELGIUM

    Responsibility for the equipping of liberated manpower, 132, 134, 165

Note: Italic numerals refer to pages in minutes of meeting.
Plain type numerals refer to pages in C.C.S. Papers.

INDEX

BLOCKADE

Operations for the defeat of Japan, 12, 168

BOMBING OPERATIONS

Employment of fighter-bombers to attack communications, entrances to tunnels and underground production plants, 193

Employment of war-weary bombers against industrial targets in Germany, 193

Establishment of liaison with the Soviet High Command with the Anglo-American strategic bombing in Germany, 181, 237, 249

Flying bomb and rocket attacks on London, 192

General Kuter's statement regarding employment of B-29's against Japan, *281*

General Marshall's statement regarding proposed measures to combat German U-boat menace, 306

General Marshall's statement regarding the effectiveness of recent Allied air operations, *257*

General Marshall's statement with regard to liaison arrangements presently necessary in the Berlin area, *271*

General Marshall and Marshal Khudyakov's statements regarding effective employment of Russian aviation in support of ground forces, *258*

German U-boat threat, 222, 231

Japanese suicide attacks, 194

Number of U.S. and British air forces on the Western and Italian Fronts and their proposed employment, *255*

Operations for the defeat of Japan, 12, 168, *219*

Possibility of German suicide attacks on vital targets, 194

Prime Minister's statement regarding diversion of air effort against German U-boat pens, 289

Principle for coordination of air with land offensives, *256*

Resumé of operations planned for the Western Front, 304

Tripartite Military Meeting discussion regarding Allied action to prevent German wthdrawal from Italy, *257*

Tripartite Military Meeting discussion with regard to liaison for coordination of air operations, *263*

Tripartite Military Meeting discussion with regard to the technique of employing air power in offensive operations, *260*

BOMBLINE

CCS agree that Sir Charles Portal and General Kuter reply separately to Marshal Khudyakov indicating impracticability of revised bombline agreement proposed by Soviet High Command, 250

CCS decision to press the Russians for agreement to the proposals set forth in FAN 477, 200

Establishment of liaison with the Soviet High Command for Anglo-American strategic bombing in Germany, 181, 237, 249

General Antonov's statement regarding bombline arrangements and employment of Russian air forces against important German targets, *272*

General Kuter's statement regarding British-U.S. principles for establishing bombline between British-U.S. and Russian forces, *269*

General Marshall's statement with regard to liaison arrangements presently necessary in the Berlin area, *271*

Tripartite Military Meeting discussion regarding bombline and liaison arrangements between the British-U.S. and Russian armies, *269*

Tripartite Military Meeting discussion with regard to liaison for coordination of air operations, *263*

BONIN ISLANDS

General Marshall and Admiral King's statements regarding operations in the Pacific, *219*

BONN

Resumé of operations planned for the Western Front, 304

SCAEF's appreciation and plan of operations for the winter and spring of 1945, 119

Note: Italic numerals refer to pages in minutes of meeting.
Plain type numerals refer to pages in C.C.S. Papers.

INDEX

BORDEAUX, FRANCE

General Smith's remarks regarding employment of French divisions, *198*

BORNEO, NORTH

General Marshall and Admiral King's statements regarding operations in the Pacific, *220*

BOUGAINVILLE

Employment of Australian troops, *221*

BREMEN-BREMERHAVEN ENCLAVE

Agreement for the American control of the Bremen-Bremerhaven enclave, 10, *235*

CCS discussion regarding American control of the Bremen-Bremerhaven enclave, *235*

Draft agreement for control of the Bremen-Bremerhaven enclave proposed by Lord Halifax and Mr. McCloy, 5

Map showing Bremen-Bremerhaven enclave, facing page 8

"BROADSWORD"

Directive to the Supreme Commander for operations in the Southeast Asia Command, 19, 163, 170

BROOKE, FIELD MARSHAL SIR ALAN

Statements in reference to:
  Accomplishments during ARGONAUT Conference, *250*
  Action to stop German withdrawals from Italy, *255*
  Agenda for the conference at Malta, *192*
  Allied operations directed toward Ljubljana Gap, *259*
  Bombline and liaison arrangements between the British-U.S. and Russian armies, *269*
  Coordination of offensive operations in Europe during the spring and summer of 1945, *253, 275*
  Coordination of operations with the Russians, *200*
  Directive to SACSEA, 211, 218
  Employment of British forces in China, *292*
  Enemy intelligence and movement of enemy forces among various fronts, *278*
  Equipment for Allied and liberated forces, 226
  Equipping of Greek forces, 244
  Flying bomb and rocket attacks on London, *193*
  Levels of supply of all petroleum products in all theaters, 240
  Liaison arrangements between the British-U.S. and Russian armies, 261
  Liaison for coordination of air operations, 263
  Movement of German forces from Norway, 260
  Naval operations in support of the land offensives in Northern Europe, 265
  Operations in Burma and China, *282*
  Operations in Southeast Asia Command, *291*
  Operations to close up to the Rhine, *289*
  Over-all review of cargo shipping, *241*
  Placing the whole effort in the North on the Western Front, *196*
  Provision of LVT's for the Mediterranean, *231*
  Reciprocal agreement on prisoners of war, 242
  Relief of tired units after crossing the Rhine, *198, 289*
  Report to the President and Prime Minister, *245, 248*
  Review of cargo shipping, 227
  SCAEF's plan for operation, 211
  Strategy in the Mediterranean Theater, *208, 255*
  Transfer of forces from the Mediterranean Theater to ETO, *208, 216, 290*
  Transfer of the Twelfth Air Force from Italy to France, 229

BUDAPEST

General Marshall and General Antonov's statements regarding bases for U.S. strategic bomber forces in the Vienna-Budapest area, *276*

Note: Italic numerals refer to pages in minutes of meeting.
Plain type numerals refer to pages in C.C.S. Papers.

INDEX

BULL, MAJOR GENERAL H. R.

Statements in reference to:
Enemy intelligence and movement of enemy forces among various fronts, 278
Projected operations in Northwest Europe, *194*
Technique of employing air power in offensive operations, *260*
Technique of employing artillery in offensive operations, *260*

BURMA (*See also* India-Burma Theater)

Directive to the Supreme Commander for operations in Southeast Asia Command, 19, 163, 170, *218*
Discussion regarding operations in Burma and China, *282*
Discussion regarding operations in Southeast Asia Command, *291*
Employment of British forces in China, *292*
General Marshall's statement regarding employment of U.S. forces outside of Burma, *212*

BURMA ROAD

Responsibility for the protection of the northern part of the Burma Road *212*

C

CCS DECISIONS (*See* Decisions)

CANADA

Transfer of forces from the Mediterranean Theater to ETO, 208, *290*

CHINA THEATER

Achievement of the Chinese forces, *292*
Basic undertakings in support of overall strategic concept, 160
British memorandum regarding allocation of resources between India-Burma and China Theaters, 101
Discussion regarding operations in Burma and China, *282*
Discussion with regard to employment of British forces in China, *292*
General Marshall's statement regarding employment of U.S. resources in Southeast Asia, *212*
General Marshall's statement with regard to importance of China in relation to U.S. action in the Pacific, *283*
General Marshall's statement with regard to the operation of U.S. air forces and the transport of supplies and equipment to China, *282*
General Marshall and Admiral King's statements regarding operations in the Pacific, *219*
Policy with regard to U.S. forces in the India-Burma Theater, 16, *218*
U.S. Army overseas strengths after V-E Day, 99

CHUSAN-NINGPO AREA

General Marshall and Admiral King's statements regarding operations in the Pacific, *220*
Operations for the defeat of Japan, 12, 169

CIVILIANS

Reciprocal agreement regarding liberated Allied prisoners of war, 175

COBLENZ

SCAEF's appreciation and plan of operations for the winter and spring of 1945, 119

COLMAR

General Bull's remarks regarding projected operations in Northwest Europe, *194*
General Smith's remarks regarding the timing factor for proposed operations, *196*
Resumé of operations planned for the Western Front, *305*

COLOGNE-BONN

General Bull's remarks regarding projected operations in Northwest Europe, *195*

Note: Italic numerals refer to pages in minutes of meeting.
Plain type numerals refer to pages in C.C.S. Papers.

INDEX

COMBINED CHIEFS OF STAFF

Plenary Meeting discussion regarding continuation of the Combined Chiefs of Staff organization after the end of the war, 296

COORDINATION WITH THE U.S.S.R.

Allied operations directed toward Ljubljana Gap, 258

CCS agree that Sir Charles Portal and General Kuter reply separately to Marshal Khudyakov indicating impracticability of revised bombline agreement proposed by Soviet High Command, 250

CCS approve certain views to be put forward to the Russians regarding liaison between the Soviet High Command and Anglo-American strategic bombing in eastern Germany, 181, 237

CCS decision to press the Russians to agree to the proposals set forth in FAN 477, 200

Discussion regarding coordination of offensive operations in Europe during the spring and summer of 1945, 200, 253, 275

General Kuter's statement regarding British-U.S. principles for establishing bombline between British-U.S. and Russian forces, 269

Marshal Stalin, the President and Prime Minister's statements with regard to coordination of effort between American-British and Russians during the winter offensives, 308

Tripartite Military Meeting discussion regarding liaison arrangements between the British-U.S. and Russian armies, 261

Tripartite Military Meeting discussion regarding bombline and liaison arrangements between the British-U.S. and Russians, 261, 269

COSSEA 200,

170

COUNTERMEASURES

Directive for effecting countermeasures against the German U-boat threat during 1945, 153

"CRICKET"

Agenda for U.S.-U.K. conferences at Malta, 129, 192, 204

CUNNINGHAM, ADM. SIR ANDREW B.

Statements in reference to:
German U-boat threat, 202, 222
Naval operations in support of the land offensives in Northern Europe, 264
Russian assault against Danzig as a measure to combat the U-boat menace, 309

D

DANZIG

Present situation regarding the German U-boat threat during 1945, 148

Prime Minister's statement with regard to submarine assembling points, 307

Statements with regard to Russian assault against Danzig as a measure to combat the U-boat menace, 309

DARDANELLES

Admiral King and the Prime Minister's statements regarding shipping to Russia via Dardanelles, 288

DATES (See Target Dates)

DECISIONS

BASIC UNDERTAKINGS

CCS approve wording for sub-paragraph h, Basic Undertakings in Support of Over-All Strategic Concept, 237

BOMBLINE

CCS agree Sir Charles Portal and General Kuter reply separately to Marshal Khudyakov indicating impracticability of revised bombline agreement proposed by Soviet High Command, 250

Note: Italic numerals refer to pages in minutes of meeting.
Plain type numerals refer to pages in C.C.S. Papers.

INDEX

DECISIONS *(Cont'd)*

COORDINATION WITH THE U.S.S.R.

CCS approve certain views regarding liaison with the Soviet High Command of Anglo-American strategic bombing in eastern Germany to be put forward to the Russians, 237

EQUIPPING LIBERATED FORCES

CCS agree to proposals for equipping Greek forces, 226

CCS note that agreement for equipping Greek forces will not interfere with equipment for Allied and liberated forces in Northwest Europe nor result in subsequent charges against U.S. resources, 244

CCS take note of reduced requirements for liberated manpower in ETO, 226

EUROPEAN THEATER OF OPERATIONS

CCS take note of SCAEF's plan for operations during spring and summer of 1945, *223*

CCS take note of CIC report of enemy situation in Europe, *213*

FIFTEENTH AIR FORCE

CCS note that U.S. Chiefs of Staff were not contemplating transfer of any formations of the Fifteenth Air Force from the Mediterranean, *201*

INDIA-BURMA AND CHINA THEATERS

CCS approve policy for the allocation of resources between India-Burma and China Theaters, *219*

LANDING SHIPS AND CRAFT

CCS approve the allocation of 400 LVT's to the Mediterranean Theater and 200 LVT's to the 21st Army Group, *235*

MEDITERRANEAN THEATER OF OPERATIONS

CCS approve directive to SACMED, *230*

PACIFIC OCEAN AREAS

CCS take note of the plans and operations proposed by the U.S. Chiefs of Staff in CCS 417/11, *222*

PETROLEUM

CCS approve policy for the levels of supply of all petroleum products in all theaters, *240*

PRISONERS OF WAR

CCS approve proposed reciprocal agreement on prisoners of war, *243*

REPORT TO THE PRESIDENT AND PRIME MINISTER

CCS approve ARGONAUT Conference Report to the President and Prime Minister, *248*

SHIPPING

CCS approve principles for guidance in the over-all review of cargo shipping, 227, *242*

CCS approve recommendation for the study of proposed civil relief shipping agreement, 227

CCS approve report on over-all review of cargo and troop shipping position for the remainder of 1945, *242*

SOUTHEAST ASIA

CCS approve directive to SACSEA, *219*

TARGET DATE

CCS approve planning date for the end of the war against Germany, *235*

CCS reaffirm planning date for the end of the war against Japan as recommended in OCTAGON, *202*

TWELFTH AIR FORCE

CCS approve movement to France of units of the Twelfth Air Force, *230*

U-BOAT WARFARE

CCS approve directive for combatting the German U-boat threat, *231*

CCS take note of British summary of the German U-boat threat and approve directive for measures to combat, *223*

ZONES OF OCCUPATION

CCS approve agreement for the American control of the Bremen-Bremerhaven enclave, *236*

DENMARK

Discussion of the possibility for naval operations in support of the land offensive in Northern Europe, *264*

Note: Italic numerals refer to pages in minutes of meeting.
Plain type numerals refer to pages in C.C.S. Papers.

INDEX

DIRECTIVES

To the Supreme Allied Commander, Mediterranean, 142
To the Supreme Allied Commander, Southeast Asia, 19
U-boat threat, 153

DOMINIONS

CCS discussion regarding reciprocal agreement on prisoners of war, 242

DUSSELDORF

SCAEF's appreciation and plan of operations for the winter and spring of 1945, 121, 123
Resumé of operations planned for the Western Front, 305

E

EASTERN FRONT

Coordination of offensive operations in the spring and summer months of 1945, 253
Discussion regarding enemy intelligence and movement of enemy forces among various fronts, 277
Discussion regarding liaison arrangements between the British-U.S. and Russian armies, 261
Estimate of the enemy situation in Europe as of 23 January 1945, 29
General Antonov's resumé of Russian intentions in Europe, 303
Marshal Stalin's statement regarding preponderance of Russian divisions over the Germans on the Eastern Front, 308
Outline of the situation existing on the Eastern Front, 300
Planning date for the end of the war with Germany, 136, 164

ECONOMY

Estimate of the enemy situation in Europe as of 23 January 1945, 33

EISENHOWER, GENERAL D. D.

Concurrence in rewording and amplification of plan for operations in ETO, 124

EQUIPMENT

(*See* Supplies and Equipment)

EUROPEAN THEATER OF OPERATIONS

CCS approve movement to France of units of the Twelfth Air Force, 230
CCS take note of CIC report of enemy situation in Europe, 213
Employment of the 47th Light Bomber Group in Northwest Europe, 210
Forces available in the ETO for spring offensive, 120
General Anderson's remark regarding need of P-47's in Northwest Europe, 209
U.S. Army overseas strengths after V-E Day, 99

EUROPE, NORTHWEST

CCS discussion regarding levels of supply of petroleum products in United Kingdom and Northwest Europe, 228
CCS discussion regarding number of days' stocks required in certain categories of oil, 234
Transfer of the Twelfth Air Force from Italy to France, 229

F

FAN 477,
185

FAN 501,
142

FIFTEENTH AIR FORCE

Transfer of the Fifteenth Air Force from the Mediterranean to ETO, 200, 201

Note: Italic numerals refer to pages in minutes of meeting.
Plain type numerals refer to pages in C.C.S. Papers.

INDEX

FIFTH ARMY

Withdrawal of forces from the Mediterranean Theater to ETO, *208*

FLEET TRAIN

British-controlled dry cargo shipping position (March-June), 67

British dry cargo shipping position after V-E Day, 87

FORCES, ALLIED

DEPLOYMENT

Permanent allocation of forces, a function of the Combined Chiefs of Staff, *201*

U.S. Army overseas strengths after V-E Day, 99

EUROPEAN THEATER

Agreed principle regarding coordination of air with land offensives, *256*

Employment of the 47th Light Bomber Group in Northwest Europe, *210*

Forces available in the ETO for spring offensive, 120

General Anderson's remark regarding need of P-47's in Northwest Europe, *209*

General Marshall's statement regarding availability of forces for crossing the Rhine, *307*

General Marshall's statement regarding number of tank divisions in General Eisenhower's command, *307*

General Marshall's statement regarding number of Allied divisions on the Western Front, *245*

General Smith's remarks regarding employment of French divisions, *198*

Marshal Stalin's statement regarding preponderance of Russian divisions over the Germans on the Eastern Front, *308*

Number of U.S. and British air forces on the Western and Italian Fronts and their proposed employment, *256*

Prime Minister's statement regarding American-British preponderance over the Germans in aircraft and armored troops, *308*

Reserves for relief of tired units in Northwest Europe, *198, 289*

Shortage of service troops, *221*

MEDITERRANEAN THEATER

CCS discussion regarding British equipping of Greek forces, *244*

Principle with regard to transfer of tactical air forces from SACMED to SCAEF, 140, 141, *229*

Transfer of the Fifteenth Air Force from the Mediterranean to European Theater of Operations, 200

Withdrawal from the Mediterranean of the Twelfth Tactical Air Force, *208, 229*

Withdrawal of forces from the Mediterranean Theater to ETO, *290*

PACIFIC OCEAN AREAS

Employment of Australian troops, *221*

REDEPLOYMENT

General Marshall's remarks regarding planning for the redeployment of forces from Europe to the Pacific, *281*

Redeployment of air forces to the Australian area, 87

SOUTHEAST ASIA

British memorandum regarding allocation of resources between India-Burma and China Theaters, 102

Employment of British forces in China, *292*

Employment of U.S. resources in Southeast Asia, *211, 218, 292*

General Marshall's statement with regard to the operations of U.S. air forces in Burma and China and the transport of supplies and equipment to China, *282*

Responsibility for the protection of the northern part of the Burma road, *212*

FORCES, ENEMY

Enemy intelligence and movement of enemy forces among various fronts, *277*

Estimate of the enemy situation in Europe as of 23 January 1945, 35

Measures to prevent movement of German forces from Norway, *259*

Number of German and Italian enemy divisions in Italy, *255*

Withdrawal of German forces from Italy, *255*

Note: Italic numerals refer to pages in minutes of meeting.
Plain type numerals refer to pages in C.C.S. Papers.

INDEX

47TH LIGHT BOMBER GROUP

Employment of the 47th Light Bomber Group in Northwest Europe, 210

FRANCE

CCS approve movement to France of units of the Twelfth Air Force, *230*
Employment of French divisions, *198*
Forces available in the ETO for spring offensive, 120
General Marshall's statement regarding strategic reasons for maintaining the goodwill of Russia and other Allies, *231*
Responsibility for the equipping of liberated manpower, 132, 134, 165

FRANKFURT, GERMANY

General Bull's remarks regarding projected operations in Northwest Europe, *194*
SCAEF's appreciation and plan of operations for the winter and spring of 1945, 117, 123, *304*

G

GDYNIA

Present situation regarding the German U-boat threat during 1945, 147

GERMANY

Allied action to prevent German withdrawal from Italy, *255, 257*
American control of the Bremen-Bremerhaven enclave, 9, *235*
Basic undertakings in support of over-all strategic concept, 159
Draft agreement for control of the Bremen-Bremerhaven enclave proposed by Lord Halifax and Mr. McCloy, 5
Employment of air forces to prevent German withdrawals from Italy, *257*
Employment of war-weary bombers against industrial targets in Germany, *193*
Establishment of liaison with the Soviet High Command for Anglo-American strategic bombing in Germany, 182, *237, 249*
Estimate of the enemy situation in Europe as of 23 January 1945, 29
Execution of the over-all strategic concept for the defeat of Germany, 160
General Antonov's resumé of Russian intentions in Europe, *303*
General Bull's remarks regarding projected operations in Northwest Europe, *194*
Map showing Bremen-Bremerhaven enclave, facing page 8
Movement of German forces from Norway, *259*
Number of German and enemy Italian divisions in Italy, *255*
Over-all objective and strategic concept for the prosecution of the war, 159
Planning date for the end of the war with Germany, 136, 164, *202, 211, 235, 265*
Present situation regarding the German U-boat threat during 1945, 146
Prime Minister's statement regarding American-British preponderance over the Germans in aircraft and armored troops, *308*
SCAEF's account of the development of operations in Northwest Europe, 109
SCAEF's appreciation and plan of operations for the winter and spring of 1945, 123, 161
The President and General Antonov's statements regarding widening the gauge of captured German railroad rolling stock, *304*
Tripartite Military Meeting discussion regarding date of the end of the war with Germany, *265*

GREECE

Directive to SACMED, 142, 166
Equipping of Greek forces, *226, 244*
Plenary discussion regarding withdrawal of forces from the Mediterranean Theater to ETO, *290*
Responsibility for the equipping of liberated manpower, 132, 134, 165

"GRENADE"

General Bull's remarks regarding projected operations in Northwest Europe, *194*

Note: Italic numerals refer to pages in minutes of meeting.
Plain type numerals refer to pages in C.C.S. Papers.

INDEX

H

HAINAN

General Marshall and Admiral King's statements regarding operations in the Pacific, *219*

HALIFAX, LORD

Draft agreement for control of the Bremen-Bremerhaven enclave proposed by Lord Halifax and Mr. McCloy, 5

HAMBURG, GERMANY

Prime Minister's statement with regard to submarine assembling points, *307*

HONSHU

Operations for the defeat of Japan, 13, 169

HOPKINS, HARRY L.

Agreement for shipment of supplies to liberated European countries during the first six months of 1945, 47

HOUFFALIZE, GERMANY

SCAEF's account of the development of operations in Northwest Europe, *114*

HUNGARY

Estimate of the enemy situation in Europe as of 23 January 1945, 41

I

INDIA-BURMA THEATER

British memorandum regarding allocation of resources between India-Burma and China Theaters, 102

Directive to the Supreme Commander for operations in the Southeast Asia Command, 19, 162, 170

General Marshall's statement regarding employment of U.S. resources in Southeast Asia, *212*

Policy with regard to U.S. forces in the India-Burma Theater, 17, *218*

Responsibility for the protection of the northern part of the Burma Road, *212*

U.S. Army overseas strengths after V-E Day, 99

INTELLIGENCE

Estimate of the enemy situation in Europe as of 23 January 1945, 29, *213*

Tripartite Military Meeting discussion regarding enemy intelligence and movement of enemy forces among various fronts, *278*

ITALIAN FRONT

Action to stop German withdrawals from Italy, *255*

Coordination of offensive operations in the spring and summer months of 1945, *253*

Number of U.S. and British air forces on the Western and Italian Fronts and their proposed employment, *256*

Tripartite Military Meeting discussion regarding enemy intelligence and movement of enemy forces among various fronts, *277*

ITALY

CCS discussion regarding withdrawal of forces from the Mediterranean Theater to ETO, *216*

CCS discussion regarding transfer of the Twelfth Air Force from Italy to France, *229*

Directive to SACMED, 142, 166

Estimate of the enemy situation in Europe as of 23 January 1945, 29

Execution of the over-all strategic concept for operations in the Mediterranean, 162

General Antonov's resumé of Russian intentions in Europe, *303*

Number of German and enemy Italian divisions in Italy, *255*

The President and Prime Minister's remarks regarding sovereignty over Trieste, *291*

Tripartite Military Meeting discussion regarding Allied action to prevent German withdrawals from Italy, *257*

IWO JIMA

Operations for the defeat of Japan, 13, 169

Note: Italic numerals refer to pages in minutes of meeting.
Plain type numerals refer to pages in C.C.S. Papers.

INDEX

J

JAPAN

Admiral King's statement with regard to effectiveness of U.S. U-boat warfare in the Pacific, *284*

Basic undertakings in support of overall strategic concept, 160

CCS reaffirm planning date for the end of the war against Japan as recommended at OCTAGON, 202

General Kuter's statement regarding employment of B-29's against Japan, *281*

General Marshall and Admiral King's statements regarding operations in the Pacific, *219*

Japanese suicide attacks, *194*

Operations for the defeat of Japan, *12*, 168

Over-all objective and strategic concept for the prosecution of the war, 159

Over-all objective in the war against Japan, 162

Planning for the entry of Russia into the war against Japan, *13*

Prime Minister and General Marshall's statements regarding postponement of main operations against Japan until after the close of the German war, *293, 294*

The President and Prime Minister's statements regarding a four-power ultimatum calling upon Japan for unconditional surrender, *296*

JAVA

Plenary discussion regarding operations in Southeast Asia Command, *291*

K

KAMCHATKA PENINSULA

Operations for the defeat of Japan, *13*, 169

KASSEL, GERMANY

Projected operations in Northwest Europe, *194*

SCAEF's appreciation and plan of operations for the winter and spring of 1945, 117 123

KHUDYAKOV, MARSHAL

Statements in reference to:
  Allied action to prevent German withdrawals from Italy, *258*
  Effective employment of Russian aviation in support of ground forces, *258*
  Enemy intelligence and movement of enemy forces among various fronts, *279*
  Liaison for coordination of air operations, *264*
  Provision of Soviet airfields for damaged British night fighters, *277*
  Technique of employing air power in offensive operations, *260*

KIEL, GERMANY

Prime Minister's statement with regard to submarine assembling points, *307*

KING, ADMIRAL E. J.

Statements in reference to:
  Allocation of forces, a function of the Combined Chiefs of Staff, *201*
  Combatting the German U-boat threat, *222*
  Effectiveness of U.S. U-boat warfare in the Pacific, *284*
  Japanese suicide attacks, *194*
  Naval operations in support of the land offensives in Northern Europe, *265*
  Operations in Burma and China, *284*
  Operations in the Pacific, *219*
  Resumé of present and future operations in the Pacific, *266, 279*
  Shipping to Russia via Dardanelles, *288*

KRA PENINSULA

Employment of U.S. resources in Southeast Asia, *292*
Plenary discussion regarding operations in Southeast Asia Command, *291*

Note: Italic numerals refer to pages in minutes of meeting.
Plain type numerals refer to pages in C.C.S. Papers.

INDEX

KURILES

General Marshall and Admiral King's statements regarding operations in the Pacific, *219*
Operations for the defeat of Japan, 13, 169

KUTER, MAJOR GENERAL L. S.

Statments in reference to:
Bombline and liaison arrangements between the British-U.S. and Russian armies, *269*
Employment of B-29's against Japan, *281*
Employment of the 47th Light Bomber Group in Northwest Europe, *210*
Impracticability of the Russian revised draft agreement regarding liaison with the Soviet High Command for strategic bombing in eastern Germany, *249*
Measures to combat the German U-boat threat, *222*
Transfer of the Fifteenth Air Force from the Mediterranean to ETO, *200*
Transfer of the Twelfth Air Force from Italy to France, *230*
Withdrawal of forces from the Mediterranean Theater to ETO, *217*

KUZNETSOV, ADMIRAL

Statements in reference to:
Naval operations in support of the land offensives in Northern Europe, *264*
Operations in Burma and China, *284*

KYUSHU ISLAND, JAPAN

General Marshall and Admiral King's statements regarding operations in the Pacific, *219*
Operations for the defeat of Japan, 12, 168

L

LAND, ADMIRAL E. S.

Statement of the CSAB on the dry cargo shipping position prior to V-E Day, 64

LANDING SHIPS AND CRAFT

Provision of LVT's for the Mediterranean, 105, *231*, *235*

LAW, RICHARD

Agreement for shipment of supplies to liberated European countries during first six months of 1945, 47

LEAHY, ADMIRAL WILLIAM D.

Statements in reference to:
Accomplishments during *ARGONAUT* Conference, *250*
Date for the end of the war with Germany, *265*
Exchange of information on river-crossing technique and equipment, *276*
Levels of supply of all petroleum products in all theaters, *240*
Liaison arrangements between the British-U.S. and Russian armies, *261*
Operations in Southeast Asia Command, *293*
Over-all review of cargo shipping, *241*
Preparation of final report to the President and Prime Minister, *244*
Reciprocal agreement on prisoners of war, *243*

LEATHERS, LORD

CCS discussion regarding over-all review of cargo shipping, *241*
Statement of the CSAB on the dry cargo shipping position prior to V-E Day, 64

LIAISON

CCS approve certain views regarding liaison with the Soviet High Command of Anglo-American strategic bombing in eastern Germany to be put forward to the Russians, *237*
CCS discussion regarding impracticability of the Russian revised draft agreement regarding liaison with the Soviet High Command for strategic bombing in eastern Germany, *249*

Note: Italic numerals refer to pages in minutes of meeting.
Plain type numerals refer to pages in C.C.S. Papers.

INDEX

LIAISON (Cont'd)

General Antonov's statement regarding bombline arrangements and employment of Russian air forces against important German targets, 272

General Kuter's statement regarding British-U.S. principles for establishing bombline between British-U.S. and Russian forces, 269

General Marshall's statement with regard to liaison arrangements presently necessary in the Berlin area, 271

Proposal for the establishment of liaison with the Soviet High Command with the Anglo-American strategic bombing in Germany, 183

Tripartite Military Meeting discussion regarding liaison arrangements between the British-U.S. and Russian armies, 261

Tripartite Military Meeting discussion regarding bombline and liaison arrangements between the British-U.S. and Russian armies 269

Tripartite Military Meeting discussion with regard to liaison for coordination of air operations, 260

LIBERATED AREAS

Agreement for shipment of supplies to liberated European countries during first six months of 1945, 47

Basic undertakings in support of overall strategic concept, 159

British-controlled dry cargo shipping position (March-June 1945), 67

British dry cargo shipping position after V-E Day, 87

CCS approve recommendation for the study of proposed civil relief shipping agreement, 227

CCS approve wording for sub-paragraph h, Basic Undertakings in Support of Over-All Strategic Concept, 237

General Marshall's statement regarding effect of suggested new category of basic undertakings on availability of shipping for military operations, 232, 288

General Somervell's remarks regarding extent of relief requirements included under military shipping, 232

Principles for guidance in allocation of combined shipping, 56

LIBERATED FORCES

Basic undertakings in support of overall strategic concept, 156

CCS agree to proposals for equipping Greek forces, 226, 244

CCS take note of reduced requirements for liberated manpower in ETO, 226

Field Marshal Brooke's statement regarding equipment for Allied and liberated forces, 226

Responsibility for the equipping of liberated manpower, 132, 134, 165

LIEGE-NAMUR SECTOR

SCAEF's account of the development of operations in Northwest Europe, 113

LINES OF COMMUNICATION

Admiral King and the Prime Minister's statements regarding shipping to Russia via Dardanelles, 288

Admiral King's statement with regard to effectiveness of U.S. U-boat warfare in the Pacific, 284

Basic undertakings in support of overall strategic concept, 160

Directive to the Supreme Comander for operations in the Southeast Asia Command, 19, 163, 170

General Antonov's resumé of Russian intentions in Europe, 303

General Marshall and Admiral King's statements regarding operations in the Pacific, 219

The President and General Antonov's statements regarding widening the gauge of captured German railroad rolling stock, 304

LJUBLJANA GAP

Strategy in the Mediterranean Theater, 208

Tripartite Military Meeting discussion regarding Allied operations directed toward Ljubljana Gap, 259

LOGISTICS

General Bull's remarks regarding projected operations in Northwest Europe, 194

General Smith's remarks regarding distribution of forces for the coming offensive, 196

Note: Italic numerals refer to pages in minutes of meeting.
Plain type numerals refer to pages in C.C.S. Papers.

INDEX

LOSS RATE

Present situation regarding the German U-boat threat during 1945, 148

"LOYALIST"

Directive to the Supreme Commander for operations in the Southeast Asia Comand, 19, 163, 170

M

McCLOY, J. J.

Draft agreement for control of the Bremen-Bremerhaven enclave proposed by Lord Halifax and Mr. McCloy, 2

MACREADY, LT. GEN. G. N.

Draft agreement for control of the Bremen-Bremerhaven enclave proposed by Lord Halifax and Mr. McCloy, 2

MAINZ-KARLSRUHE

SCAEF's appreciation and plan of operations for the winter and spring of 1945, 117, 123

MAINZ-MANNHEIM

General Bull's remarks regarding projected operations in Northwest Europe, *194*

MALACCA, STRAITS OF

Directive to the Supreme Commander for operations in the Southeast Asia Command, 19, 163, 170
Plenary discussion regarding operations in Southeast Asia Command, *291*

MALAYA PENINSULA

Directive to the Supreme Commander for operations in the Southeast Asia Command, 19, 163, 170
Employment of U.S. resources in Southeast Asia, *292*

General Marshall's statement regarding employment of U.S. resources in Southeast Asia, 212, 213
Plenary discussion regarding operations in Southeast Asia Command, *291*

MANPOWER

CCS take note of reduced requirements for liberated manpower in ETO, *226*
Estimate of the enemy situation in Europe as of 23 January 1945, 35
Planning date for the end of the war with Germany, 136, 164, *202, 235*

MAPS

Map showing Bremen-Bremerhaven enclave, facing page 8

MARITIME PROVINCES

General Marshall and Admiral King's statements regarding operations in the Pacific, *221*

MARSHALL, GENERAL G. C.

Statements in reference to:
Advantage of more than one line of advance on the Western Front, *198*
Agenda for the conference at Malta, *192*
American control of the Bremen-Bremerhaven enclave, *236*
Availability of forces for crossing the Rhine, *307*
Bases for U.S. strategic bomber forces in the Vienna-Budapest area, *276*
Bombline and liaison arrangements between the British-U.S. and Russian armies, *271*
British equipping of Greek forces, *244*
Continuation of the CCS organization after the end of the war, *297*
Coordination of offensive operations in Europe during the spring and summer of 1945, *254, 275*
Coordination of operations with the Russians, *200*
Effect of suggested new category of basic undertakings on availability of shipping for military operations, *232, 288*

Note: Italic numerals refer to pages in minutes of meeting.
Plain type numerals refer to pages in C.C.S. Papers.

INDEX

MARSHALL, GENERAL G. C. *(Cont'd)*

    Effectiveness of recent Allied air operations, *257*

    Employment of British forces in China, *293*

    Employment of fighter-bombers to attack communications, entrances to tunnels and underground production plants, *193*

    Employment of U.S. forces outside of Burma, *212*

    Employment of U.S. resources in Southeast Asia, *212*

    Enemy intelligence and movement of enemy forces among various fronts, *278*

    Final report to the President and Prime Minister, *248*

    Flying bomb and rocket attacks on London, *192*

    Importance of China in relation to U.S. action in the Pacific, *283*

    Levels of supply of petroleum products in U.K. and Northwest Europe, *228*

    Liaison arrangements between the British-U.S. and Russians, *262*

    Liaison arrangements presently necessary in the Berlin area, *271*

    Liaison for coordination of air operations, *262*

    Measures to combat the German U-boat threat, *222*

    Number of Allied divisions on the Western Front, *245*

    Number of German and enemy Italian divisions on the Italian Front, *306*

    Number of tank divisions in General Eisenhower's command, *307*

    Operations in Burma and China, *282*

    Operations in Southeast Asia Command, *292*

    Operations in the Pacific, *219*

    Operation of U.S. Air Force and the transport of supplies and equipment to China, *282*

    Planning date for the end of the war with Germany, *202, 211, 266*

    Planning for the redeployment of forces from Europe to the Pacific, *281*

    Possibility of German suicide attacks on vital targets, *194*

    Postponement of main operations against Japan until after the close of the German war, *294*

    Proposed directive to SACSEA, *212, 218*

    Proposed measures to combat German U-boat menace, *306*

    Reciprocal agreement on prisoners of war, *243*

    Removal of forces from the Mediterranean Theater to ETO, *208, 217*

    Responsibility for the protection of the northern part of the Burma Road, *212*

    Results achieved by the Chinese forces, *292*

    Resumé of operations planned for the Western Front, *304*

    Review of cargo shipping, *227*

    Strategic reasons for maintaining the goodwill of Russia and other Allies, *231*

    Strategy in the Mediterranean Theater, *208*

    Technique of employing air power in offensive operations, *261*

    Transfer of the Fifteenth Air Force from the Mediterranean to ETO, *201*

    Transfer of the Twelfth Air Force from Italy to France, *229*

    Withdrawal from the Mediterranean of a part of the Twelfth Tactical Air Force, *208*

MEDITERRANEAN THEATER OF OPERATIONS

    CCS discussion regarding withdrawal of forces from the Mediterranean Theater to ETO, *207, 216*

    Directive to SACMED, 142, 166, *230*

    Employment of the 47th Light Bomber Group in Northwest Europe, *210*

    Execution of the over-all strategic concept for operations in the Mediterranean, *162*

    Field Marshal Brooke and General Marshall's statements regarding strategy in the Mediterranean Theater, *208*

    Number of German and enemy Italian divisions on the Italian Front, *306*

    Plenary discussion regarding strategy in the Mediterranean, *290*

    Principle with regard to transfer of tactical air forces from SACMED to SCAEF, 140, 141, *229*

    Provision of LVT's for the Mediterranean, 105, *231, 235*

    Responsibility for the equipping of liberated manpower, 132, 134, 165

Note: Italic numerals refer to pages in minutes of meeting.
Plain type numerals refer to pages in C.C.S. Papers.

INDEX

MEDITERRANEAN THEATER OF OPERATIONS (Cont'd)

The President and Prime Minister's remarks regarding sovereignty over Trieste, 291
Transfer of the Fifteenth Air Force from the Mediterranean to ETO, 200, 201
Tripartite Military Meeting discussion regarding Allied operations directed toward Ljubljana Gap, 258, 259
Withdrawal from the Mediterranean of a part of the Twelfth Tactical Air Force, 207, 229, 230

"MEDLOC"

British-controlled troop shipping position after V-E Day, 92
Position of British-controlled troop shipping position (March-June 1945), 79

MONSCHAU

SCAEF's account of the development of operations in Northwest Europe, 112

MOSELLE

SCAEF's appreciation and plan of operations for the winter and spring of 1945, 121, 124

N

NAF 841,
188

NETHERLANDS

Tripartite Military Meeting discussion of the possibility for naval operations in support of the land offensive in Northern Europe, 264

NEW GUINEA

Employment of Australian troops, 221

NORWAY

Estimate of the enemy situation in Europe as of 23 January 1945, 40
General Antonov's resumé of Russian intentions in Europe, 303
Measures to prevent movement of German forces from Norway, 259

O

OKHOTSK, SEA OF

Operations for the defeat of Japan, 13, 169

OKINAWA (See Ryukyu Islands)

OVER-ALL OBJECTIVE

In the war against the Axis, 160
In the war against Japan, 162

P

PACIFIC OCEAN AREAS

Admiral King's statement with regard to effectiveness of U.S. U-boat warfare in the Pacific, 284
General Kuter's statement regarding employment of B-29's against Japan, 281
General Marshall's remarks regarding planning for the redeployment of forces from Europe to the Pacific, 281
Operations for the defeat of Japan, 12, 168, 219
Resumé of present and future operations in the Pacific, 219, 279
Resumé of situation in the Far East and operations in that area, 266
U.S. Army overseas strength after V-E Day, 99

PETROLEUM

Agreement on levels of supply of all petroleum products in all theaters, 23, 165, 171, 234, 240
CCS discussion regarding levels of supply of petroleum products in United Kingdom and Northwest Europe, 228
Estimate of the enemy situation in Europe as of 23 January 1945, 34

Note: Italic numerals refer to pages in minutes of meeting.
Plain type numerals refer to pages in C.C.S. Papers.

INDEX

PHILIPPINE ISLANDS

Employment of Australian troops, 221
General Marshall and Admiral King's statements regarding operations in the Pacific, 219
Operations for the defeat of Japan, 13

PLANNING

CCS reaffirm planning date for the end of the war against Japan as recommended at OCTAGON, 202
Planning date for the end of the war with Germany, 136, 164, 202, 211, 235
Planning for the entry of Russia into the war against Japan, 13

POLAND

Estimate of the enemy situation in Europe as of 23 January 1945, 29
Responsibility for the equipping of liberated manpower, 132

PORTAL, SIR CHARLES

Statements in reference to:
    Agreed principle regarding coordination of air with land offensives, 256
    Allocation of forces, a function of the Combined Chiefs of Staff, 201
    Bombline and liaison arrangements between the British-U.S. and Russian armies, 271
    Bombline arrangements and employment of Russian air forces against important German taregts, 274
    Employment of fighter-bombers to attack communications, entrances to tunnels and underground production plants, 193
    Employment of U.S. resources in Southeast Asia, 292
    Employment of war-weary bombers against industrial targets in Germany, 193
    Flying bomb and rocket attacks on London, 193
    Impracticability of the Russian revised draft agreement regarding liaison with the Soviet High Command for strategic bombing in eastern Germany, 249
    Liaison arrangements presently necessary in the Berlin area, 272
    Liaison for coordination of air operations, 263
    Measures to prevent movement of German forces from Norway, 259
    Measures to combat the German U-boat threat, 222
    Number of U.S. and British air forces on the Western and Italian Fronts and their proposed employment, 256
    Operations in Burma and China, 282
    Operations in Southeast Asia Command, 292
    Proposed directive to SACSEA, 213, 218
    Provision of Soviet airfields for damaged British night fighters, 277
    Reciprocal agreement on prisoners of war, 243
    Strategy in the Mediterranean, 290
    The German U-boat threat, 203
    Transfer of the Fifteenth Air Force from the Mediterranean to ETO, 200
    Transfer of the Twelfth Air Force from Italy to France, 229
    Withdrawal of forces from the Mediterranean Theater to ETO, 216, 290

PRESIDENT OF THE UNITED STATES

Report to President and Prime Minister of the agreed summary of conclusions reached by the CCS at the ARGONAUT Conference, 159, 244, 248, 296
Statements in reference to:
    Continuation of the Combined Chiefs of Staff organization after the end of the war, 297
    Coordination of effort between American-British and Russians during the winter offensives, 308
    Four-power ultimatum calling upon Japanese unconditional surrender, 296
    Operations planned for the Western Front, 304
    Results achieved by the Chinese forces, 292
    Widening the gauge of captured German railroad rolling stock, 304

Note: Italic numerals refer to pages in minutes of meeting.
Plain type numerals refer to pages in C.C.S. Papers.

INDEX

PRIME MINISTER OF THE UNITED KINGDOM

Report to President and Prime Minister of the agreed summary of conclusions reached by the Combined Chiefs of Staff at the *ARGONAUT* Conference, 159, *244, 248, 296*

Statements in reference to:

American-British preponderance over the Germans in aircraft and armored troops, *308*

Continuation of the Combined Chiefs of Staff organization after the end of the war, *296*

Coordination of effort between American-British and Russians during the winter offensives, *309*

Diversion of air effort against German U-boat pens, *289*

Employment of British forces in China, *292*

Employment of U.S. resources in Southeast Asia *292*

Exchange of information with U.S.S.R. regarding amphibious operations, *307*

Four-power ultimatum calling upon Japanese unconditional surrender, *296*

General Eisenhower's proposed operation to close up to the Rhine, *289*

Operations in Southeast Asia Command, *291*

Operations planned for the Western Front, *304*

Postponement of main operations against Japan until after the close of the German war, *293, 294*

Reserves in Northwestern Europe to replace tired divisions, *289*

Results achieved by the Chinese forces, *292*

Shipping required for imports to Great Britain, *288*

Shipping to Russia via Dardanelles, *288*

Sovereignty over Trieste, *291*

Submarine assembling points, *307*

U.S.-British occupation of Austria, *290, 291*

Withdrawal of forces from the Mediterranean Theater to ETO, *290*

PRIORITY

CCS discussion regarding over-all review of cargo shipping, *241*

General Kuter's statement regarding employment of B-29's against Japan, *281*

General Marshall's remarks with regard to planning for the redeployment of forces from Europe to the Pacific, *281*

Principles for guidance in allocation of combined shipping, 56, *227*

Shortage of service troops, *221*

PRISONERS OF WAR

Reciprocal agreement regarding liberated Allied prisoners of war 177, *242, 243*

PRODUCTION

Basic undertakings in support of over-all strategic concept, 164

Effectiveness of recent Allied air operations on enemy production, *257*

Estimate of the enemy situation in Europe as of 23 January 1945, 33

Planning date for the end of the war with Germany, 136, 164, *202, 235, 265*

PSYCHOLOGICAL WARFARE

Estimate of the enemy situation in Europe as of 23 January 1945, 32

R

REDEPLOYMENT

Basic undertakings in support of over-all strategic concept, 159

General Marshall's remarks with regard to planning for the redeployment of forces from Europe to the Pacific, *281*

Over-all review of cargo and troop shipping position for the remainder of 1945, 97, *241*

Position of British-controlled troop shipping position (March-June 1945), 79

Redeployment of air forces to the Australian area, 87

Shortage of service troops, *221*

Note: Italic numerals refer to pages in minutes of meeting.
Plain type numerals refer to pages in C.C.S. Papers.

INDEX

RELIEF AND REHABILITATION

Agreement for shipment of supplies to liberated European countries during first six months of 1945, 47

CCS approve recommendation for the study of proposed civil relief shipping agreement, 227

General Somervell's remarks regarding extent of relief requirements included under military shipping, *232*

Principles for guidance in allocation of combined shipping, 56

REPORT TO PRESIDENT AND PRIME MINISTER

CCS approve *ARGONAUT* Conference Report to the President and Prime Minister, 159, *248*

Basic undertakings in support of overall strategic concept, 156, 159

Plenary meeting discussion with regard to, *288*

The President and Prime Minister's acceptance of the report of the Combined Chiefs of Staff on the *ARGONAUT* Conference, *296*

RHINE RIVER

General Bull's remarks regarding projected operations in Northwest Europe, *194*

General Marshall's statement regarding availability of forces for crossing the Rhine, *307*

General Smith's remarks with regard to crossing of the Rhine, *196*

Plenary discussions regarding General Eisenhower's proposed operation to close up to the Rhine, *289*

Resumé of operations planned for the Western Front, 305

SCAEF's account of the development of operations in Northwest Europe, 109

SCAEF's appreciation and plan of operations for the winter and spring of 1945, 116, 123

RIDDELL-WEBSTER, GEN. SIR THOMAS

Statement in reference to levels of supply of petroleum products in United Kingdom and Northwest Europe, *228*

ROCKETS AND FLYING BOMBS

Employment of fighter-bombers to attack communications, entrances to tunnels and underground production plants, *193*

Estimate of the enemy situation in Europe as of 23 January 1945, 39

Statements regarding flying bomb and rocket attacks on London, *192*

ROER RIVER

Resumé of operations planned for the Western Front, 305

SCAEF's account of the development of operations in Northwest Europe, 111

RUHR

General Bull's remarks regarding projected operations in Northwest Europe, *194*

Resumé of operations planned for the Western Front, 305

SCAEF's account of the development of operations in Northwest Europe, 109

RUSSIA (*See* U.S.S.R.)

RUSSIAN FRONT (*See* Eastern Front)

RYUKYU ISLANDS

Operations for the defeat of Japan, 13, 169, *219*

S

SAAR

SCAEF's account of the development of operations in Northwest Europe, 111

SAAR-LAUTERN

SCAEF's account of the development of operations in Northwest Europe, 111

ST. NAZAIRE

General Smith's remarks regarding employment of French divisions, *198*

Note: Italic numerals refer to pages in minutes of meeting.
Plain type numerals refer to pages in C.C.S. Papers.

INDEX

SCAF 179,
109

SCAF 180,
116

SCAF 194,
123

SCHNORKEL

Admiral Cunningham and Sir Charles Portal's statements regarding the German U-boat threat, *202*
Present situation regarding the German U-boat threat during 1945, 146

SHIPBUILDING, CONVERSIONS

British-controlled troop shipping position after V-E Day, 92
U.S. dry cargo shipping position after V-E Day, 89
U.S. troop shipping position after V-E Day, 95

SHIPPING

Admiral King and the Prime Minister's statements regarding shipping to Russia via Dardanelles, *288*
Agreement for shipment of supplies to liberated European countries during first six months of 1945, 47
CCS approve recommendation for the study of proposed civil relief shipping agreement, 227
CCS approve report on over-all review of cargo and troop shipping position for the remainder of 1945, *242*
Directive for effecting countermeasures against the German U-boat threat, 153
General Marshall's statements regarding effect of suggested new category of basic undertakings on availability of shipping for military operations, *232, 288*
General Somervell's remarks regarding extent of relief requirements included under military shipping, *232*
Over-all review of cargo shipping, 55

Over-all shipping deficiencies, 53, 55, 61
Present situation regarding the German U-boat threat during 1945, 146
Prime Minister and General Marshall's statements regarding postponement of main operations against Japan until after the close of the German war, *293, 294*
Provisional forecast of combined dry cargo and troop shipping position after V-E Day on 1 July 1945, 86, 164
Statement of the CSAB on the dry cargo shipping position prior to V-E Day, 64

SHIPPING, CARGO

British-controlled dry cargo shipping position (March-June 1945), 67
British dry cargo shipping position after V-E Day, 87
CCS approve principles for guidance in the over-all review of cargo shipping, 227
CCS discussion regarding over-all review of cargo shipping, *227, 241*
Over-all review of cargo and troop shipping position for the remainder of 1945, 60
Present situation regarding the German U-boat threat during 1945, 146
U.S. dry cargo shipping position (March-June 1945), 74
U.S. dry cargo shipping position after V-E Day, 89

SHIPPING, PERSONNEL

British-controlled troop shipping position after V-E Day, 92
British-controlled troop shipping position (March-June 1945), 79
Over-all review of cargo and troop shipping position for the remainder of 1945, 60
Present situation regarding the German U-boat threat during 1945, 146
U.S. troop shipping position (March-June 1945), 85
U.S. troop shipping position after V-E Day, 95

SIEGFRIED LINE

General Smith's remarks regarding vulnerability of the Siegfried line, *199*

Note: Italic numerals refer to pages in minutes of meeting.
Plain type numerals refer to pages in C.C.S. Papers.

INDEX

SILESIA

    Estimate of the enemy situation in Europe as of 23 January 1945, 29

SLOVAKIA

    Estimate of the enemy situation in Europe as of 23 January 1945, 41

SMITH, LT. GEN. W. B.

    Statements in reference to:
        Crossing of the Rhine, *196*
        Distribution of forces for the coming offensive, *196*
        Employment of French divisions, *198*
        SCAEF's plan for operation, *211*
        Timing factor for proposed operations, *196*
        Vulnerability of the Siegfried line, *199*
        Withdrawal from the Mediterranean of a part of the Twelfth Tactical Air Force, *209*
        Withdrawal of forces from the Mediterranean Theater to ETO, *217*

SOMERVELL, LT. GEN. B. B.

    Statements in reference to:
        Levels of supply of petroleum products in United Kingdom and Northwest Europe, 228
        Number of days' forward stocks required in certain categories of oil, *234*
        Over-all review of cargo shipping, *242*

SOUTHEAST ASIA

    Directive to the Supreme Commander for operations in the Southeast Asia Command, 19, 163, 170, *211*, 218
    Discussion regarding operations in Southeast Asia Command, *291*
    General Marshall's statement regarding employment of U.S. resources in Southeast Asia, *212, 213*
    Policy with regard to U.S. forces in the India-Burma Theater, 17
    Responsibility for the protection of the northern part of the Burma Road, *212*

SOVEREIGNTY

    The President and Prime Minister's remarks regarding sovereignty over Trieste, *291*

STALIN, MARSHAL

    Statements in reference to:
        Attrition of tanks in Russian central campaign, *307*
        Coordination of efforts between American-British and Russians during the winter offensives, *308*
        Preponderance of Russian divisions over the Germans on the Eastern Front, *308*
        Russian assault against Danzig as a measure to combat the U-boat menace, *309*

STRASBOURG

    General Smith's remarks regarding the timing factor for proposed operations, *196*
    Resumé of operations planned for the Western Front, *305*
    SCAEF's account of the development of operations in Northwest Europe, 114

STRATEGIC AIR FORCES

    Transfer of the Fifteenth Air Force from the Mediterranean to ETO, *200*

STRATEGY

    Agreed principle regarding coordination of air with land offensives, *256*
    BASIC POLICIES
    Basic undertakings in support of over-all strategic concept, 156, 159
    Execution of the over-all strategic concept for the defeat of Germany, 160
    Execution of the over-all strategic concept for operations in the Mediterranean, 162
    Over-all objective in the war against Japan, 162
    Over-all objective and strategic concept for the prosecution of the war, 159
    Report to the President and Prime Minister of the agreed summary of conclusions reached by the Combined Chiefs of Staff at the *ARGONAUT* Conference, 159

Note: Italic numerals refer to pages in minutes of meeting.
Plain type numerals refer to pages in C.C.S. Papers.

INDEX

STRATEGY *(Cont'd)*

IN THE EUROPEAN THEATER OF OPERATIONS

Coordination of offensive operations in the spring and summer months of 1945, *253*

Field Marshal Brooke and General Smith's statements regarding SCAEF's plan for operation, *211*

General Antonov's resumé of Russian intentions in Europe, *303*

General Bull's remarks regarding projected operations in Northwest Europe, *194*

General Marshall's remarks regarding advantage of more than one line of advance on the Western Front, *198*

General Marshall's statement regarding availability of forces for crossing the Rhine, *307*

General Smiths' remarks regarding distribution of forces for the coming offensive, *196*

General Smith's remarks regarding the timing factor for proposed operations, *196*

Plenary discussion regarding General Eisenhower's proposed operation to close up to the Rhine, *289*

Resumé of operations planned for the Western Front, *304*

SCAEF's account of the development of operations in Northwest Europe, 109

SCAEF's appreciation and plan of operations for the winter and spring of 1945, 116, 123, *223*

Sir Alan Brooke's remarks regarding placing the whole effort in the North, *197*

Tripartite Military Meeting discussion regarding coordination of offensive operations in Europe during the spring and summer of 1945, *275*

IN THE MEDITERRANEAN THEATER OF OPERATIONS

CCS discussion regarding withdrawal of forces from the Mediterranean Theater to ETO, *216*

Directive to SACMED, 142, 166, *230*

Employment of air forces to prevent German withdrawals from Italy, *257*

Field Marshal Brooke and General Marshall's statements regarding strategy in the Mediterranean Theater, *208*

Plenary discussion regarding strategy in the Mediterranean, *290*

IN THE PACIFIC OCEAN AREAS

General Marshall and Admiral King's statements regarding operations in the Pacific, *219*

Operations for the defeat of Japan, 12, 168, *219*

IN SOUTHEAST ASIA

Directive to the Supreme Commander for operations in the Southeast Asia Command, 19, 163, 170, *211, 218*

General Marshall's statement regarding employment of U.S. resources in Southeast Asia, *212*

Plenary discussion regarding operations in Southeast Asia, *291*

SUMATRA

Plenary discussion regarding operations in Southeast Asia, *291*

SUPPLIES AND EQUIPMENT

Agreement on levels of supply of all petroleum products in all theaters, 23, 165, 171, *240*

CCS agree to proposals for equipping Greek forces, *226, 244*

CCS discussion regarding levels of supply of petroleum products in United Kingdom and Northwest Europe, *228*

CCS discussion regarding number of days' stocks required in certain categories of oil, *234*

CCS take note of reduced requirements for liberated manpower in ETO, *226*

Responsibility for the equipping of liberated manpower, 132, 134, 165

Sir Alan Brooke's statement regarding equipment for Allied and liberated forces, *226*

Statement regarding attrition of tanks in Russian central campaign, *307*

T

TACTICAL AIR FORCES

Principle with regard to transfer of tactical air forces from SACMED to SCAEF, 140, 141, *230*

Note: Italic numerals refer to pages in minutes of meeting.
Plain type numerals refer to pages in C.C.S. Papers.

INDEX

TANKS

General Marshall's statement regarding number of tank divisions in General Eisenhower's command, 307

Statement regarding attrition of tanks in Russian central campaign, 307

TANKERS

Present situation regarding the German U-boat threat during 1945, 150

TARGET DATES

Operations for the defeat of Japan, 13, 169

Planning date for the end of the war with Germany, 136, 164

Planning date for the end of the war with Japan, 202

TECHNIQUE

Admiral Leahy and General Antonov's statements regarding exchange of information on river-crossing technique and equipment, 276

Discussion with regard to the technique of employing air power in offensive operations, 260

Discussion with regard to the technique of employing artillery in offensive operations, 260

The Prime Minister's statement regarding exchange of information with U.S.S.R. regarding amphibious operations, 307

TOKYO PLAIN

General Marshall and Admiral King's statements regarding operations in the Pacific, 219

Operations for the defeat of Japan, 12, 168

TRIESTE

The President and Prime Minister's remarks regarding sovereignty over Trieste, 291

TROOPLIFT (See Shipping, Personnel)

TWELFTH TACTICAL AIR FORCE

CCS discussion regarding withdrawal of forces from the Mediterranean Theater to ETO, 216

CCS discussion regarding transfer of the Twelfth Air Force from Italy to France, 229

Withdrawal from the Mediterranean of a part of the Twelfth Tactical Air Force, 208, 229

TWENTIETH AIR FORCE

General Kuter's statement regarding employment of B-29's against Japan, 281

21ST ARMY GROUP

Provision of LVT's, 105, 235

U

U-BOAT WARFARE

Admiral Cunningham and Sir Charles Portal's statements regarding the German U-boat threat, 202

Admiral King's statement with regard to effectiveness of U.S. U-boat warfare in the Pacific, 284

CCS discussion regarding measures to combat the German U-boat threat, 222

Directive for effecting countermeasures against the German U-boat threat, 153, 231

Estimate of the enemy situation in Europe as of 23 January 1945, 29

Execution of the over-all strategic concept for the defeat of Germany, 160

General Marshall's statement regarding proposed measure to combat German U-boat menace, 306

Present situation regarding the German U-boat threat during 1945, 146, 222

Prime Minister's statement regarding diversion of air effort against German U-boat pens, 289

Prime Minister's statement with regard to submarine assembling points, 307

Statements with regard to Russian assault against Danzig as a measure to combat the U-boat menace, 309

Note: Italic numerals refer to pages in minutes of meeting.
Plain type numerals refer to pages in C.C.S. Papers.

INDEX

U.S.S.R.

Admiral King and the Prime Minister's statement regarding shipping to Russia via Dardanelles, *288*

Basic undertakings in support of overall strategic concept, 160

CCS agree Sir Charles Portal and General Kuter reply separately to Marshal Khudyakov indicating impracticability of revised bombline agreement proposed by Sovet High Command, *250*

CCS decision to press the Russians to agree to the proposals set forth in FAN 477, 200

Effective employment of Russian aviation in support of ground forces, *258*

Field Marshal Brooke and General Marshall's statements regarding coordination of operations with the Russians, *200*

General Antonov's resumé of Russian intentions in Europe, *303*

General Marshall's statement regarding strategic reasons for maintaining the goodwill of Russia and other Allies, *231*

General Marshall and Admiral King's statements regarding operations in the Pacific, *219*

Outline of the situation existing on the Eastern Front, *300*

Over-all objective and strategic concept for the prosecution of the war, 159

Planning for the entry of Russia into the war against Japan, 13

Proposal for the establishment of liaison with the Soviet High Command over Anglo-American strategic bombing in Germany, 183, *237*

Reciprocal agreement regarding liberated Allied prisoners of war, 177, *242*

Sir Charles Portal's statement regarding provision of Soviet airfields for damaged British night fighters, *277*

The President and General Antonov's statements regarding widening the gauge of captured German railroad rolling stock, *304*

The President and Prime Minister's statements regarding issuing a four-power ultimatum calling upon Japanese unconditional surrender, *296*

Tripartite Military Meeting discussion regarding bombline and liaison arrangements between the British-U.S. and Russian armies, *269*

Tripartite Military Meeting discussion regarding liaison arrangements between the British-U.S. and Russian armies, *261*

Tripartite Military Meeting discussion with regard to liaison for coordination of air operations, *262*

UNITED KINGDOM

British-controlled dry cargo shipping position (March-June 1945), 67

British-controlled troop shipping position after V-E Day, 92

British dry cargo shipping position after V-E Day, 87

CCS discussion regarding levels of supply of petroleum products in United Kingdom and Northwest Europe, *228*

CCS discussion regarding number of days' stocks required in certain categories of oil, *234*

Position of British-controlled troop shipping position (March-June 1945) 79

The Prime Minister's statement regarding shipping required for imports to Great Britain, *288*

V

VLR BOMBERS

(*See* Twentieth Air Force)

"VERITABLE"

General Bull's remarks regarding projected operations in Northwest Europe, *194*

VIENNA, AUSTRIA

General Marshall and General Antonov's statements regarding bases for U.S. strategic bomber forces in the Vienna-Budapest area, *276*

VOSGES

SCAEF's account of the development of operations in Northwest Europe, 111

Note: Italic numerals refer to pages in minutes of meeting.
Plain type numerals refer to pages in C.C.S. Papers.

INDEX

W

WESTERN FRONT

Coordination of offensive operations in the spring and summer months of 1945, *253*

Enemy intelligence and movement of enemy forces among various fronts, *277*

Estimate of the enemy situation in Europe as of 23 January 1945, 29

General Antonov's resumé of Russian intentions in Europe, *303*

General Bull's remarks regarding projected operations in Northwest Europe, *194*

General Marshall's remarks regarding advantage of more than one line of advance on the Western Front, *198*

General Marshall's statement regarding number of Allied divisions on the Western Front, *245*

General Marshall's statement regarding number of tank divisions in General Eisenhower's command, *307*

General Smith's remarks regarding the timing factor for proposed operations, *196*

Liaison arrangements between the British-U.S. and Russian armies, *261*

Number of U.S. and British air forces on the Western and Italian Fronts and their proposed employment, *256*

Planning date for the end of the war with Germany, 136, 164

Resumé of operations planned for the Western Front, *304*

Sir Alan Brooke's remarks regarding placing the whole effort in the North, *196*

Sir Alan Brooke's remarks regarding relief of tired units after crossing the Rhine, *198*

WESTWALL

Estimate of the enemy situation in Europe as of 23 January 1945, 31

WILSON, FIELD MARSHAL

Statements in reference to:
Strategy in the Mediterranean, *290*
Withdrawal of forces from the Mediterranean Theater to ETO, *290*

Y

YUGOSLAVIA

Directive to SACMED, 141, 167

Estimate of the enemy situation in Europe as of 23 January 1945, 41

The President and Prime Minister's remarks regarding sovereignty over Trieste, *291*

Z

ZONES OF OCCUPATION

Agreement for the American control of the Bremen-Bremerhaven enclave, 2, 236

Draft agreement for control of the Bremen-Bremerhaven enclave proposed by Lord Halifax and Mr. McCloy, 2

Map showing Bremen-Bremerhaven enclave, facing page 8

Note: Italic numerals refer to pages in minutes of meeting.
Plain type numerals refer to pages in C.C.S. Papers.

www.ingramcontent.com/pod-product-compliance
Lightning Source LLC
Chambersburg PA
CBHW060335010526
44117CB00017B/2836